I0803135

IMAGES
of America

LAND O' LAKES

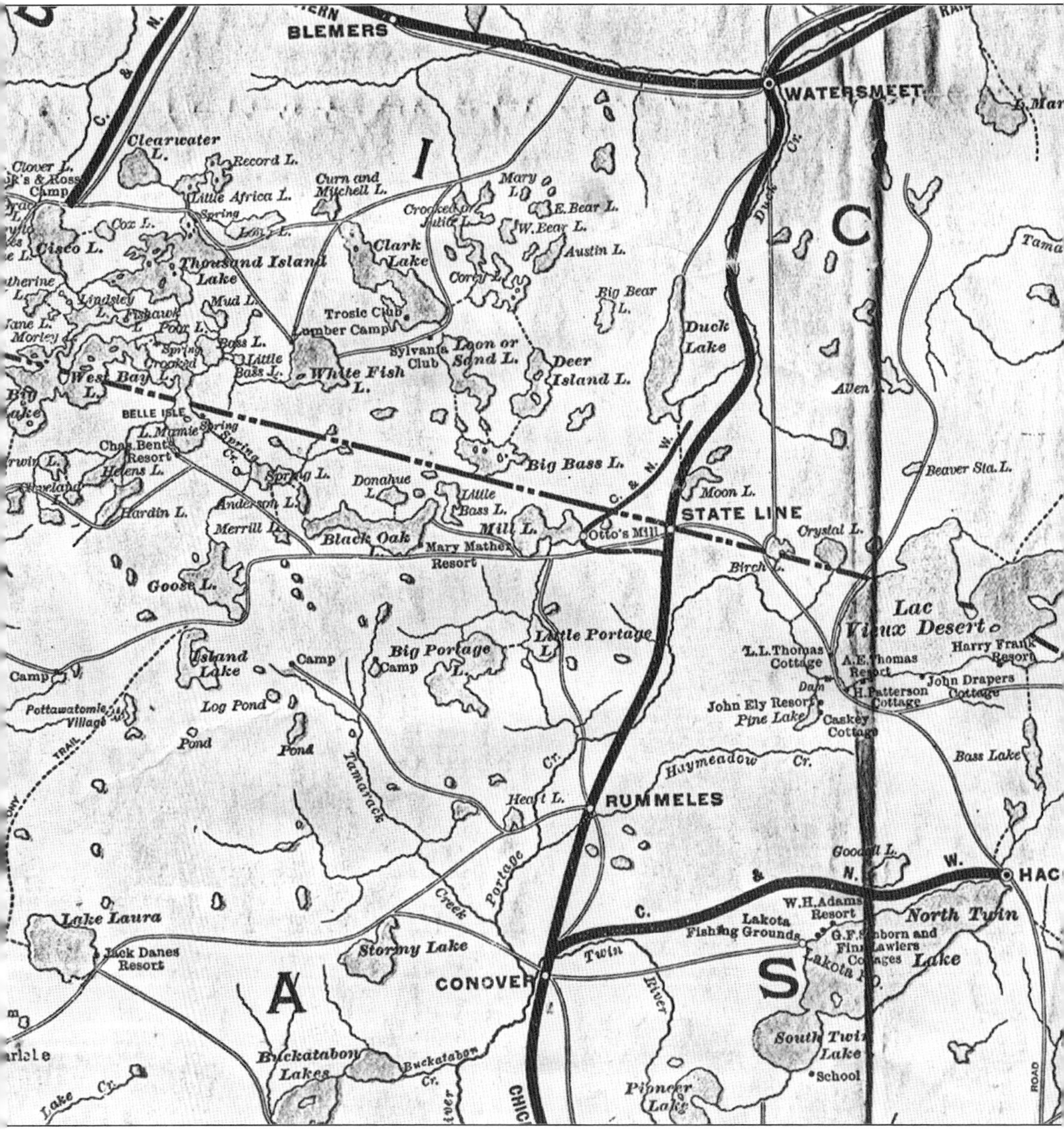

In 1903, the Northwestern Line Railway published a map of "Hunting and Fishing Resorts of Northern Wisconsin and Michigan." The map included the former Sylvania Club on Clark Lake and the Charles Bent Resort on Mamie Lake, which remains today. The dark lines are rail routes, and the other lines denote wagon roads and trails. Note the rail spur that runs west from State Line to Otto's Mill then north to the lumber camp on Duck Lake. (Courtesy of the Land O' Lakes Historical Society.)

On the Cover: Before motorized outboard engines, boating in the Land O' Lakes region meant rowing or paddling. Such occasions were often formal, daylong affairs, including a shore lunch of fresh fish. Most of the outings were organized by area resorts or fishing guides. These canoeists were guests of the Black Oak Lake Resort in 1928. (Courtesy of the Land O' Lakes Historical Society.)

IMAGES
of America

LAND O' LAKES

Jon Helminiak

ARCADIA
PUBLISHING

ISBN 978-0-7385-8316-7

Published by Arcadia Publishing
Charleston, South Carolina

Printed in the United States of America

Library of Congress Control Number: 2010940863

For all general information, please contact Arcadia Publishing:
Telephone 843-853-2070
Fax 843-853-0044
E-mail sales@arcadiapublishing.com
For customer service and orders:
Toll-Free 1-888-313-2665

Visit us on the Internet at www.arcadiapublishing.com

To the pioneering men and women of Donaldson,
State Line, and Land O' Lakes.

They wore moccasins, boots, or were barefoot.
Some were refined, many were rough.
Some were born here, most traveled hundreds of miles to arrive.
Some lived quietly, but others planned, built, and led.
But all of them found beauty and fulfillment
Here at the "top of Wisconsin."

CONTENTS

ACKNOWLEDGMENTS

I am grateful to the following people and organizations that helped make this book possible:

The Land O' Lakes Historical Society board of directors, led by president Sally (Dussault) Schlaak, are an enthusiastic group of people who are passionate about preserving and sharing the history of Land O' Lakes.

Janet Geronime, archivist for the Land O' Lakes Historical Society, is dedicated, meticulously organized, and proud of the collection.

Jack LaChance Jr. is a Land O' Lakes attorney and great-grandson of Peter LaChance, who constructed the first building and store in State Line in 1895.

Barbara and Harold Nehring—Barbara was a founding member of the Land O' Lakes Historical Society and one of the fist organizers of Land O' Lakes historical photographs, documents, and interviews with long-term residents. Barbara and her husband, Harold, have been longtime owners of the Trading Post International. Barbara's proofreading of the text was extremely helpful.

Rob Andersen, owner of the Hillside Resort and Loose Moose Pub (formerly the Tia Juana); Lee Bennett, former pilot, flight instructor, and operator of the Land O' Lakes airport from 1958 to 1964; Carol Becker, daughter of former Land O' Lakes chairwoman Violet Becker; Dick Boehmer, grandson of Lillian, and Bert Carlson—former owners of Carlson's Big Lake Cabins; Gerd Klausmeyer, seasonal Phelps resident and postcard collector; Paul McLeod, former instructor at the Conserve School and historical society researcher; Nagel Lumber Yard—no photographs were available, but this company has my gratitude for its many years of service to Land O' Lakes, including donations of lumber for the construction of the current library; Barb (Gremban) Renc, Land O' Lakes Historical Society volunteer; Cindy Pekrul, Land O' Lakes resident and postcard collector; Tom Reed, president of Headwaters State Bank; Lisa and Paul Stemen, former owners of Bent's Camp Resort; Mike Stopczynski, owner of Stops Refrigeration, Inc., and son of Al and Angie Stopczynski, former owners of the Black Oak Inn; Laurie Taylor, archivist assistant for the Land O' Lakes Historical Society; the Turnquist family, longtime Land O' Lakes residents; the *Vilas County News Review*; Sandy Wait, executive secretary of the Land O' Lakes Chamber of Commerce; the Wisconsin State Historical Society; and, finally, my parents, Raymond and Marilyn, for introducing my sister Lyn and me to Land O' Lakes and the north woods. Our summer vacations at the Gateway Lodge and Stormy Lake are forever remembered and cherished.

Preface

Land O' Lakes is deceiving. Today's casual visitor would not know of its fascinating history, one rich with entertainment, colorful personalities, and visionary entrepreneurs. Most small towns would envy what happened here through the years.

The process of writing and assembling this book has been both intriguing and educational. During my research, every resident I met with was welcoming and helpful. They spoke pridefully about Land O' Lakes, their families, and the old days. Their personalities are as robust as the town pioneers you will meet in this book.

As you read, please note the following: unless otherwise credited, the photographs in this book are courtesy of the Land O' Lakes Historical Society. With only a few exceptions, the historical photographs cover the period from approximately 1880 to 1980, a span of 100 years. As with many oral and written histories, different dates and various names are often associated with specific events. The dates and names provided here are those that have been recorded most consistently.

Because of lack of written records and photographs, or the space restrictions of this book, I may have not recognized every event, business, or personality associated with Land O' Lakes history. Perhaps future editions of this book can include them.

I hope these photographs and words will inspire current and future Land O' Lakes residents and visitors to carry on its proud heritage.

INTRODUCTION

For years, Land O' Lakes was the most fashionable destination in northern Wisconsin. The morning train brought women in billowing skirts and men in suits and hats. In the summer, families and businessmen often arrived via a North Central Airlines DC-3 airliner. Most came to relax, fish, boat, or swim. Guests at the Gateway Inn and Lodge might also golf, play tennis, ski, bowl, watch a ski jumping competition, and even gamble. At night, they could have a drink at the Gateway's Red Deer cocktail lounge and then be seated for dinner. Formal dress was required. The menu was eclectic, with offerings such as Wisconsin jumbo frog legs, Lake Superior trout, or calve's liver sauteed with bacon.

After dinner, there was big-city entertainment, such as Bob Hope, Lawrence Welk and his band, or a tuxedo-clad jazz trio. In its prime, Land O' Lakes was *the place to be* in the north woods. It had it all: natural beauty, fine dining, entertainment, multiple sporting options, and regular air and rail transportation from Milwaukee and Chicago. The Land O' Lakes recreation scene was featured in newspapers from Chicago and Milwaukee to Detroit and Minneapolis.

Although the Gateway Inn and Lodge were the fulcrum of the Land O' Lakes tourism industry, there were other attractions as well. The High Hat Club was a favorite downtown supper club, operated for many years by the first person born in the old town of State Line, Cora (Dickman) Harris, and her husband, Chet. The Wannigan Club (now the Bear Trap Inn) and LaChance's Bar (current site of the Rusty Nail Tavern) attracted a regular flow of locals and visitors. The Tia Juana (currently the Loose Moose) nightclub claimed to serve "the world's best barbecue ribs" and hosted many early-morning gatherings after the last-call drinks were downed at the Gateway.

One day in 1930, Charlie Haase arrived in town and built a log tavern and inn, naming it Barefoot's. Soon it earned a national reputation as one of the most unique nightclubs and restaurants in the Great Lakes region.

But like many small towns, the history of Land O' Lakes is one of cycles. There were decades of thriving businesses, a robust flow of tourists, and big-city entertainment. Then came the years when Land O' Lakes had to reorganize, recover, and start over.

The first boom came during the logging years of 1890 to 1910, when the towns of Donaldson and State Line (the precursors to Land O' Lakes) bustled with activity and new settlers. Young men, some with families, came to work as lumberjacks for the many lumber mills. The Brown Brothers logging camp just north of Spring Lake and the Salsich & Wilson camp near Black Oak Lake were active for about a decade. The first permanent town of Donaldson built up around the Mason-Donaldson Lumber Camp on the south shore of Mill Lake. Donaldson consisted of about 30 homes, a school, a community building, and a meeting hall.

When the loggers finished their work, the immense trees were gone, and so were the jobs. Then forest fires laid to ashes hundreds of thousands of cut-over acres, leaving the landscape desolate and scarred. Since the land had little commercial value, the Yale Land Company of Minneapolis bought much of the logging company property. They aggressively sought buyers of what they promoted as a "bountiful land," promising that it was perfect for farming but little else.

Despite the ravages of lumbering and fires, the lakes and rivers remained pristine. Rumors spread that a man could catch his fishing "limit in a minute." The promise of bountiful angling fueled an economic recovery, led by the growth of resorts, some of which were converted from former lumber camp facilities. Conditions were primitive; it took about four hours to drive from State Line to Bent's Camp Resort with a team of horses on a very rough tote road. Some guests reported that it was easier to walk, than ride on a dilapidated wagon with no springs. By the late 1930s, approximately 14 resorts operated within a 12-mile radius of Land O' Lakes. The town was again a desirable destination. In 1926, the post office designation was changed from State Line to Land O' Lakes, based on a petition from George St. Clair, town clerk and owner of the Black Oak Lake Resort.

And then, in 1937, one man appeared who changed everything. His name was John H. King. King, a self-made man who put himself through business school by shining shoes and selling newspapers, built himself a fortune by correctly predicting the future popularity of the motion picture industry. By 1928, King (whose real name was John Kunsky) built and owned 28 movie theaters in Detroit, many of which were the most elegant in the nation. Several seated up to 3,300 people, and most remain today, including the Fisher and Redford Theaters.

Driving through Land O' Lakes in 1936 en route to his property on Snap Jack Lake in upper Michigan, King stopped at Harrington's café and gas station on the northwest corner of Highways 45 and B. Discovering it was for sale, he bought the property, and a year later, construction of the King's Gateway Inn began. Completed in 1938, the inn boasted a billiard hall, bowling alleys, a dining room, gambling, the Tap Room bar, and the Red Deer Cocktail Lounge. A year later, King built the Gateway Lodge across the street, followed by a ski hill, golf course, and an airport. At the time, he was 62 years old. John King's Gateway complex became the crown of the rapidly expanding tourist industry in Land O' Lakes.

During the high-interest, high-inflation period of the 1970s, the Gateway Inn struggled to be financially viable and was repeatedly sold, bought, and sold again. Many longtime resorts closed, because owners or prospective buyers could not afford the soaring property taxes or high interest rates. The railway ended passenger service in 1964 and freight service in 1974. North Central Airlines cancelled its seasonal flights in 1965. The fuel crisis of the early 1970s forced people to postpone their vacation drive to the north woods. Once again, it seemed like Land O' Lakes was being abandoned.

By the early 1980s, the economy improved and the tourists returned. Builders constructed record numbers of seasonal homes, and demand for prime north woods real estate soared. Resorts and restaurants experienced record bookings, and newly groomed trails for snowmobilers and cross-country skiers brought needed winter income.

But the fires came again. This time they claimed several of the town's most popular entertainment venues. Both Barefoot Charlie's Restaurant and Night Club and Archdale's Merrill Inn (located across from the present Forest Lake Country Store) burned to the ground in 1988. The venerable downtown Hi-Hat Club and Restaurant also burned in the 1980s. The lumberyard, situated downtown along the railroad tracks, was destroyed by an intense fire that required many hours to extinguish. The loss of these favorite attractions, in such a short time span, plunged Land O' Lakes into an economic and emotional letdown. The owners of the burned establishments, perhaps knowing that they could not replicate the unique interiors and ambiance, did not rebuild.

But the ebb and flow of Land O' Lakes is only a thimble of the region's history. Geology, Native Americans, and the French all influenced northern Wisconsin long before the first lumberjacks arrived at the Mill Lake lumber camp.

Over millions of geologic years ago, three mountain ranges rose and fell here. Later, glaciers over a mile thick covered the area. When the last glacier receded about 12,000 years ago, sand and gravel was molded into hilly terrain and basins were scoured out, which filled with glacial melt water. Those basins remain today as our lakes. A glacier also created a rare subcontinental divide, 15 miles west of town. Here, waters either flow west to the Mississippi River and the Gulf of Mexico, or east to the Atlantic via drainage into Lake Superior. Land O' Lakes rests 1,700 feet above sea level, making it one of the highest points in Wisconsin. (For perspective, Milwaukee is approximately 760 feet above sea level.)

In the 1600s, the area was inhabited by the Lac Vieux Desert band of Chippewa, also called Ojibwa, Indians. They lived in teepees and wigwams made of birch bark, hunted white-tailed deer and small game, and were skilled craftsmen, making clothing of hides adorned with porcupine quills, feathers, and furs. They planted beans, potatoes, and squash and also fished with nets and, at spawning time, with spears.

The first Europeans to encounter the Ojibwa were French traders, missionaries, and voyageurs who wintered on the shore of Lac Vieux Desert as early as 1672. Because it was the source of the Wisconsin River, Lac View Desert was the door to the Mississippi River and the Gulf of Mexico, and therefore a popular rendezvous point. The French named the lake Lac Vieux Desert, meaning "Lake of the Old Desert or Deserted Planting Ground," and sent the first maps of the region back to Paris. The Jesuit priest Jacques Marquette, explorer Louis Joliet, and Slovene Catholic missionary Frederic Baraga were said to have visited the lake on their journeys. In 1842, the Lac Vieux Desert Band of Chippewa sold 86 acres of their land to the US government, and this was eventually the site of the town of State Line.

In 1852, the first known white settler, G.L Draper, moved to Lac Vieux Desert with his six children. The first trading post was built on the Draper property in 1857 by Joshua Fox. It also served as the region's first post office and bank.

In 1884, Leonard Thomas, who married G. L. Draper's daughter, opened the Thomas Resort on the southwest shore of Lac Vieux Desert. It offered room and board to fishermen and was one of the first resorts in the region; it remains today as the Sunrise Lodge. In 1895, Canadian-born Peter LaChance arrived from Watersmeet and bought land from the present Bel-Air Motel to the town hall. He built a store and a family home in the vicinity of the present site of the Rusty Nail Tavern. That same year, Charles Bent began a fishing camp on Maimie Lake.

By 1893, the railroad reached State Line. The lumber companies arrived to harvest the immense white pines, and the development of Land O' Lakes, said to be at the "top of Wisconsin," had begun.

One

In the Beginning

Native Americans, Loggers, Donaldson, and State Line

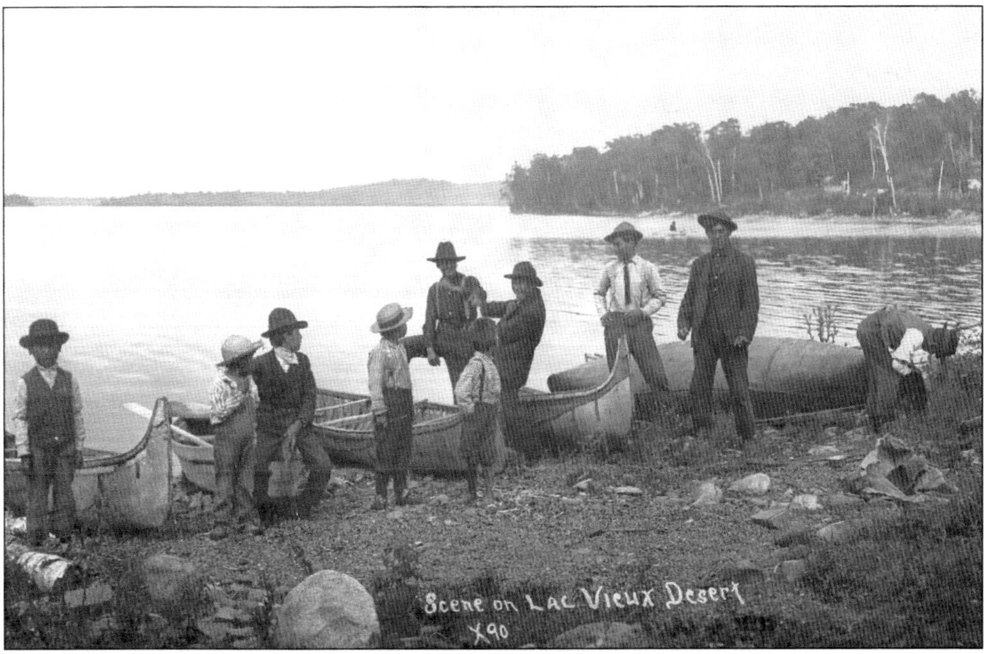

John Caskey, son of Agnes and Sylvester Caskey, who were among the first white settlers in the region, recalled, "All winter and all summer the Chippewa and the whites worked together to help one another. They shared their food, their work, their sorrows and their joys—neither would have survived without the other." This c. 1908 photograph was taken on Lac View Desert. Note the handcrafted birch bark canoes. (Courtesy of Gerd Klausmeyer.)

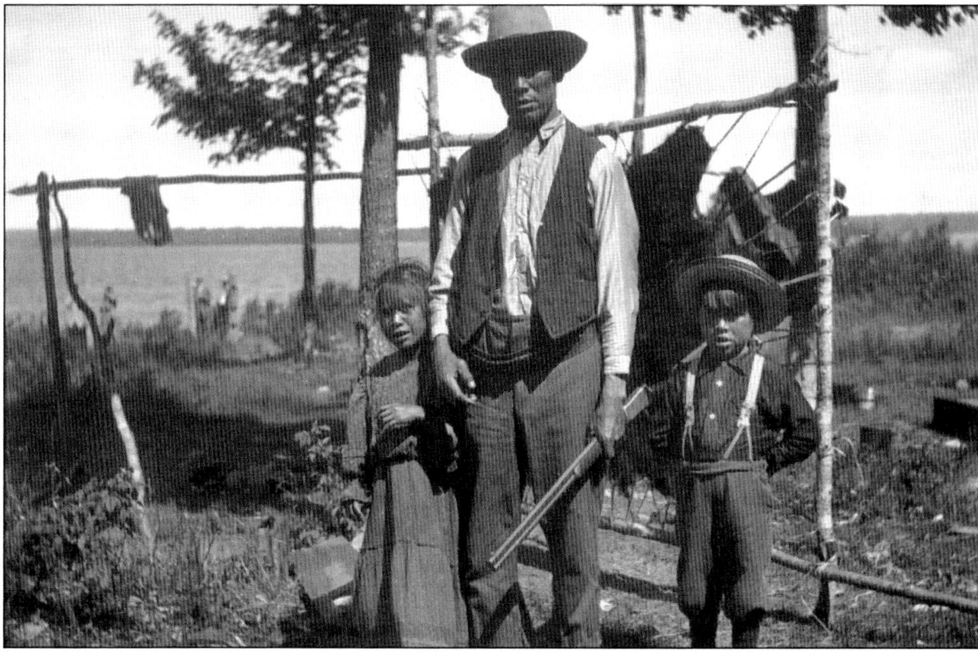

An unidentified Chippewa man stands with his two children next to a bear hide stretched on poles, with Lac Vieux Desert in the background. The French traded with the Chippewa, giving cloth, blankets, pots, beads, gunpowder, bullets, and tobacco in exchange for pelts of beaver mink, skunk, and fox. (Courtesy of Wisconsin Historical Society.)

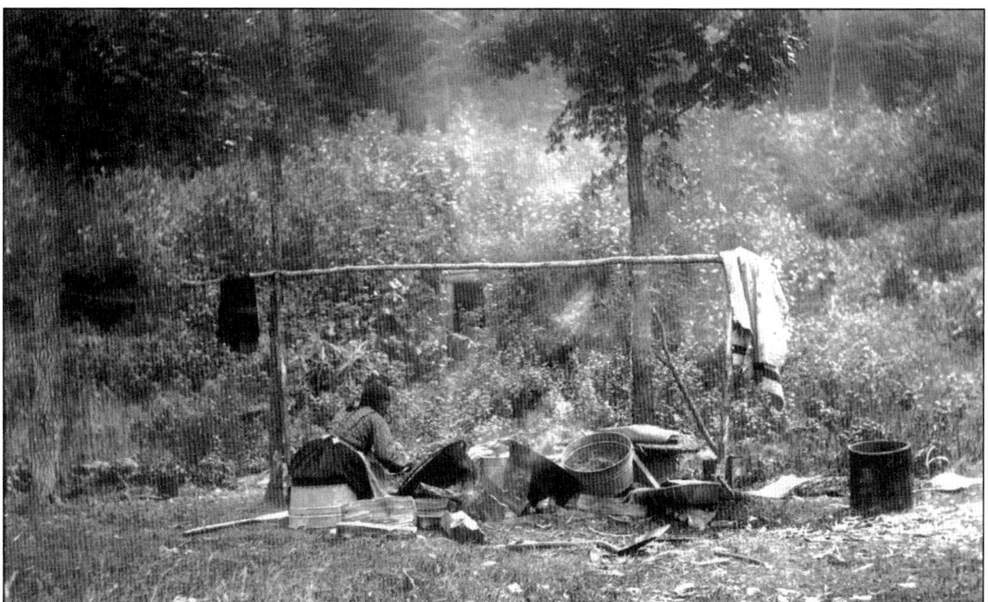

An unidentified Chippewa woman parches wild rice near Lac Vieux Desert. The Lac Vieux Desert Band of Lake Superior Chippewa were first encountered in northern Wisconsin by early French missionaries and fur traders in the 1600s. (Courtesy of Wisconsin Historical Society.)

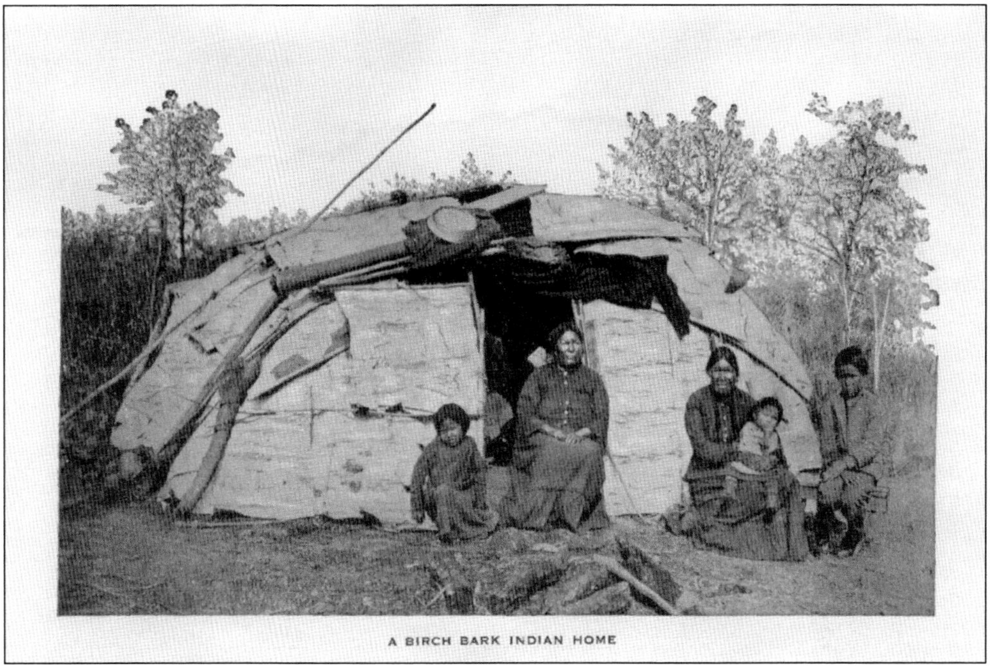

A typical Chippewa birch bark home is pictured near Lac Vieux Desert in 1903. The early French in the area recorded that the Chippewa were dressed "in exquisite clothing from deer, beaver and other animal skins, and adorned themselves with quills, feathers, and furs."

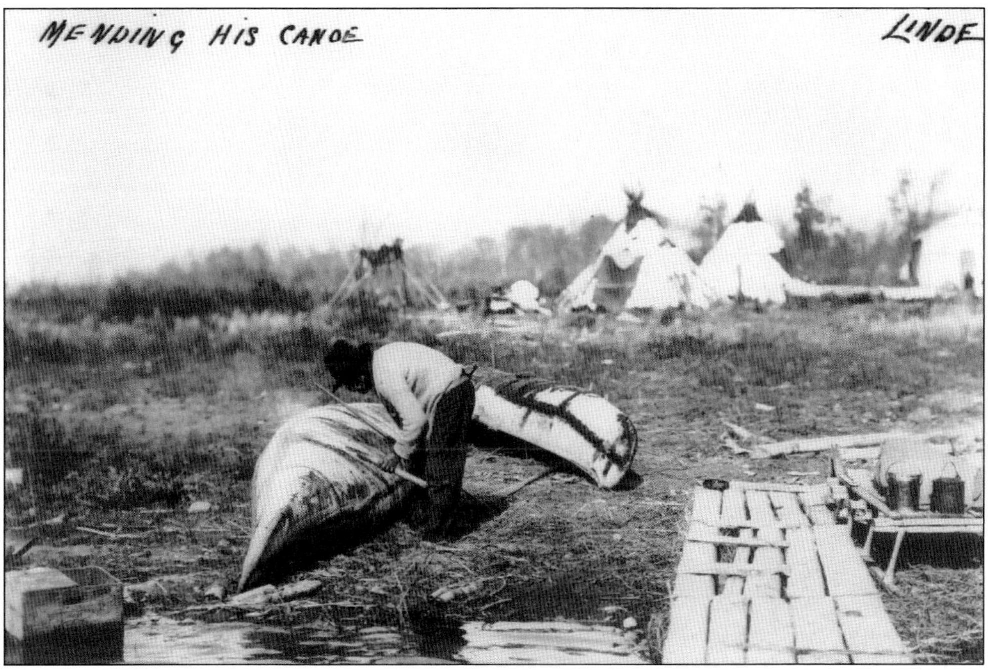

The Lac Vieux Desert Band of Lake Superior Chippewa included skilled craftsmen who made canoes, tepees, and wigwams from birch bark. This photograph shows an unidentified Chippewa man repairing a tribal canoe along the shore of Lac Vieux Desert, a lake that provided them with walleye, muskellunge, bass, and panfish.

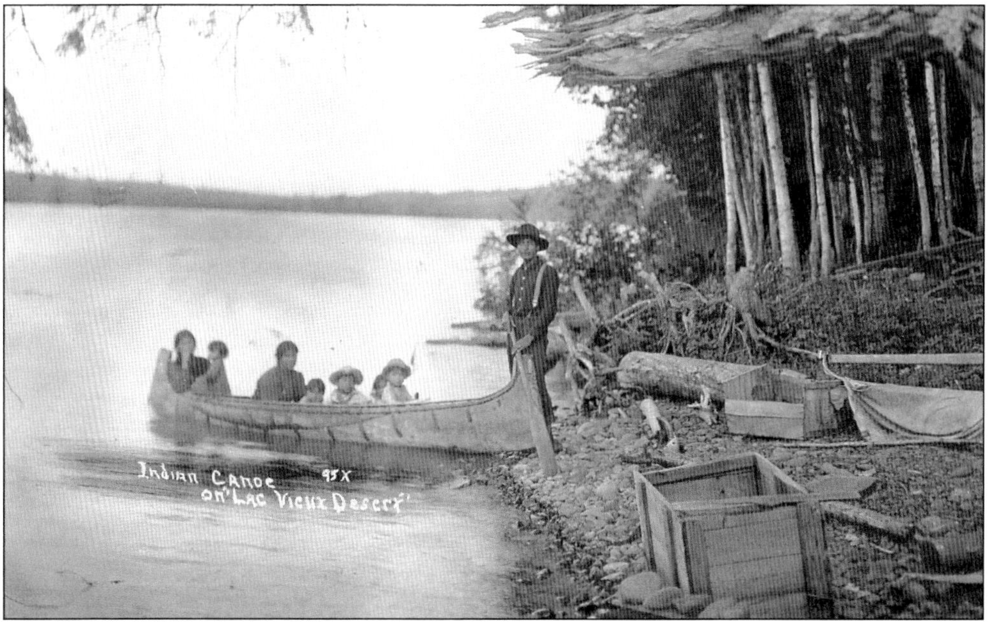

The journals of French explorers stated that a large Chippewa village was located on the north shore of Lac Vieux Desert. Relations between the French and early white settlers were hospitable and mutually beneficial. This unidentified Chippewa man and his family were photographed on Lac Vieux Desert around 1900. (Courtesy of Gerd Klausmeyer.)

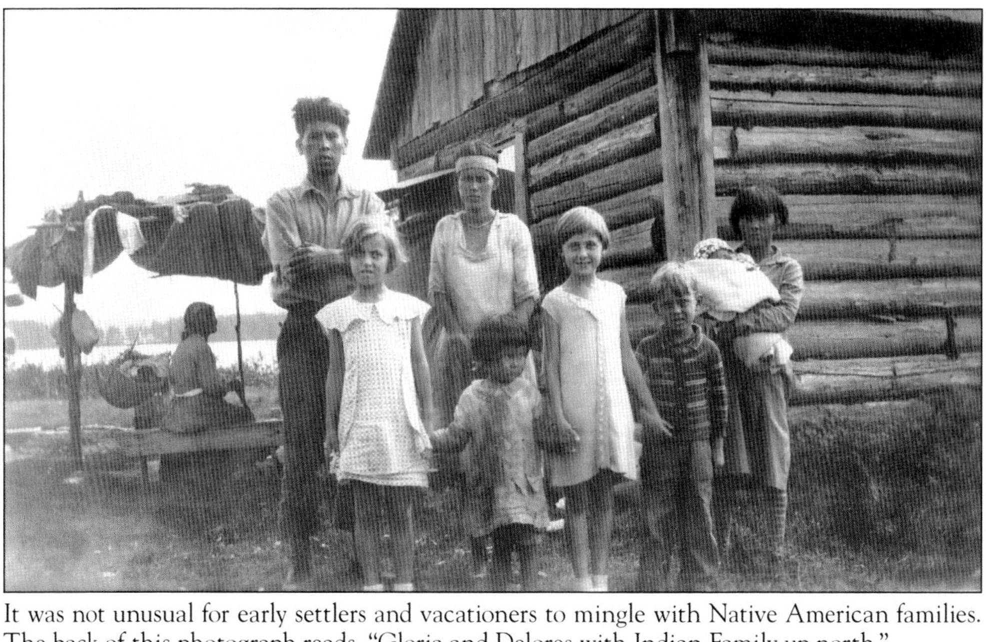

It was not unusual for early settlers and vacationers to mingle with Native American families. The back of this photograph reads, "Gloria and Delores with Indian Family up north."

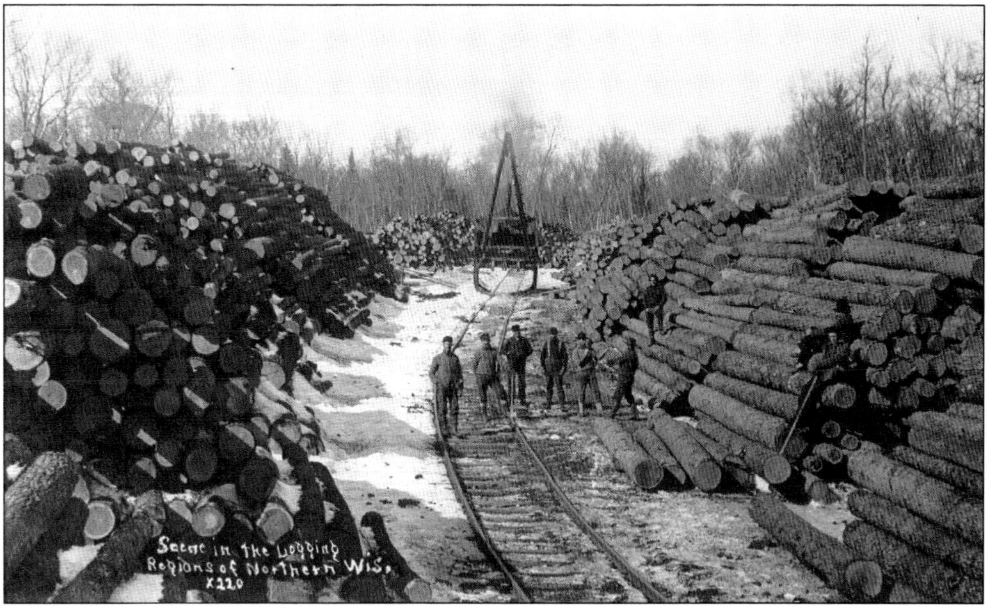

Around 1900, timber was so thick that one 40-acre parcel along the tote road (presently Highway B) produced one million board feet of lumber. Local lumber camps included the Brown Brothers north of Spring Lake, the Pine Camp seven miles west of State Line, Mason-Donaldson and Otto's camps on Mill Lake, the Duck Lake Camp, and the Wisconsin River Camp.

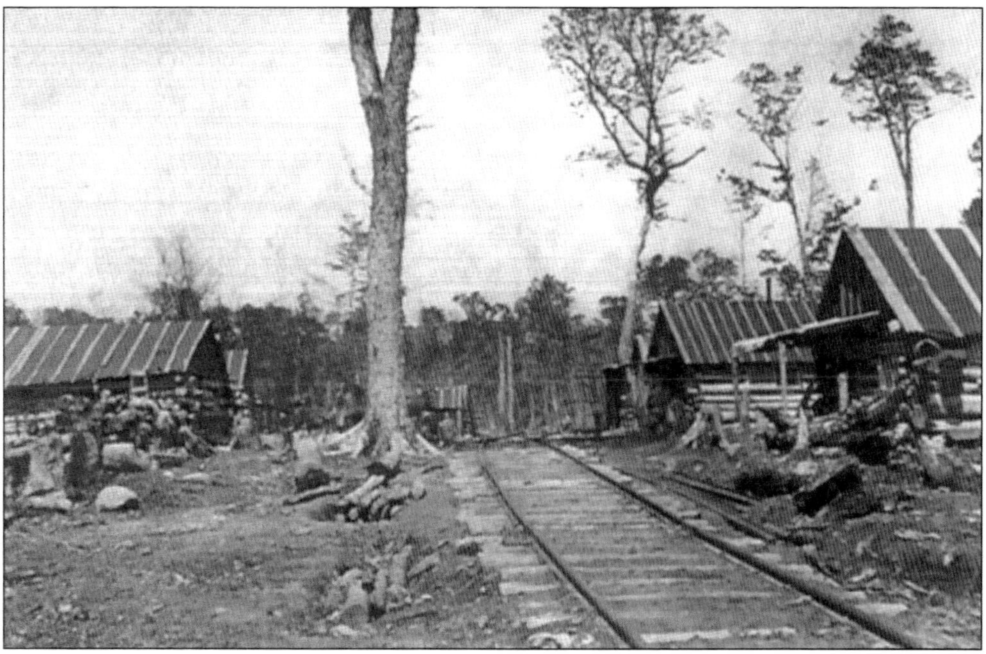

The Brown Brothers logging camp was located just north of Spring Lake and operated until about 1910. Its railroad spur began at State Line and ran west to the camp.

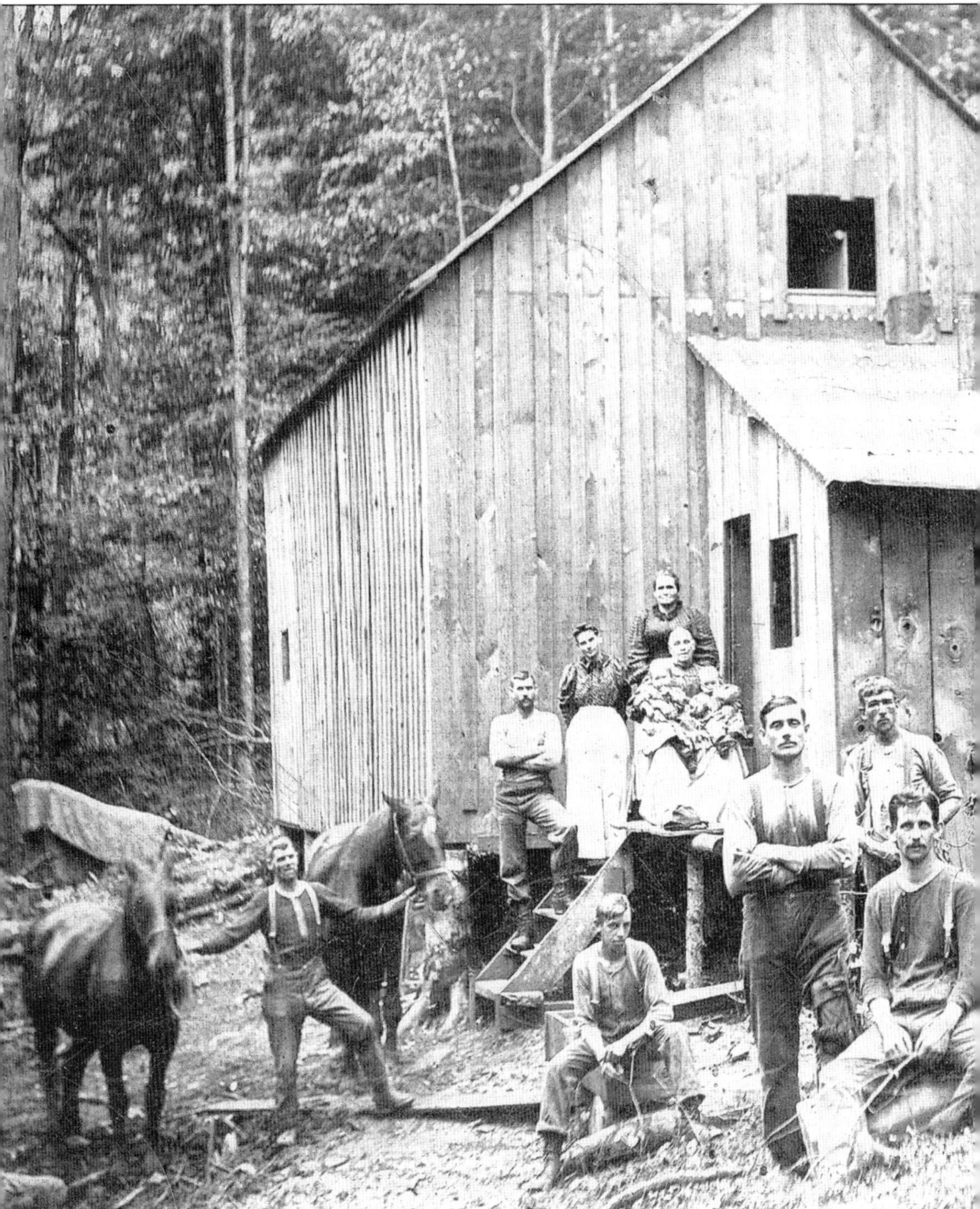

The life of a north woods lumberjack was not glamorous. Work began at sunrise, and trees were felled with axes and handsaws. Logs were pulled from the forest by horses harnessed to railroad cars or sleighs. Lumber camps included a dining room with long tables and benches, sleeping quarters with bunk beds, and a large room that served as a social hall and clothes drying area.

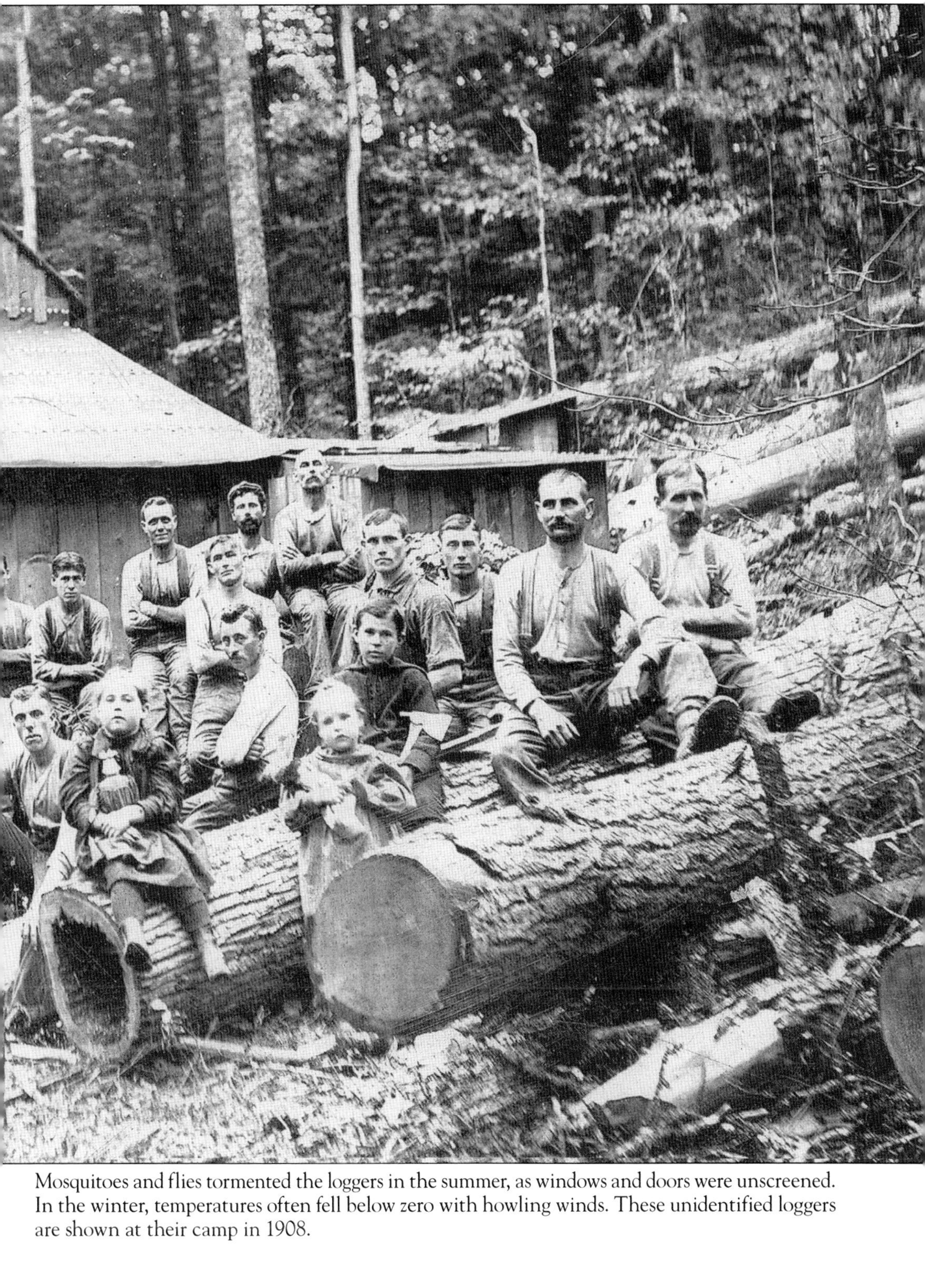

Mosquitoes and flies tormented the loggers in the summer, as windows and doors were unscreened. In the winter, temperatures often fell below zero with howling winds. These unidentified loggers are shown at their camp in 1908.

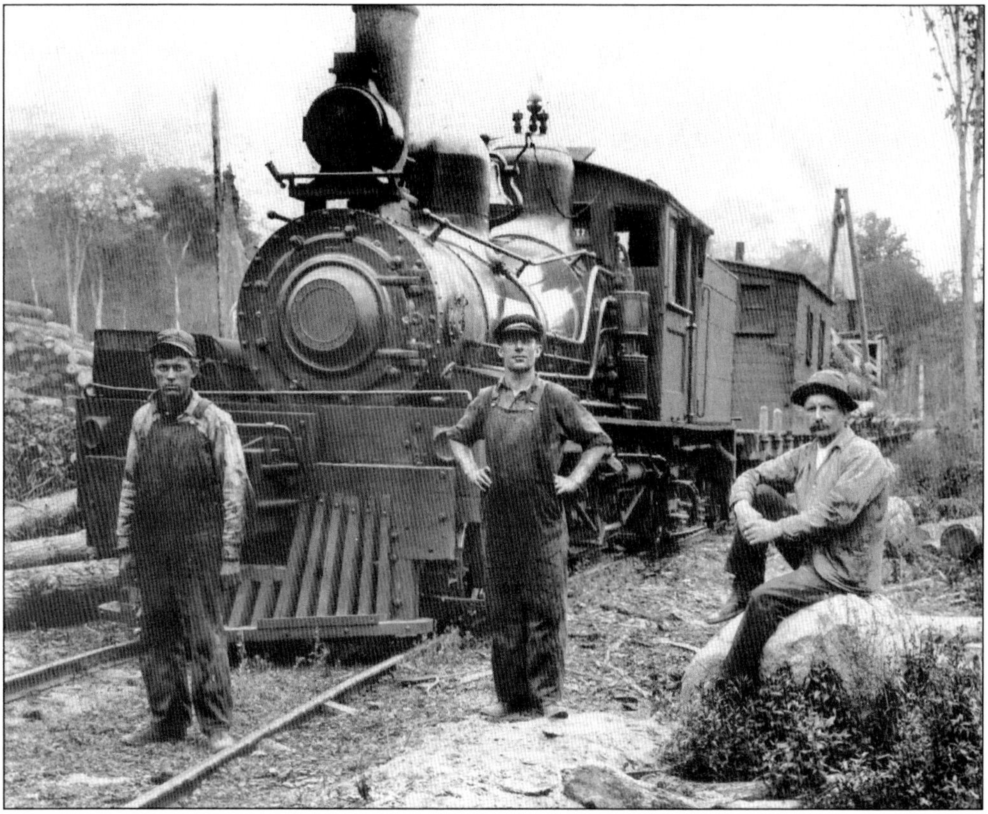

Lumber companies built several railroad networks around Donaldson and State Line. Rudolph Otto built the first one in 1895 from his camp on Mill Lake to Duck Lake. A few years later, the Salsich & Wilson Lumber company laid tracks from Star Lake north to the south shore of Black Oak Lake. In 1901, the Brown Brothers built a spur from State Line west to their lumber camp just north of Spring Lake. This c. 1910 photograph depicts a typical logging train.

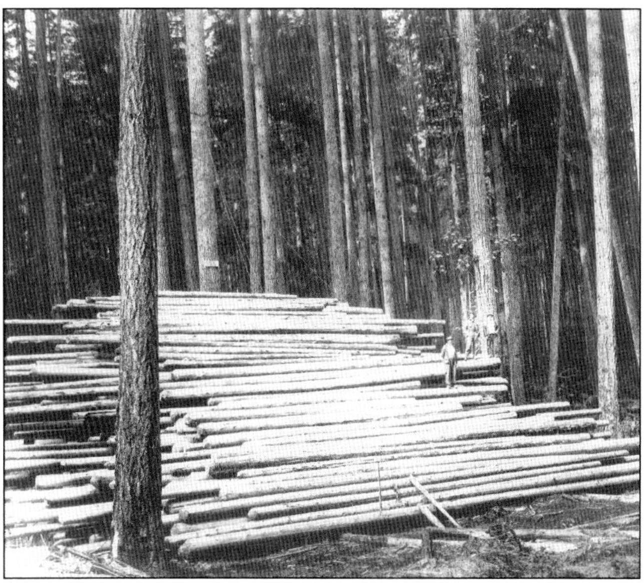

This photograph depicts the magnitude of the forests around Donaldson and State Line in the early 1900s. At the conclusion of the logging era, the region was decimated of trees. This method of clear-cutting left only unusable branches and stumps. Dry summers and forest fires eventually laid to ashes all remaining vegetation. Fireweed was the first to recover, followed by birch and aspen. By the 1930s, hardwood and pine reappeared, and deer and other animals returned to the new woods.

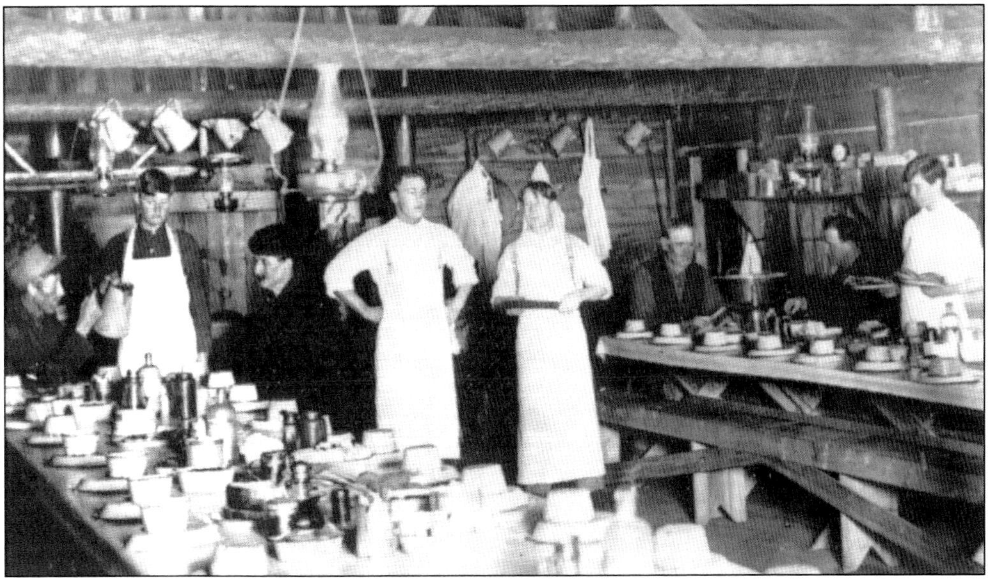

Lumber camps served ample food to the loggers, especially at breakfast. Donuts, pancakes, pies, eggs, and strong coffee prepared the men for a long morning of physical, outdoor labor. Days began early, and some camps enforced a "no talking" rule at breakfast to keep the tired and sometimes hungover loggers civil.

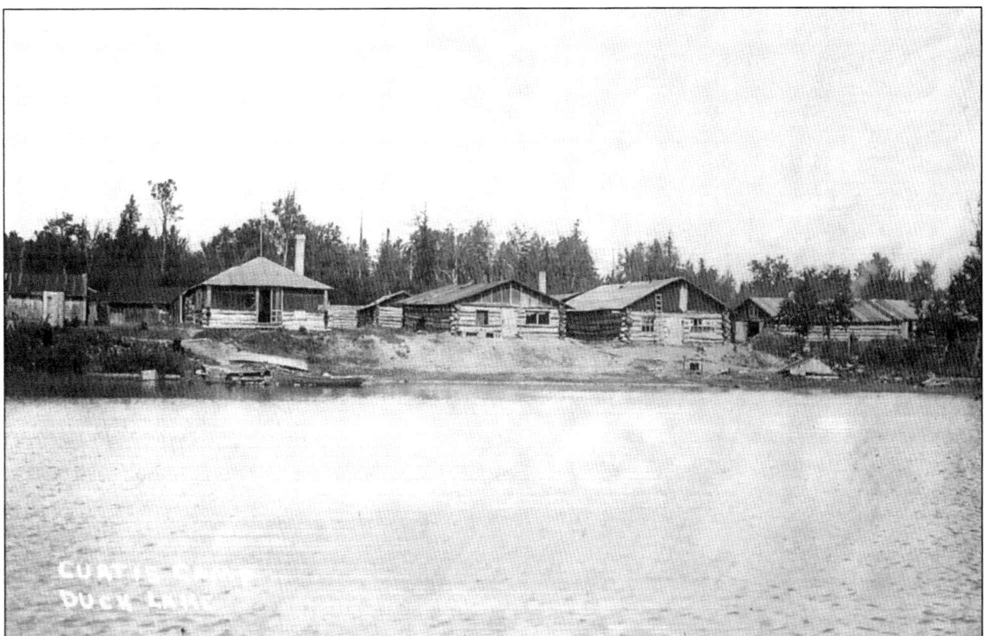

The Curtis Camp, a logging camp located on Duck Lake north of State Line, operated for several years around 1900.

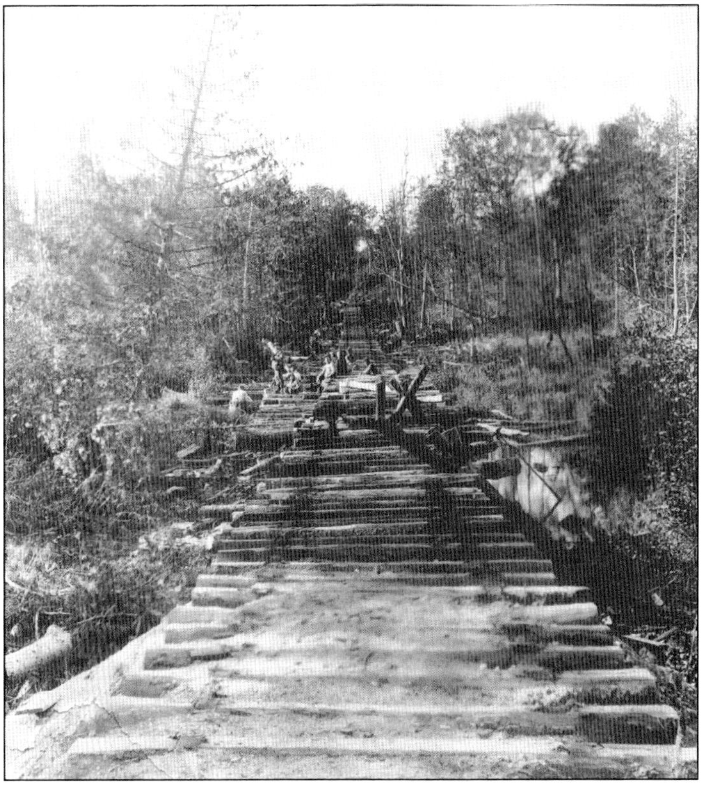

Log roads were sometimes constructed to ease the transportation of the huge white pine trunks from the forest to the nearest railroad spurs. There they would be loaded on to railcars and taken to mills.

One of the first homes and trading posts was built in 1874 on Lac Vieux Desert by G.L Draper, the area's first white settler. Leonard Thomas bought the structure in 1876 after he married Draper's daughter. Thomas went on to build the area's first resort, the Thomas Resort, on Lac Vieux Desert in 1884. (Courtesy of Wisconsin Historical Society.)

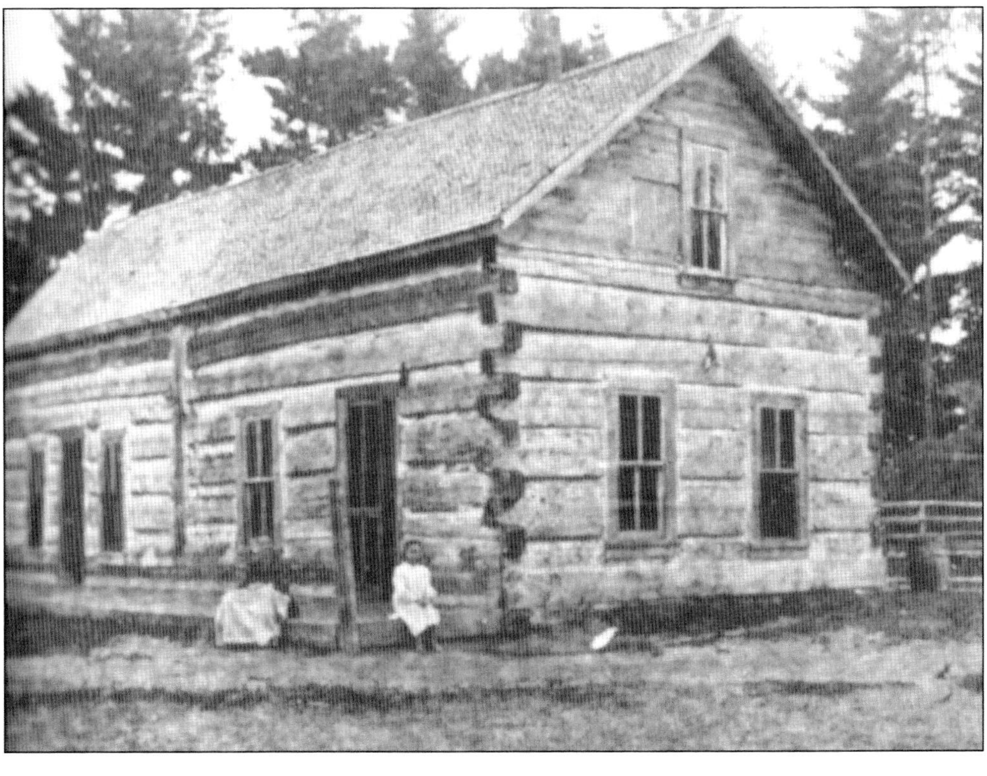

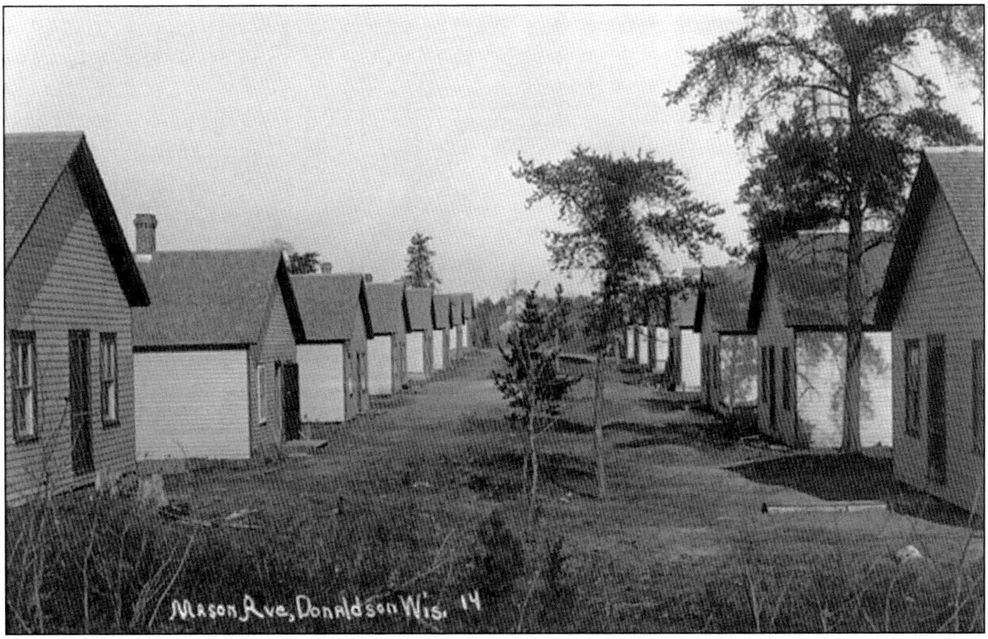

This is one of the few remaining photographs of Donaldson, Wisconsin. Donaldson boasted a school, community building (which was also used as a church), and meeting hall. Most of the 30 Donaldson homes were moved east to State Line after the Mason-Donaldson Lumber Camp was destroyed by fire in 1908.

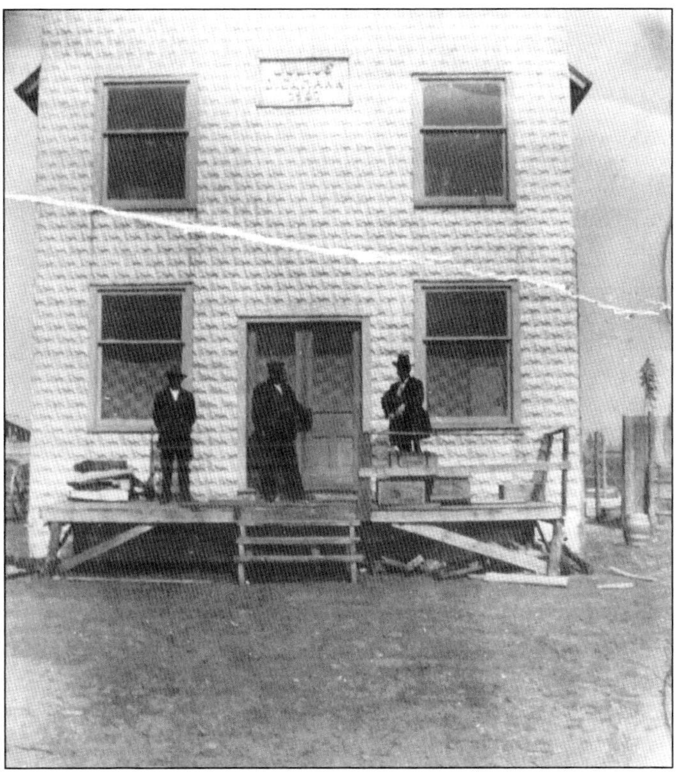

The Donaldson home of Lena and Julius Dickman was completed in 1903 on their farm located between Donaldson and State Line. Dickman eventually moved this house to State Line, where it remains today, just west of the library.

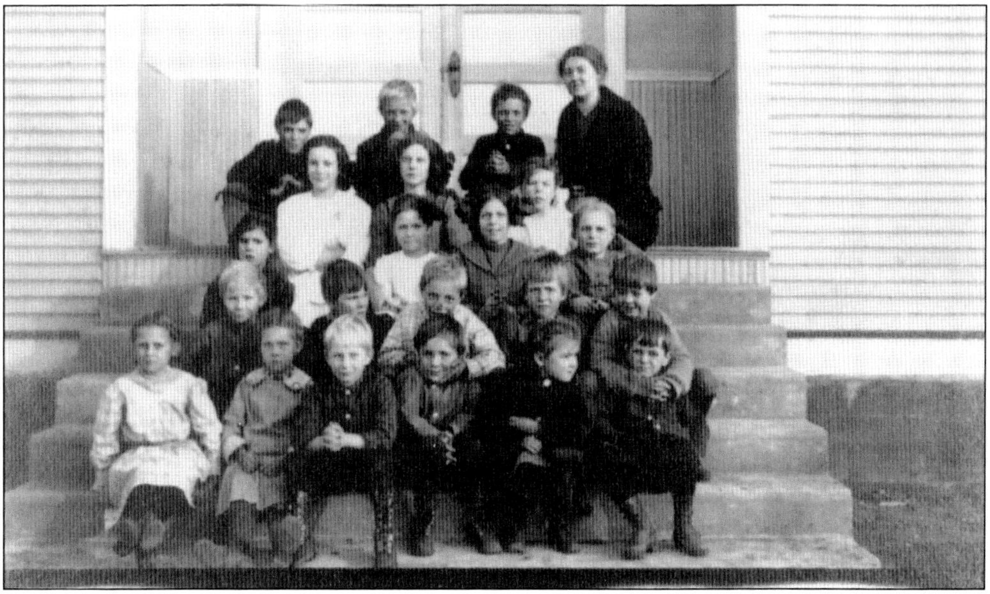

Children sit for a 1914 class photograph on the front steps of the Donaldson School with teacher Esther Knowles Morgan. When the residents of Donaldson moved to State Line, World War I lieutenant colonel John Van Natta bought the Donaldson land and converted the school into sleeping rooms for hunters and fishermen. Today, only the concrete steps and the foundation of the school remain, along the road to the Land O' Lakes recycling center.

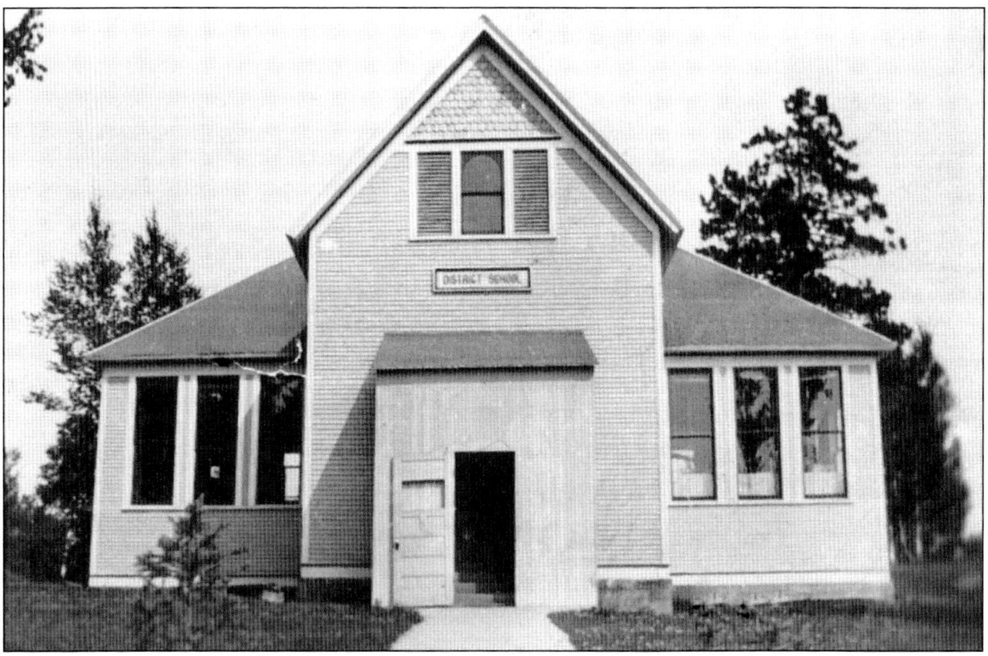

This photograph shows the Donaldson School in 1916 after the vestibule was added around the front steps. The sign above it reads "District School." Built in 1907 to educate the children of Donaldson, a town that developed around the nearby Mason-Donaldson Lumber Camp, the school had two rooms—one for grades one through four and the other for grades five through eight. It was razed in 1942.

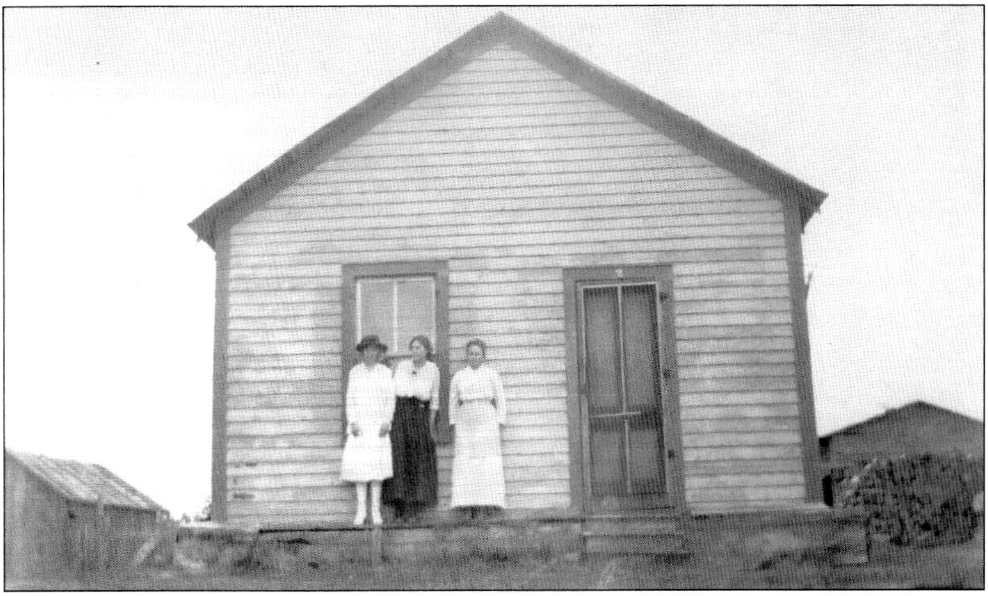

This Donaldson home belonged to the Knoble family. Vera Knoble, the student who received the award certificate below, stands on the left.

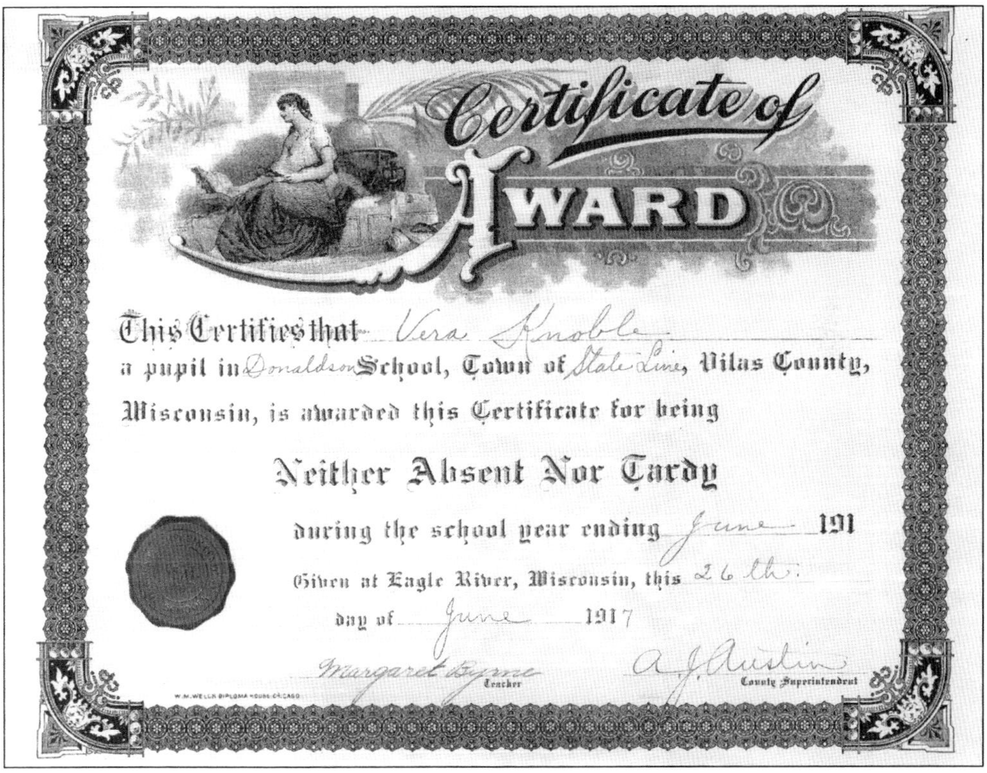

Certificate of AWARD

This Certifies that Vera Knoble
a pupil in Donaldson School, Town of State Line, Vilas County,
Wisconsin, is awarded this Certificate for being

Neither Absent Nor Tardy

during the school year ending June 191
Given at Eagle River, Wisconsin, this 26th
day of June 1917

Margaret Byrne
Teacher

A. J. Austin
County Superintendent

This Donaldson School award certificate was presented to pupil Vera Knoble for being "Neither Absent Nor Tardy" during the school year ending in June 1917. The Knoble family was among the first permanent settlers in the town of Donaldson, about two miles west of State Line, in the vicinity of the current Bear Trap Inn.

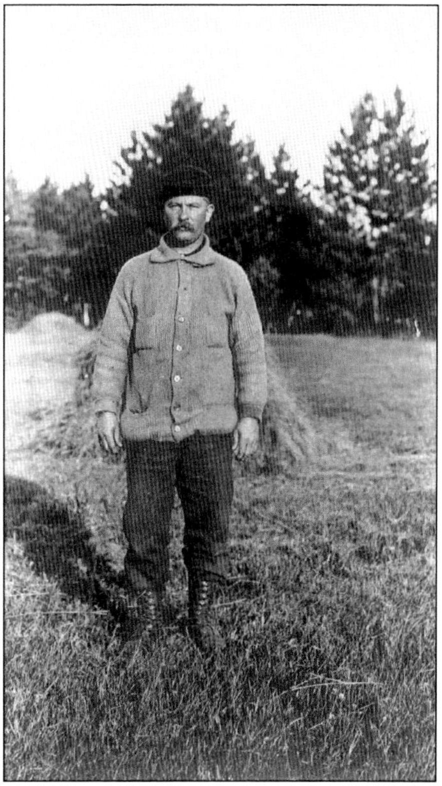

John Knoble, a resident of Donaldson, was a highly respected fishing and hunting guide. He was described as "a very picturesque character of the north woods and a fine marksman who was long on stories and cussing."

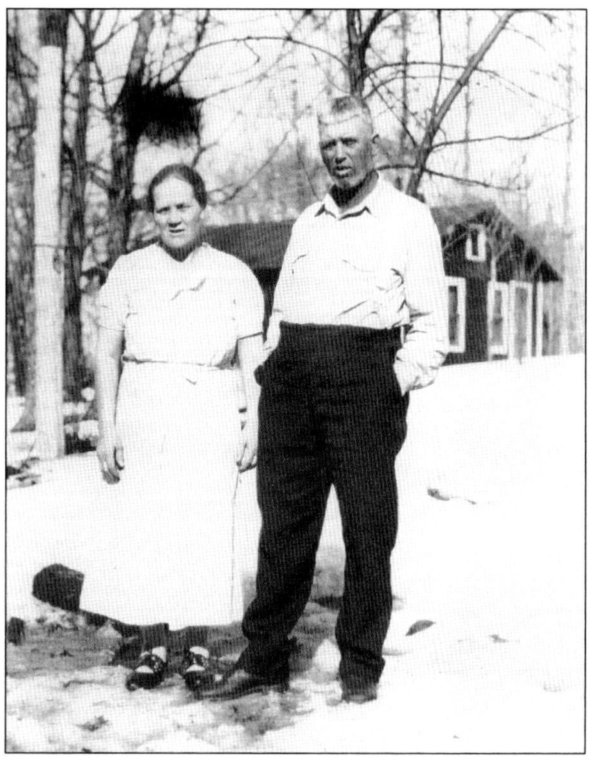

Agnes and Sylvester Caskey were among the first white settlers in the Land O' Lakes region. Around 1890 at the age of 10, Sylvester left his southern Wisconsin home and followed the Indian paths along the Wisconsin River until he reached its source on Lac Vieux Desert. There he settled and in 1904 married Agnes, a Swedish woman who worked for Harry Patterson's trading post. In 1925, Sylvester and Agnes built Sylvan Rest Cottages on the south shore of Lac Vieux Desert.

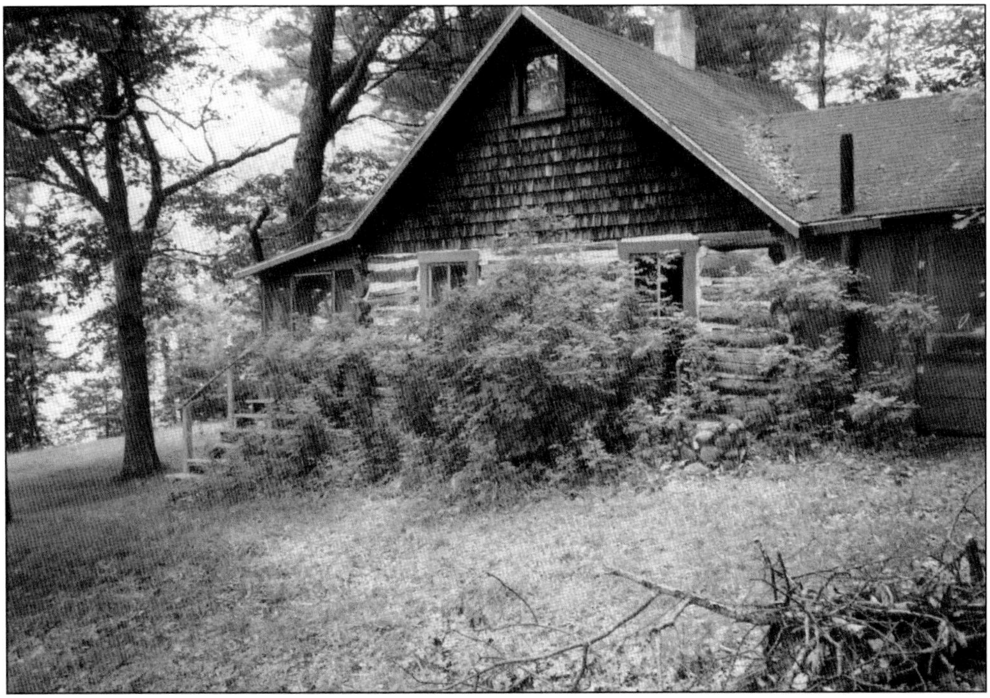

After Agnes and Sylvester Caksey were married, they built a log cabin along Lac Vieux Desert in 1905. The cabin remains today, as shown in this photograph.

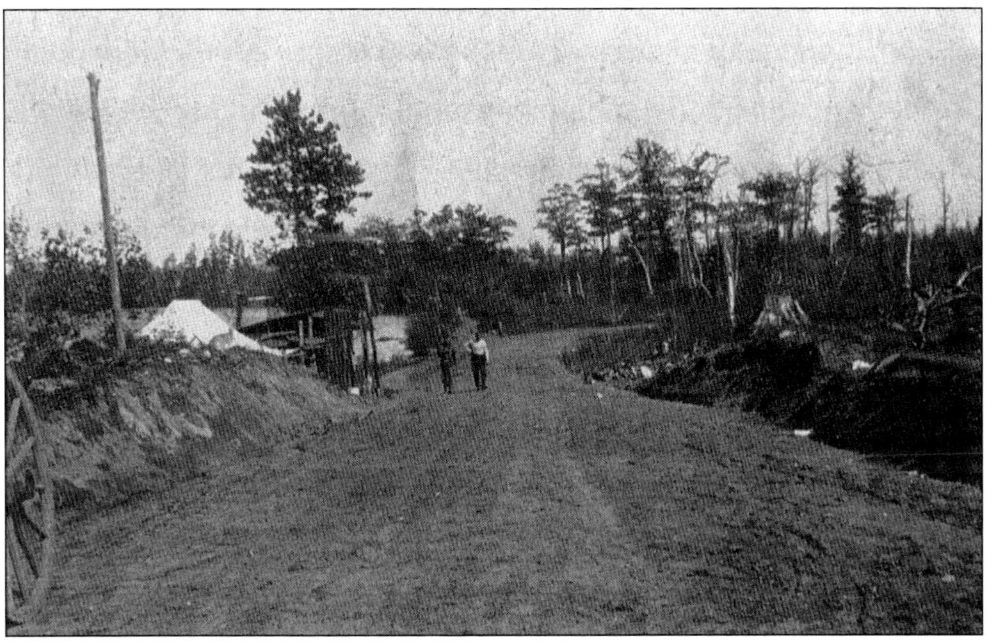

Roads in the early 20th century were either dusty, muddy, washed out, littered with horse manure, or so rutted from rains that they became temporarily impassible. The poor suspensions of wagons and early automobiles made for a rough and slow ride. Many found it was easier and faster to walk or ride a horse. This 1913 photograph shows the main tote road (presently Highway B) as it passes by the current public beach on the south shore of Black Oak Lake.

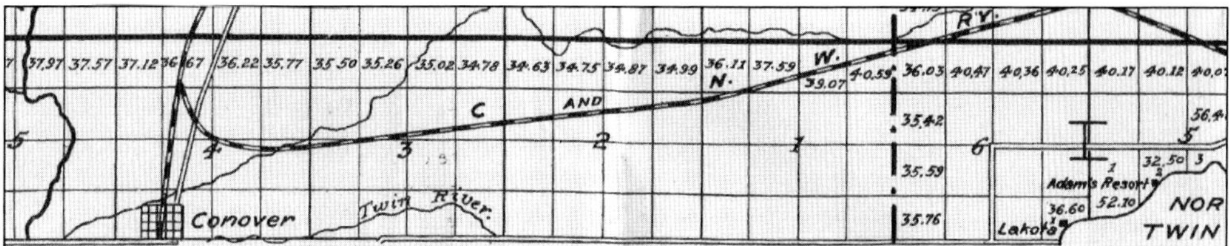

The Yale Tract

These lands now offered for sale comprise 12,000 acres of what is termed cut over lands, on which once grew one of the largest and densest forests in Northern Wisconsin. Most of the territory was covered with pine timber, frequently, however, interspersed with abundant quantities of sugar maple, birch, basswood, oak, poplar, hemlock and spruce. The pine has now been cut. The reasons why these lands have never been settled before are easily understood when the homeseeker realizes that this entire region has been dominated absolutely by the lumbering industry. Lumbermen discouraged settlers from coming into their districts. One small fire started by the settler clearing up his land was liable to destroy millions of dollars worth of timber.

However, all this is changed. The lands have passed into other hands. Farms have been opened up and cleared and the results in crops have been both amazing and enriching to the owners.

The possibilities for the farmer, fruit grower and stock raiser, that are offered on the Yale Tract, are apparent and will appeal to any intelligent man on inspection.

Considering the location, the superior quality of the soil, the water from ever-flowing crystal springs and streams on the lands, the diversity of profitable crops, the timber, the ready cash markets, the good wagon roads, the school and church privileges and last but not least the exceptional inducements offered to actual settlers to locate on these lands, a combination of advantages is afforded, which, we know can not be equalled elsewhere in the country today. Each of the above features will be truthfully treated further along in this folder, and any additional information desired will be honestly given.

THE LOCATION OF THE YALE TRACT

Study carefully the small map on this folder. You will observe, first, that this territory lies farther east and south than any of the cheap lands now offered for sale.

The Yale Tract is surrounded by such cities as Minneapolis and St. Paul to the west; Chicago, Milwaukee, Madison and others to the south; and Duluth, Ashland and the great copper and iron country to the north and east.

You will also observe that the Northwestern railway line runs directly north from Chicago to the Upper Peninsula of Michigan. That peninsula, without doubt, is today the richest area in iron and copper on the globe. The Chicago, Milwaukee & St. Paul also runs

After the lumber companies finished their work, they sold 12,000 acres of their land to the Yale Land Company of Minneapolis, Minnesota. Known as the Yale Tract, the land was divided into tracts between 20 and 320 acres that were offered to new owners. With no viable timber, the primary value of the land, according to the Yale Company, was said to be for farming, with "onions, beets, parsnips, carrots and potatoes doing equally well." The wagon roads were deemed "excellent," and existing train service assured that the lands were accessible from large cities. This brochure dates from around 1910.

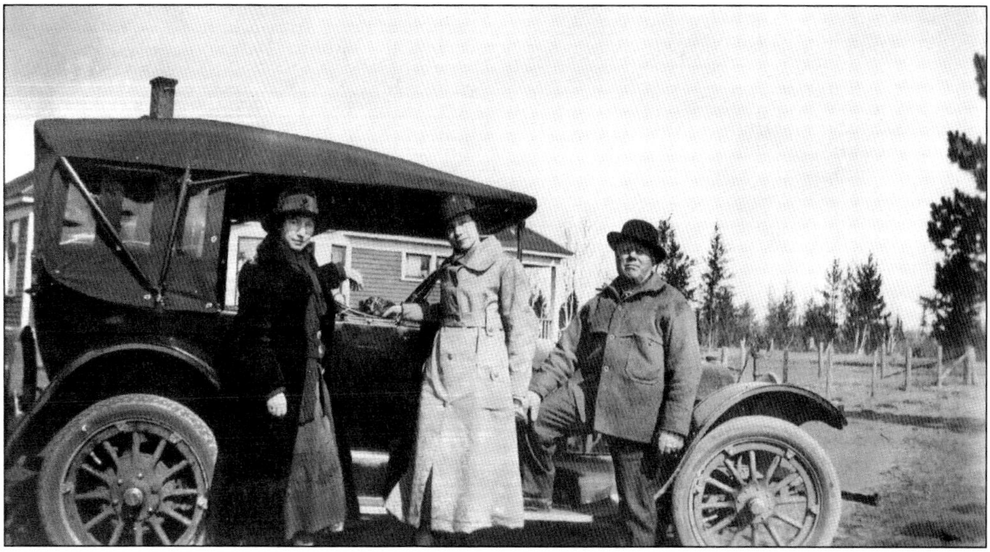

Peter LaChance (right) was born in Quebec, Canada, in 1865 and arrived in northern Wisconsin 28 years later. He purchased property that stretched from the present Bel-Air Motel west to the current town hall and built the town's first store. Pictured around 1922 with Peter are his wife, Mary (far left), and daughter-in-law Lulu (Dussault) LaChance. (Courtesy of the Jack LaChance Family Archives.)

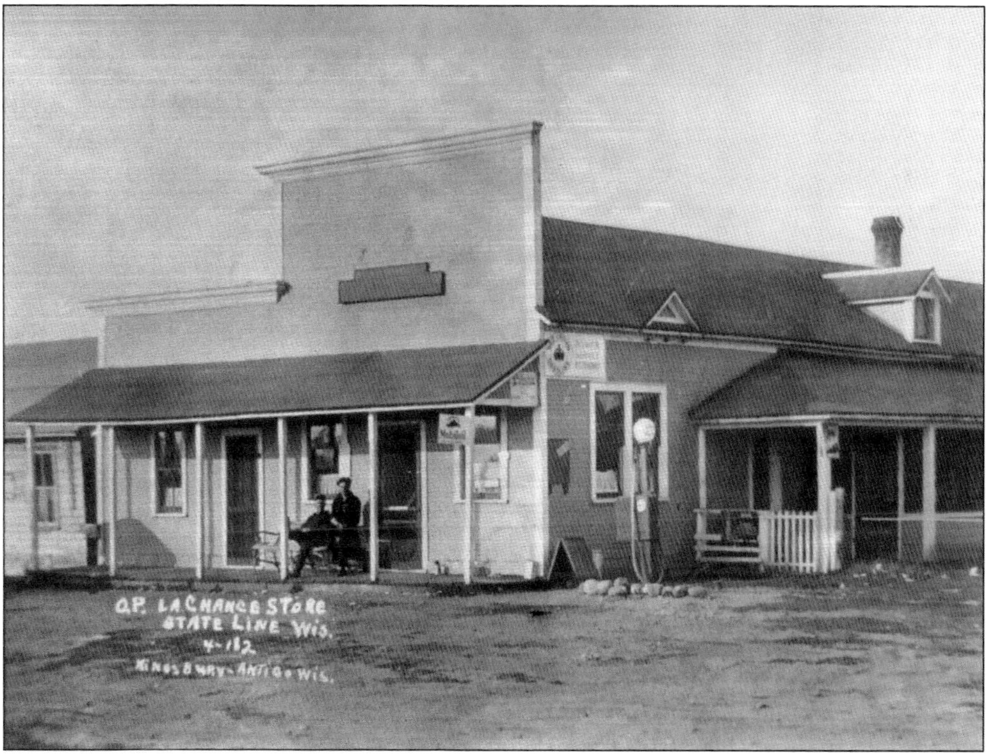

The first store in State Line was built by Peter LaChance in 1895 and housed a saloon, pool hall, telegraph office, and beauty parlor. This building burned in 1926 and was rebuilt by his son Oliver on the same location a year later. (Courtesy of the Jack LaChance Family Archives.)

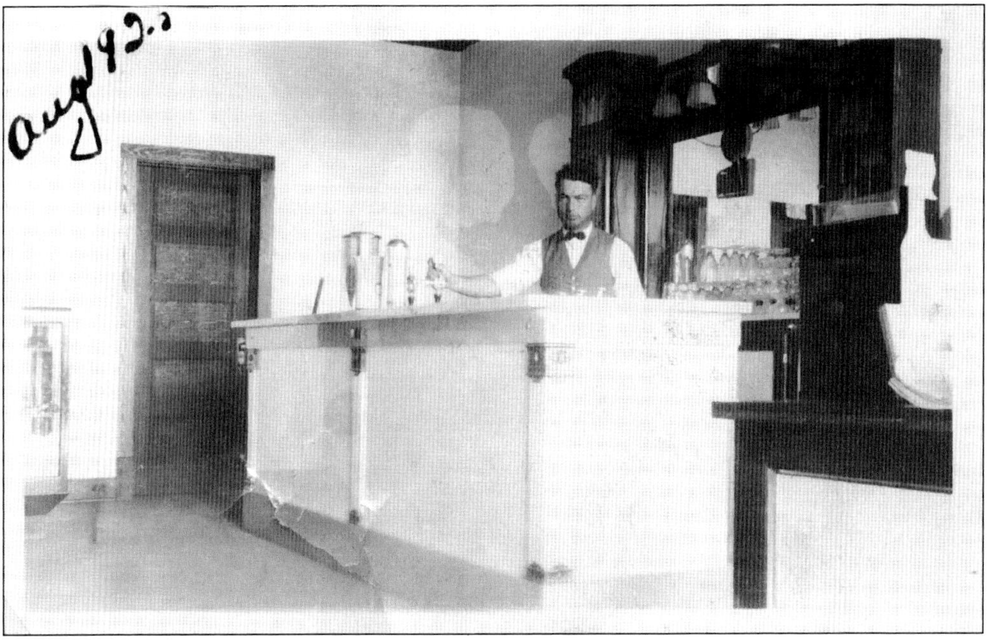

Around 1925, Oliver LaChance stands behind the bar of the original LaChance store, built by his father, Peter, in 1895. (Courtesy of the Jack LaChance Family Archives.)

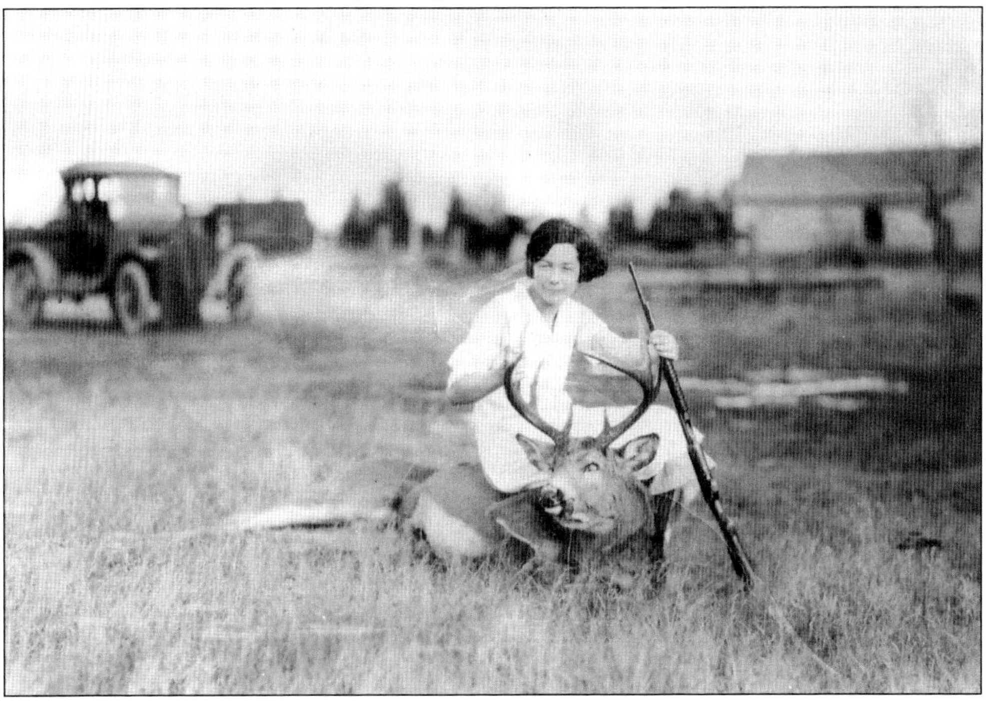

In 1934, one did not have to leave town to find wild game. At age 15, Lorraine LaChance, daughter of Oliver LaChance, shot a 10-point white-tailed buck near the LaChance home in "downtown" State Line. As of this book's publication date, Lorraine is currently 90 years old, healthy, and makes regular summer visits to Land O' Lakes from her residence in Tucson, Arizona. (Courtesy of the Jack LaChance Family Archives.)

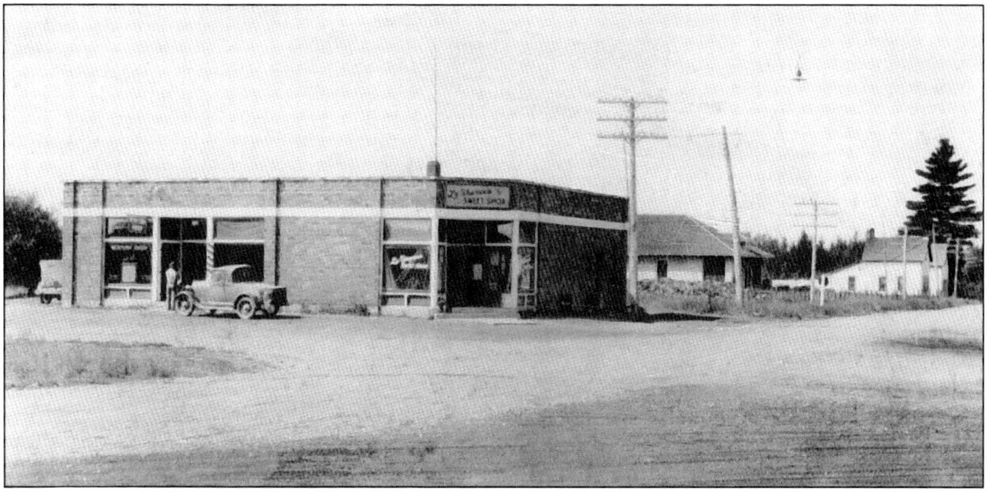

This photograph offers an excellent view of downtown State Line, looking west, in 1930. The buildings are, from left to right, Oliver LaChance's Tavern and Ice Cream Parlor, the LaChance family home, and boardinghouses owned by the LaChance family. The LaChance family owned much of property in State Line, north of today's Highway B. (Courtesy of the Jack LaChance Family Archives.)

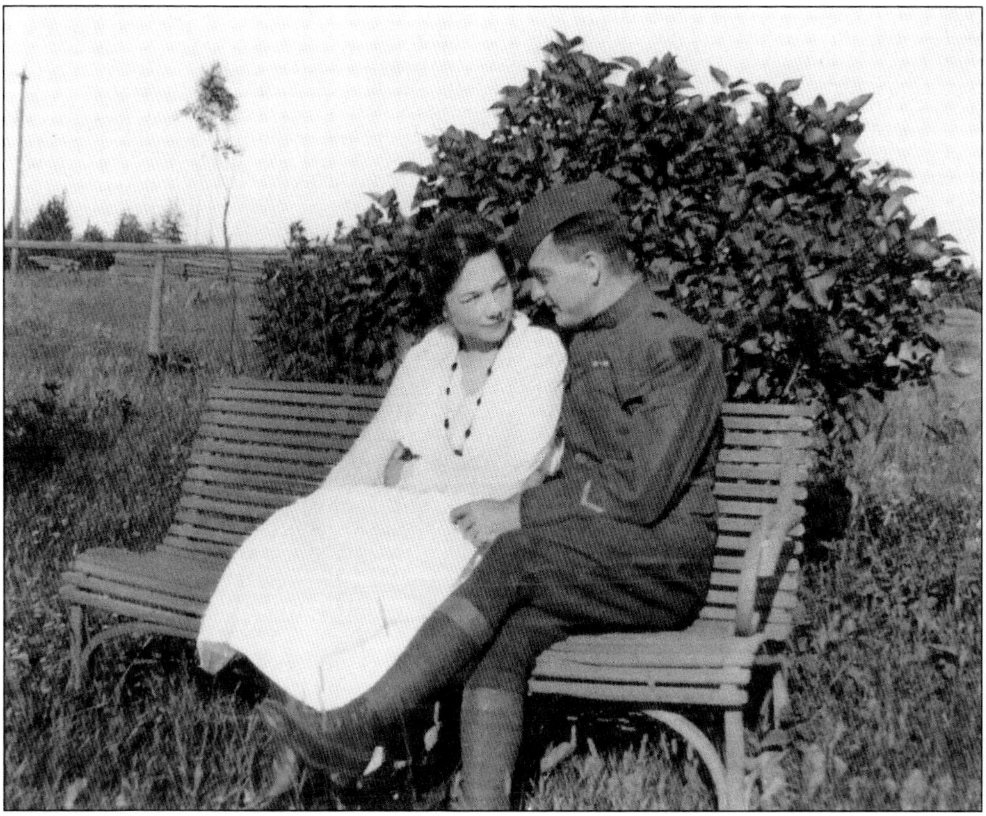

On July 18, 1919, Oliver LaChance returned to State Line after serving overseas in World War I. He is pictured with his wife, Lulu (Dussault) LaChance, behind the family home. (Courtesy of the Jack LaChance Family Archives.)

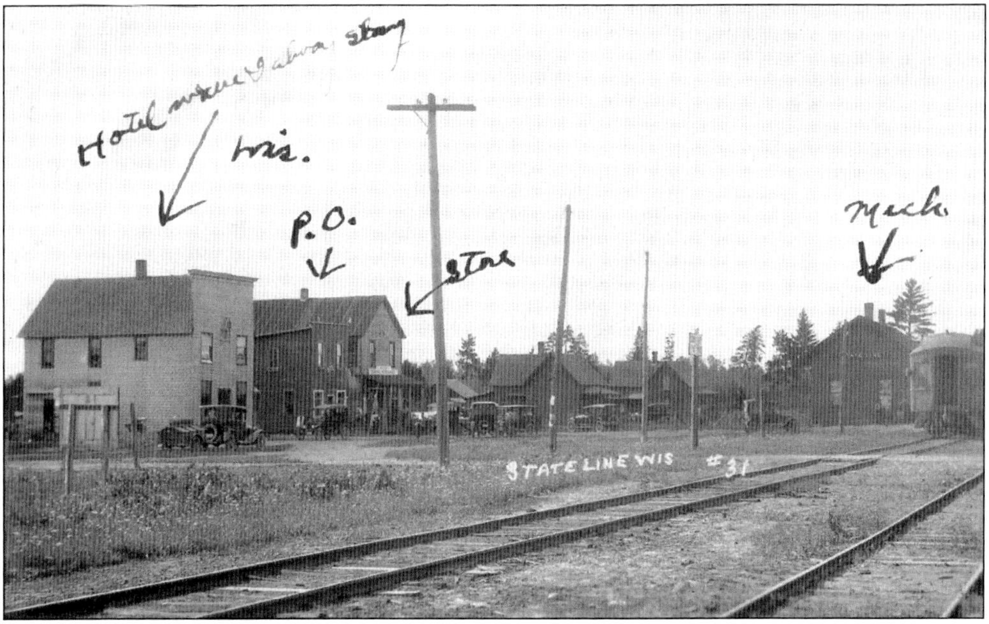

Viewed looking north, this is what downtown State Line looked like in 1920. The railroad depot on the right is in the approximate location of the current Land O' Lakes library. The buildings on the left, from front to back, are the Dickman Hotel and Bar, post office, Hutchinson's Store, and the Section House. Both the Dickman building and one of the Section Houses remain today as a retail store and private residence, respectively.

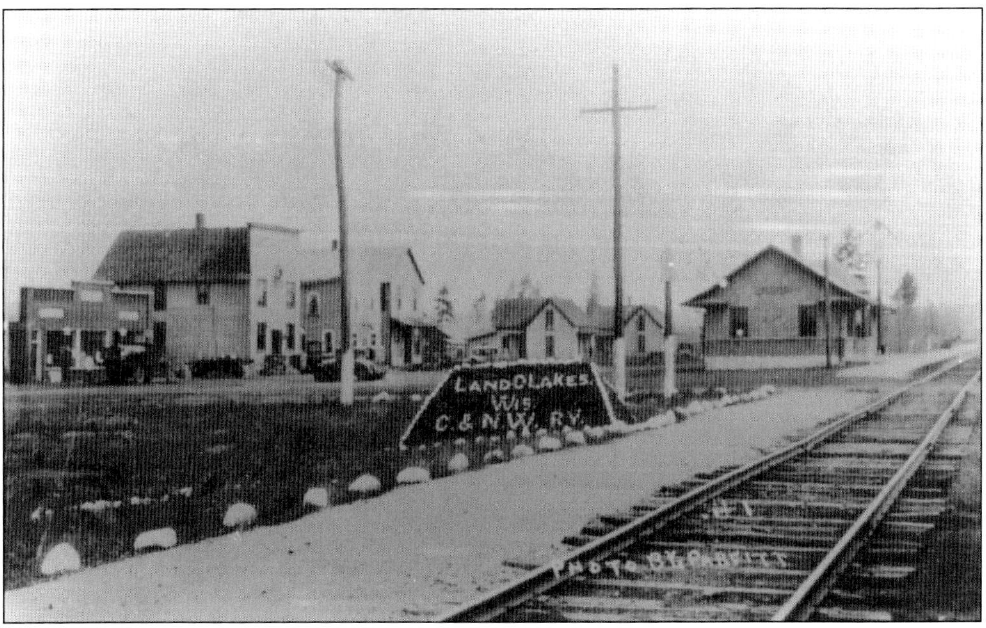

This is the same view as the photograph above, 10 years later in 1930. Note the addition of landscaping and Dickman's garage on the far left. The railroad depot is also new, having replaced the original building that burned in 1926. The town population in 1930 was 302 people.

When the train arrived, postmaster Washburn "Wash" Bates wheeled the mail to the post office across the street from the depot. Bates was the only postmaster of State Line and the first postmaster of Land O' Lakes when the town postal designation changed in 1926. He died in 1935 at age 75.

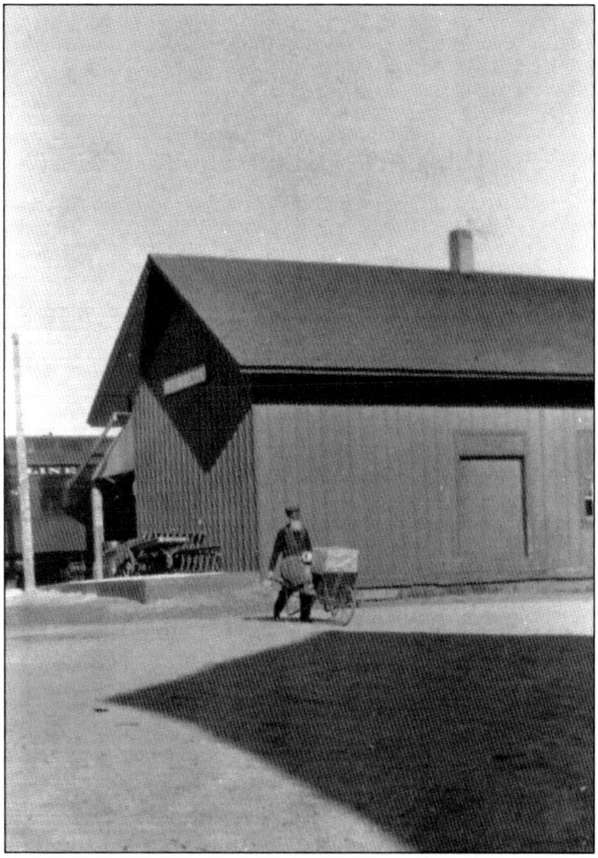

Pictured at the State Line Post Office in 1923 are, from left to right, Lena Benson Torres, Ella Bates (sister of George St. Clair, founder of the Black Oak Lake Resort), and postmaster Washburn "Wash" Bates.

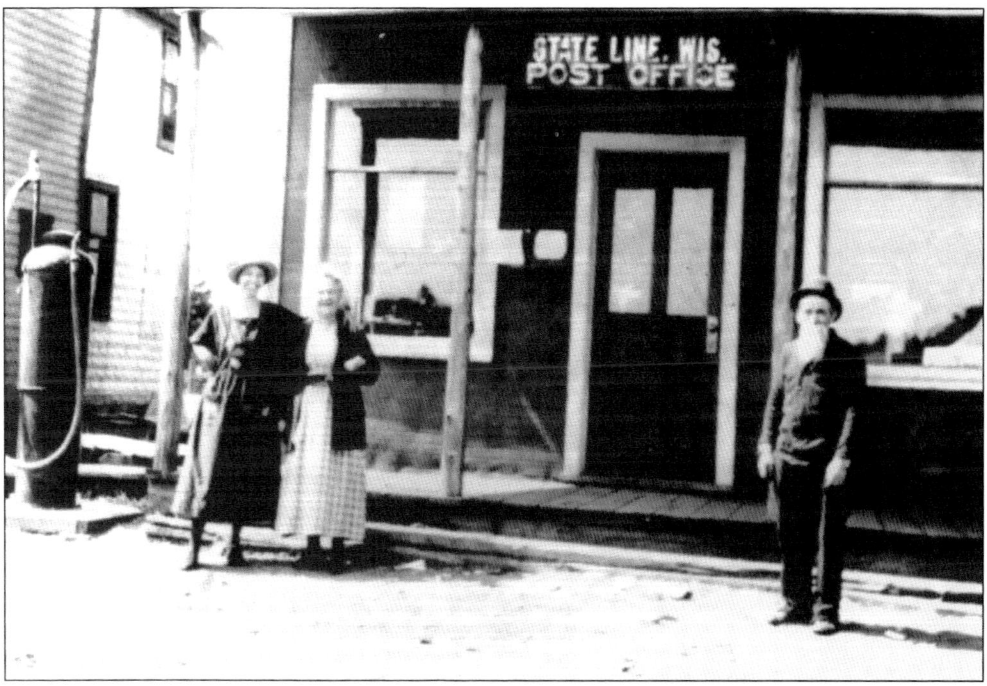

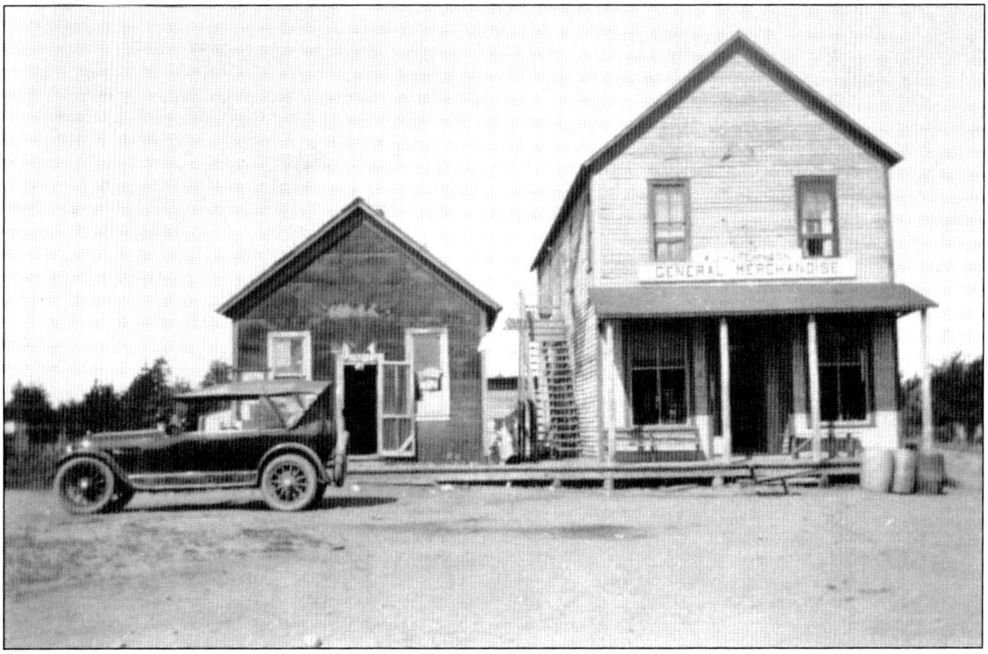

The sign above the large building reads, "J Hutchinson General Merchandise." During the early 1920s, Hutchinson's was one of only two stores in State Line, the other being operated by Peter LaChance at the present site of the Rusty Nail Tavern. The building next to Hutchinson's Store was torn down in the 1990s.

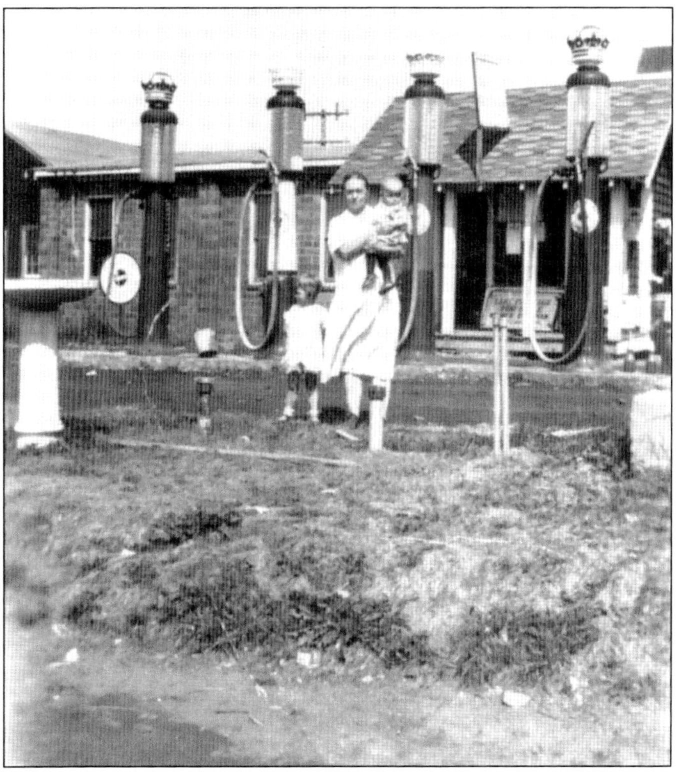

On August 6, 1910, Cora Dickman, standing by her mother, Lena, was the first child born in the town of State Line. Her parents, Lena and Julius Dickman, were one of the original families in Donaldson and State Line, and they raised six sons and two daughters. Cora's mother holds her sister Julia. Cora lived her entire life in Land O' Lakes and passed away in 2003 at age 92.

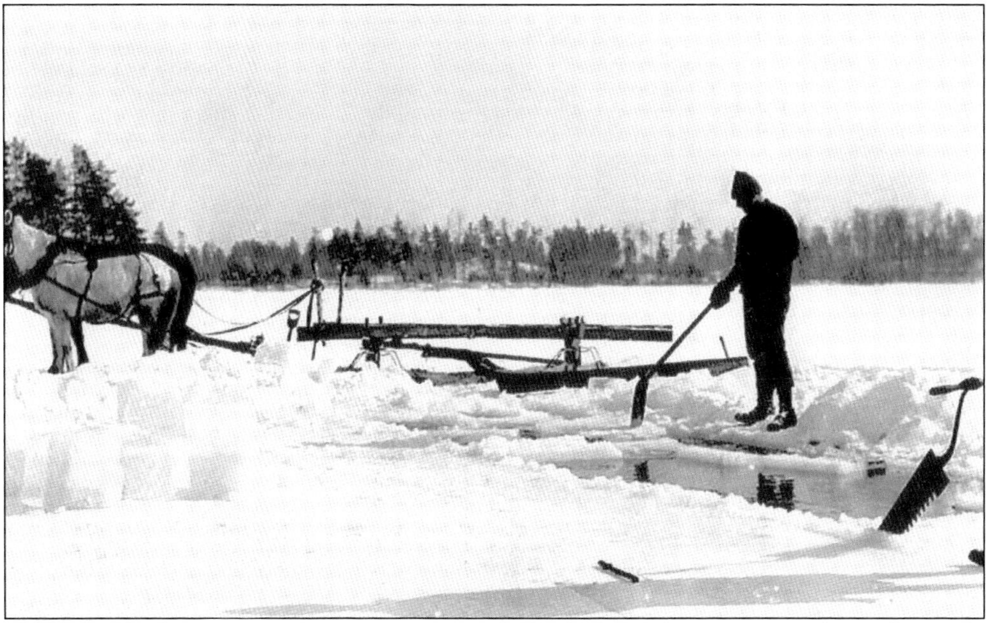

Ice blocks, cut from area lakes, were transported to icehouses to keep perishable goods fresh year-round. Before electric refrigeration, the demand for ice, both locally and in larger cities to the south, provided seasonal jobs for many State Line residents. This crew, pictured in the 1920s, works on Black Oak Lake.

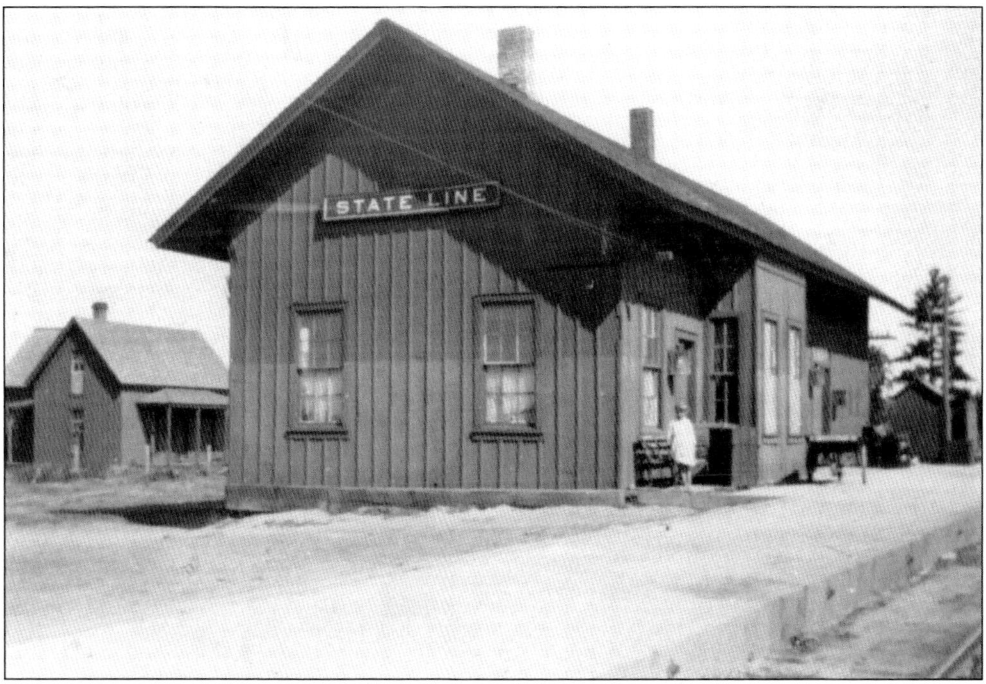

In 1916, when this photograph was taken, nearly everyone who arrived or departed State Line did so via this railroad depot. Cars were still a novelty, and roads were merely wagon trails. The post office building is on the left, and Cora Dickman stands next to the depot. At this time, the population of State Line was 70 people.

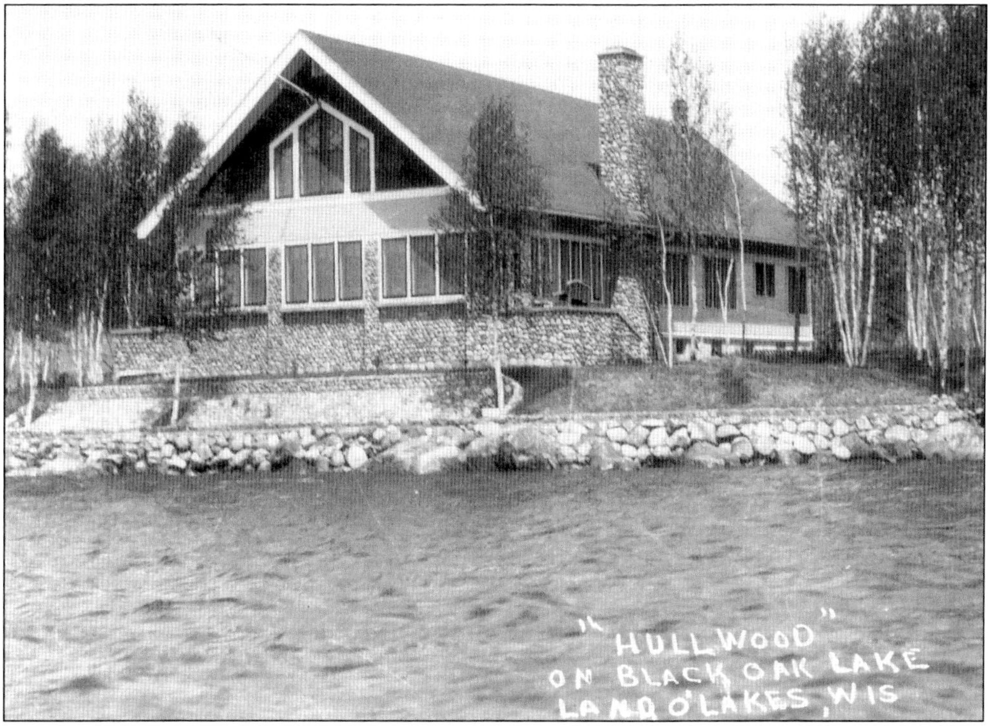

"Hullwood" was the first permanent cabin on Black Oak Lake, built by Ross Woodhull in 1921 on land purchased from the Brown Brothers Logging Company. The cabin and property were eventually sold to Jim Lowenstine, who razed "Hullwood" in 1989. Today, the Conserve School campus occupies the property, which was bequeathed by Lowenstine for the construction of a private high school.

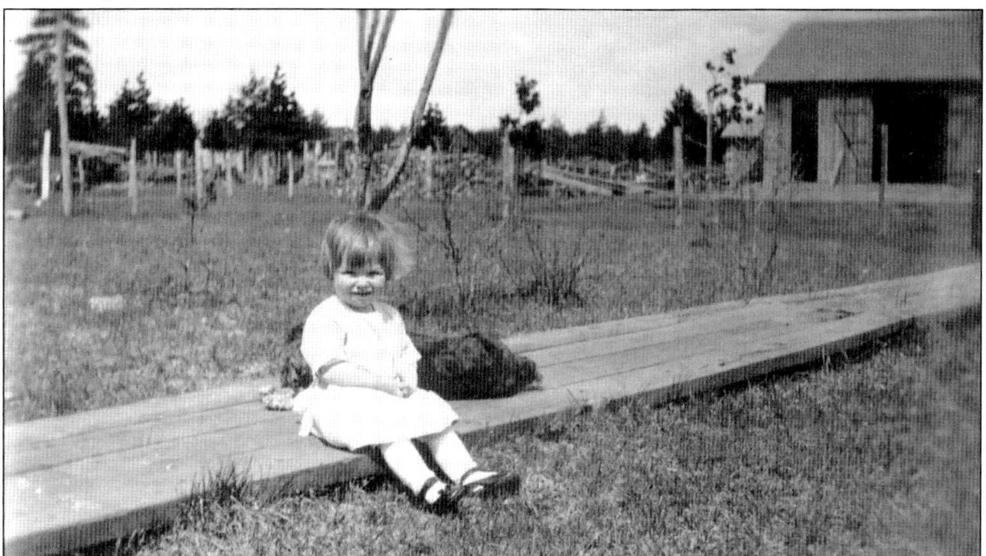

Around 1920, Oliver LaChance built the first sidewalk in State Line. It stretched from his store, west to his home, and past his boardinghouses. Pictured is his daughter Lorraine in 1922. (Courtesy of the Jack LaChance Family Archives.)

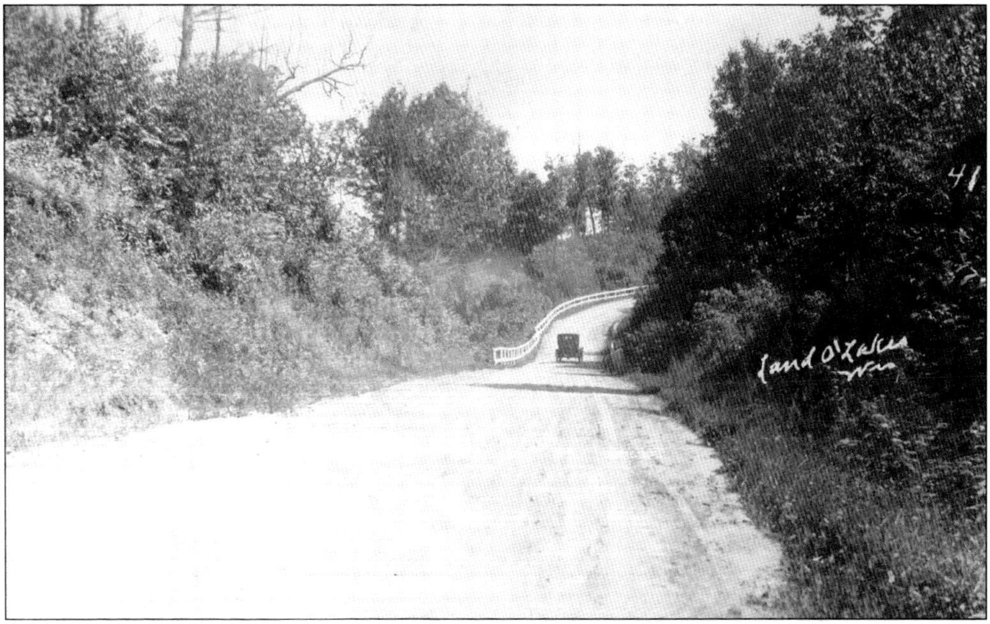

Indian and wagon trails were eventually widened and groomed to accommodate automobiles. Publicity brochures described the new roads as "having enough clay in the soil to make them hard and solid, and enough sand to make them dry even in rainy weather." This photograph depicts Highway B, west of Black Oak Lake.

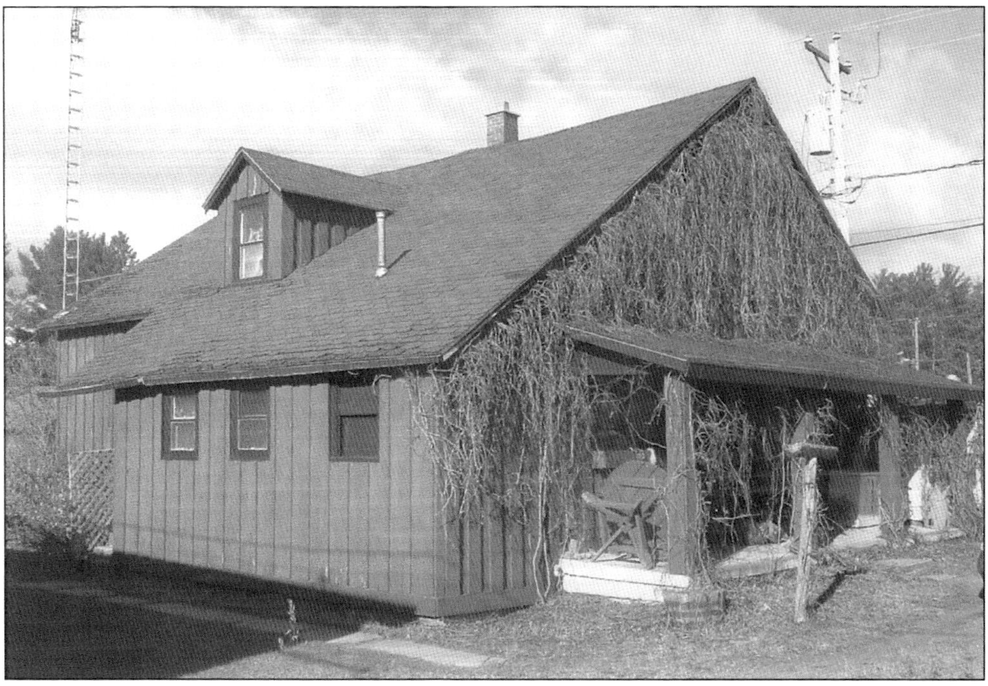

This building was constructed by Oliver LaChance in 1920 and was a popular nightspot for nearly two decades, with a saloon and dance hall on the lower level and boarding rooms on the second floor. Saturday night dances brought girls from Watersmeet, and Lulu LaChance earned a reputation for serving hearty dinners. (Photograph by author.)

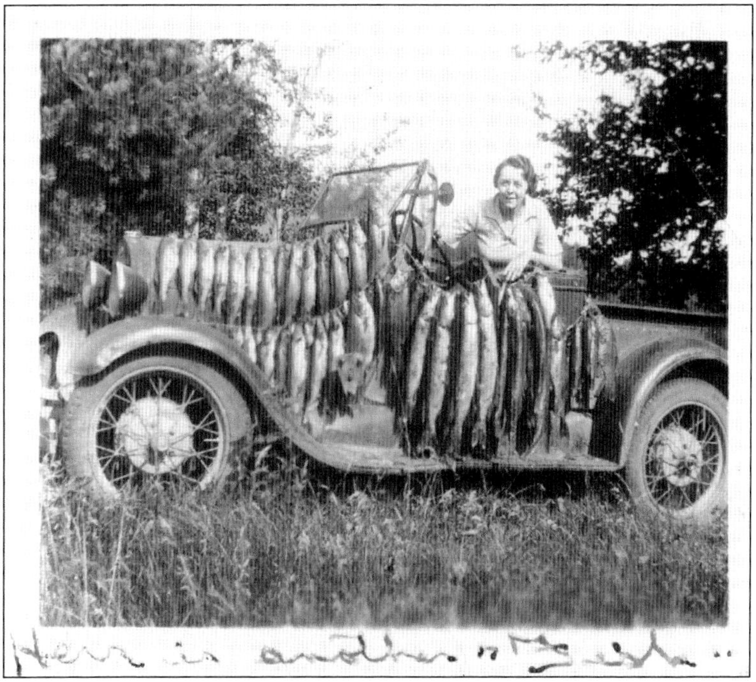

Photographs like this one of a Ford Model A draped with pike, walleye, and bass enticed sportsmen to vacation on the lakes surrounding State Line. Fishermen were promised they would catch their "limit in a minute," and the sport's popularity spawned the growth of many new fishing camps.

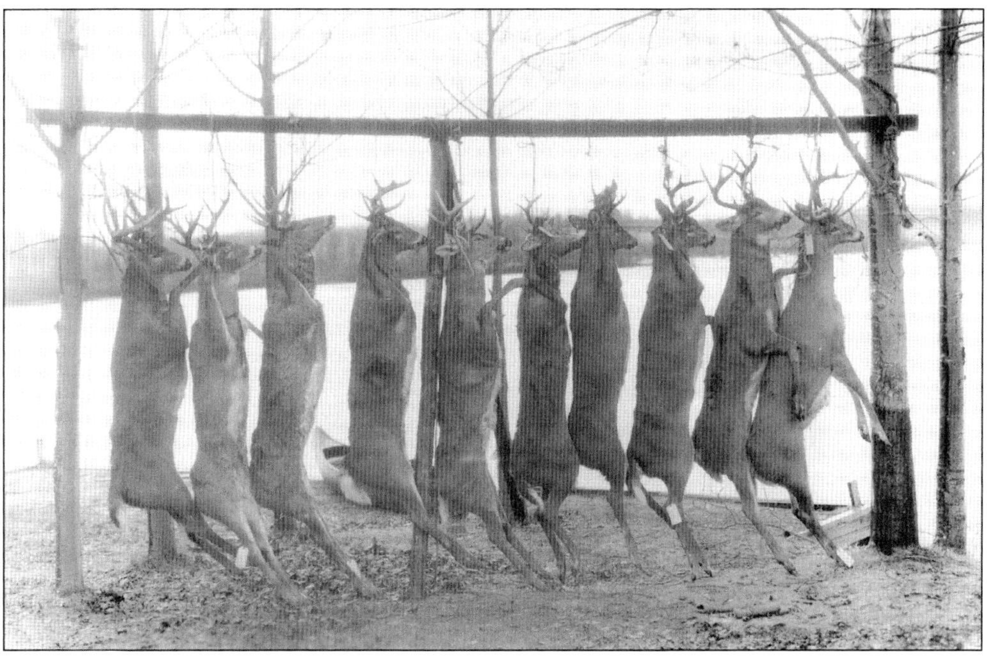

Ten white-tailed bucks hang from a "meat pole" at Bent's Camp Resort. Ample white-tailed deer brought hunters into the region, often in large groups for the annual "deep camp" tradition. Venison was a staple at most area resorts, and during Prohibition, it was traded for bootlegged liquor brought in from Chicago. Venison was a delicacy in many Chicago restaurants.

Operated by the first three generations of the LaChance family from 1895 until the 1950s, the LaChance Store, Tavern, Restaurant, and Ice Cream Parlor was the meeting place and social center of Land O' Lakes. This menu is from the early 1930s. (Courtesy of the Jack LaChance Family Archives.)

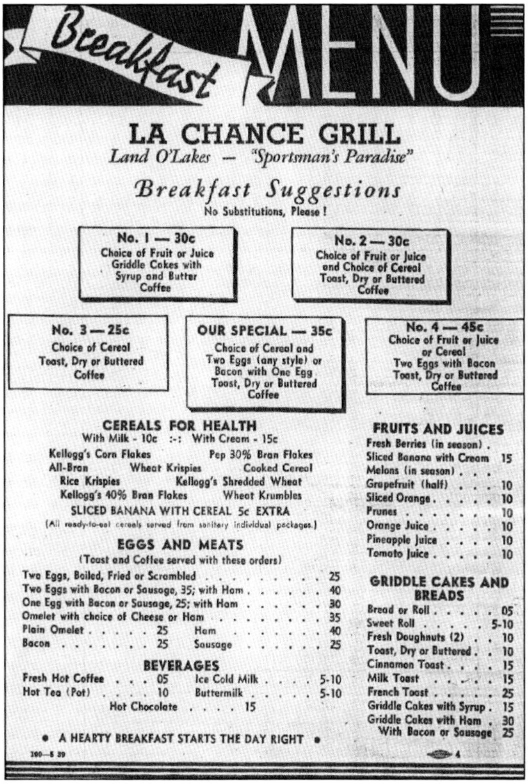

Breakfast MENU

LA CHANCE GRILL

Land O'Lakes — "Sportsman's Paradise"

Breakfast Suggestions

No Substitutions, Please!

No. 1 — 30c
Choice of Fruit or Juice
Griddle Cakes with Syrup and Butter
Coffee

No. 2 — 30c
Choice of Fruit or Juice and Choice of Cereal
Toast, Dry or Buttered
Coffee

No. 3 — 25c
Choice of Cereal
Toast, Dry or Buttered
Coffee

OUR SPECIAL — 35c
Choice of Cereal and Two Eggs (any style) or Bacon with One Egg
Toast, Dry or Buttered
Coffee

No. 4 — 45c
Choice of Fruit or Juice or Cereal
Two Eggs with Bacon
Toast, Dry or Buttered
Coffee

CEREALS FOR HEALTH

With Milk - 10c :-: With Cream - 15c

Kellogg's Corn Flakes — Pep 30% Bran Flakes
All-Bran — Wheat Krispies — Cooked Cereal
Rice Krispies — Kellogg's Shredded Wheat
Kellogg's 40% Bran Flakes — Wheat Krumbles

SLICED BANANA WITH CEREAL 5c EXTRA

(All ready-to-eat cereals served from sanitary individual packages.)

EGGS AND MEATS

(Toast and Coffee served with these orders)

Two Eggs, Boiled, Fried or Scrambled	25
Two Eggs with Bacon or Sausage, 35; with Ham	40
One Egg with Bacon or Sausage, 25; with Ham	30
Omelet with choice of Cheese or Ham	35
Plain Omelet	25
Ham	40
Bacon	25
Sausage	25

BEVERAGES

Fresh Hot Coffee	05
Ice Cold Milk	5-10
Hot Tea (Pot)	10
Buttermilk	5-10
Hot Chocolate	15

FRUITS AND JUICES

Fresh Berries (in season)	
Sliced Banana with Cream	15
Melons (in season)	
Grapefruit (half)	10
Sliced Orange	10
Prunes	10
Orange Juice	10
Pineapple Juice	10
Tomato Juice	10

GRIDDLE CAKES AND BREADS

Bread or Roll	05
Sweet Roll	5-10
Fresh Doughnuts (2)	10
Toast, Dry or Buttered	10
Cinnamon Toast	15
Milk Toast	15
French Toast	25
Griddle Cakes with Syrup	15
Griddle Cakes with Ham	30
With Bacon or Sausage	25

• A HEARTY BREAKFAST STARTS THE DAY RIGHT •

300—5 39 4

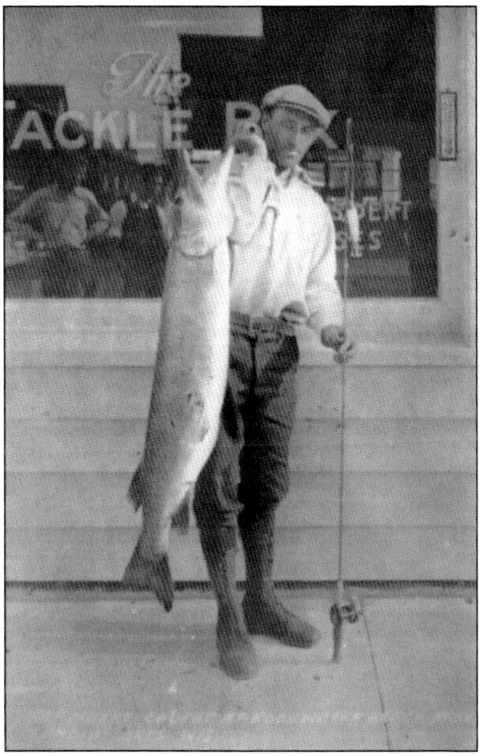

This photograph appeared in a 1930 brochure promoting tourism in Land O' Lakes. It read, in part, "For those who seek health and relief from frayed nerves there are sanctuaries deep in the woods beside still waters that restore the soul."

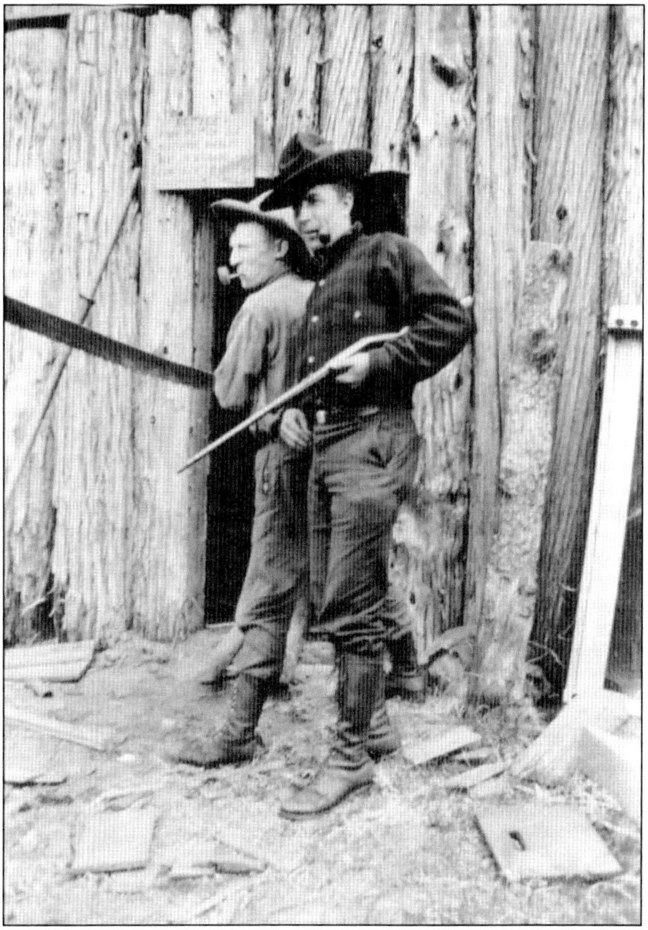

Dressed in wool shirts and pants, hats, and lace-up leather boots, these "real men" of Land O' Lakes pose outside of an icehouse in 1930. When dusted with sawdust and properly stacked, ice blocks cut from winter lakes kept perishable goods fresh through the summer. The sign above the man on the left reads, "Fish put on ice must have owners name or they will be confiscated."

Early fishing trips coordinated by the local guides and resorts usually included a shore lunch of the morning's catch. Men and women dressed for such affairs, viewing them as social functions with good friends and family.

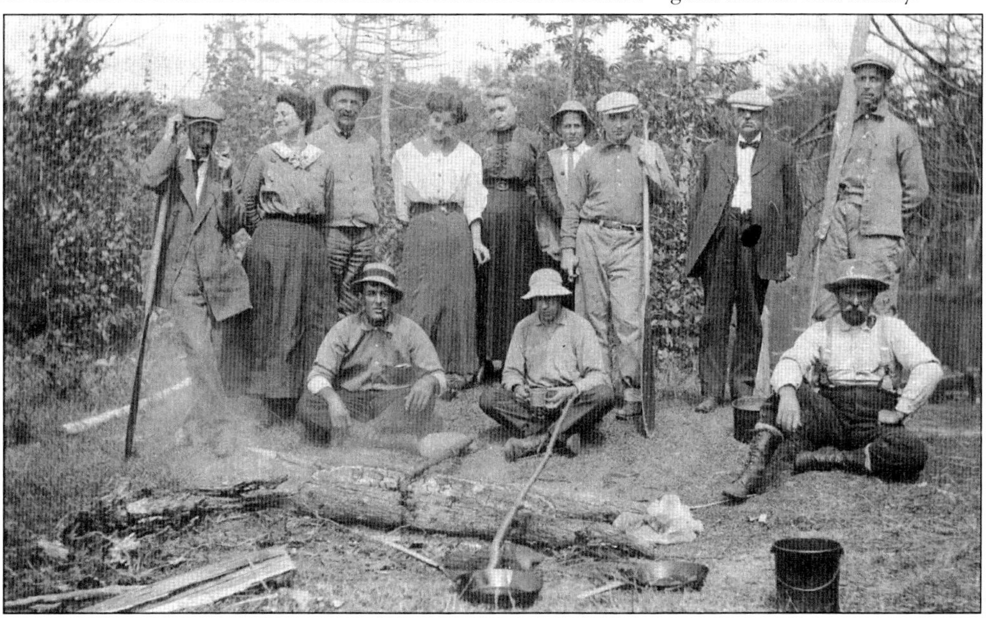

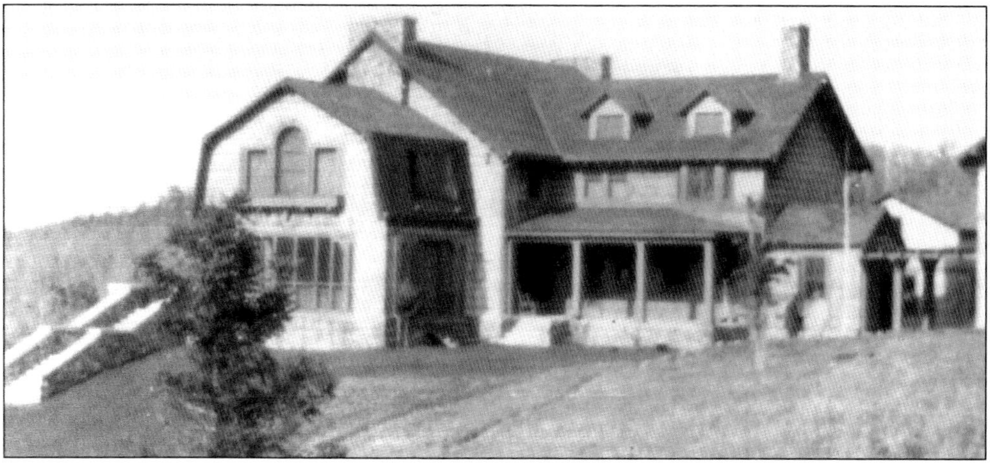

In 1916, the 20-room mansion "Summerwind" was completed along West Bay Lake by Robert P. LaMont, the future secretary of commerce in the Hoover administration. In 1980, *Life* magazine named "Summerwind" as one of the most haunted places in the United States. Although LaMont was skeptical of "ghosts," an apparition appeared in his kitchen, which he shot at with his revolver. In the 1970s, contractors refused to work on the home, citing missing tools and rooms changing shape. The mansion burned to the ground after a lightening strike and fire in June 1988.

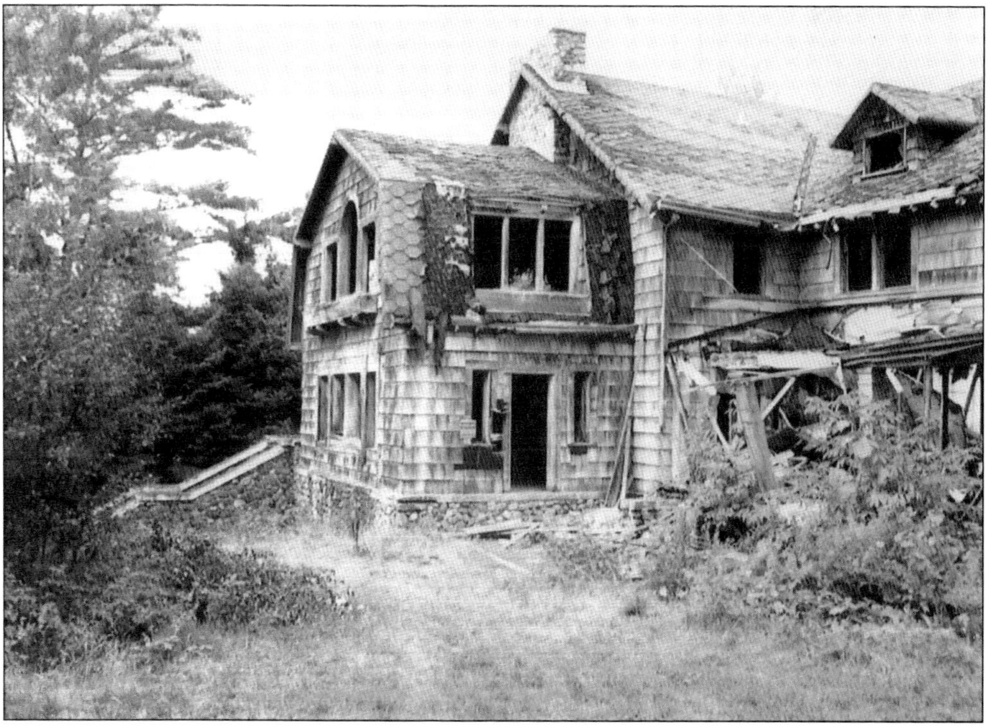

By the early 1980s, "Summerwind" was dilapidated and abandoned. After LaMont's death in 1948, the mansion had various owners, most of whom had their ambitious renovation plans thwarted by paranormal circumstances. In 1970, the last occupants, Ginger and Arnold Hinshaw, discovered a mummified skull in a crawl space and reported that closed windows and doors mysteriously reopened overnight. The wife eventually attempted suicide, and the husband was driven mad. They moved out six months later.

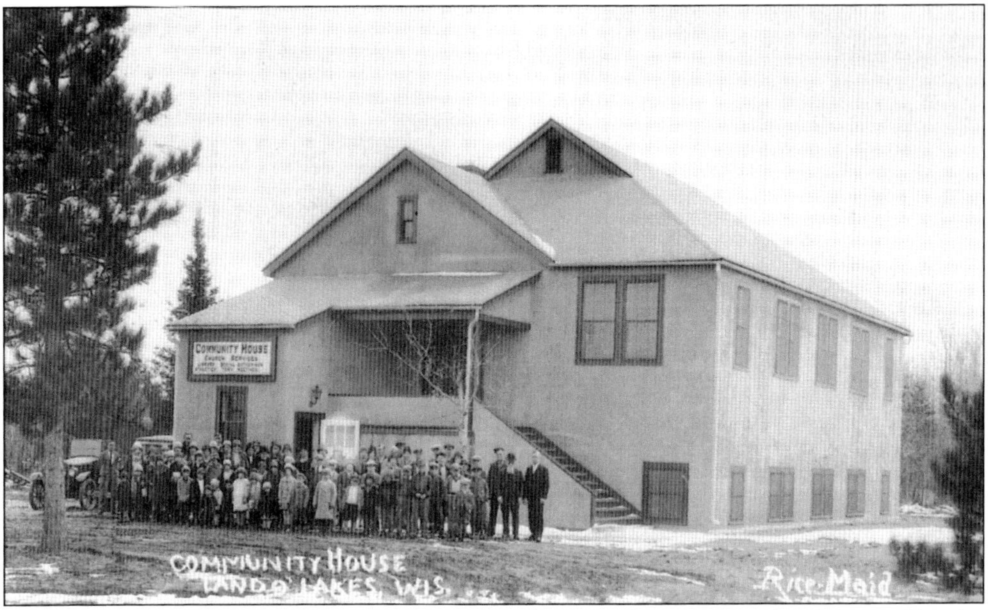

The Land O' Lakes Community House (town hall) was built in 1927 on land donated by the Ferry-Hill family. All four of the current Land O' Lakes churches held services in the Community House until funds were raised for their own facilities. Standing outside the building is a 1930 Sunday school class.

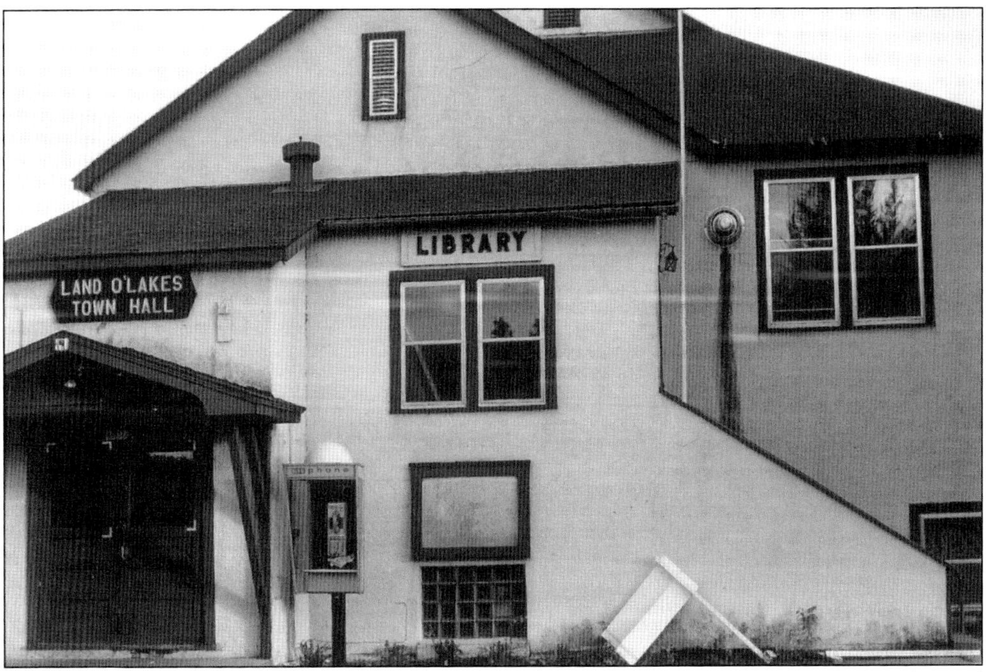

For 70 years, the Land O' Lakes Town Hall, originally known as the Community House, housed the town library, church services, official town business, local lake association meetings, dances, plays, card parties, and basketball games. Situated directly east of the current firehouse, it was razed in 2001.

Two

Land O' Lakes is Born

Early Stores, Restaurants, Clubs, Main Street, and People

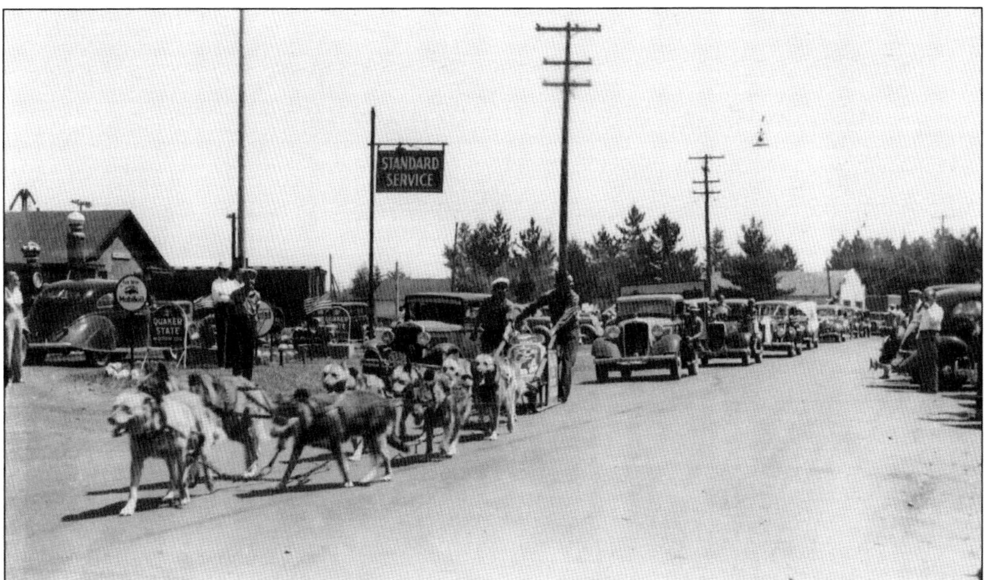

The Land O' Lakes Fourth of July parade in 1942 was led by Julius "Dude" Dodge and his dog team. Dodge founded and owned the Tia Juana Restaurant and Night Club at the junction of Highways B and E and often used his dog team for transportation during the winter and for entertaining tourists and residents in the summer.

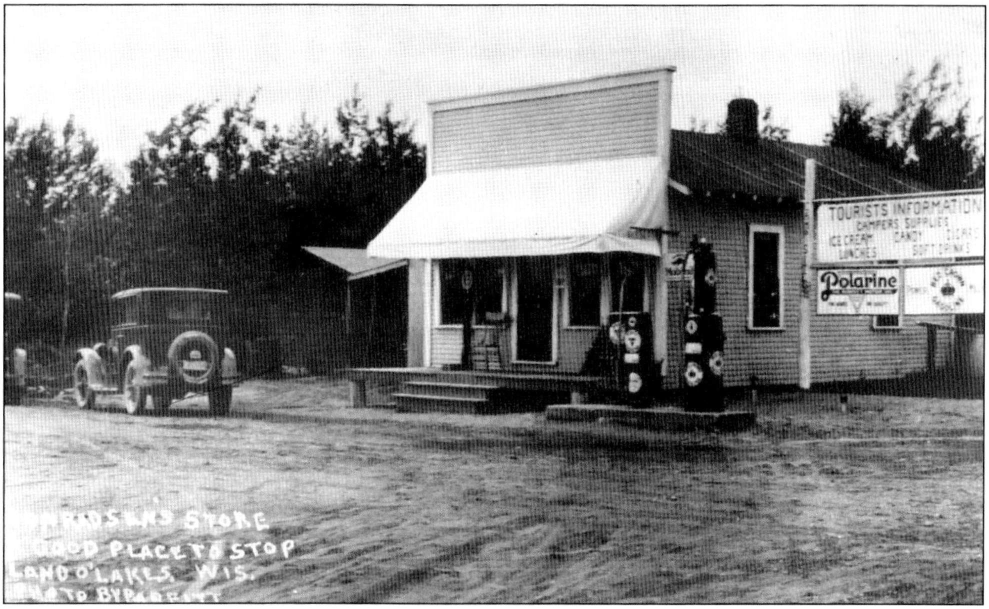

Gus Conradsen operated a gas station, café, and information center at the junction of what is now the northwest corner of State Highway 45 County Highway B (above). In the early 1930s, Conradsen sold his operation to a man named Harrington who rebuilt a more modern facility (below). In 1937, the property was purchased by John King, who built a bowling alley, barroom, and eventually the Gateway Inn.

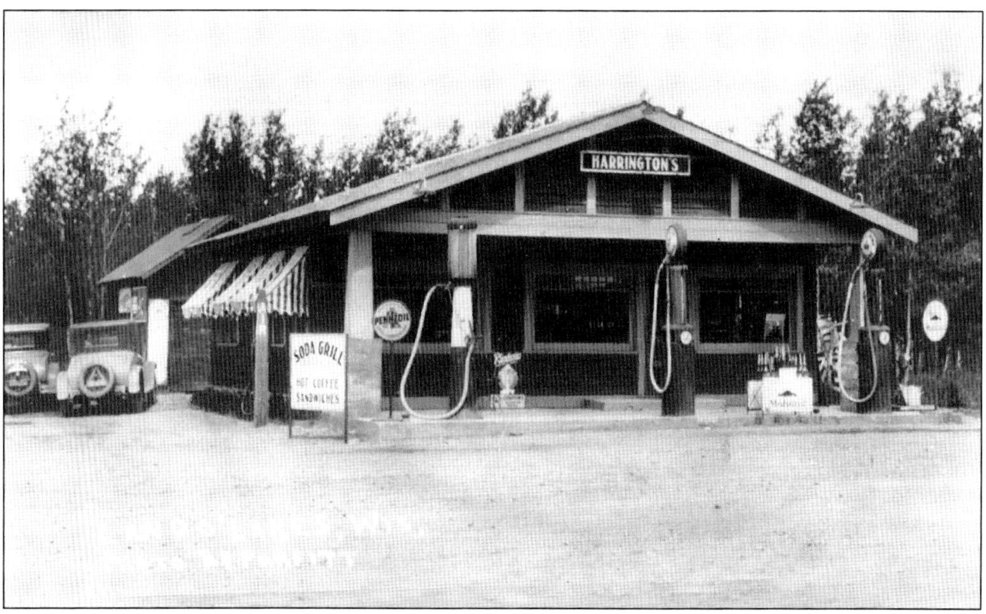

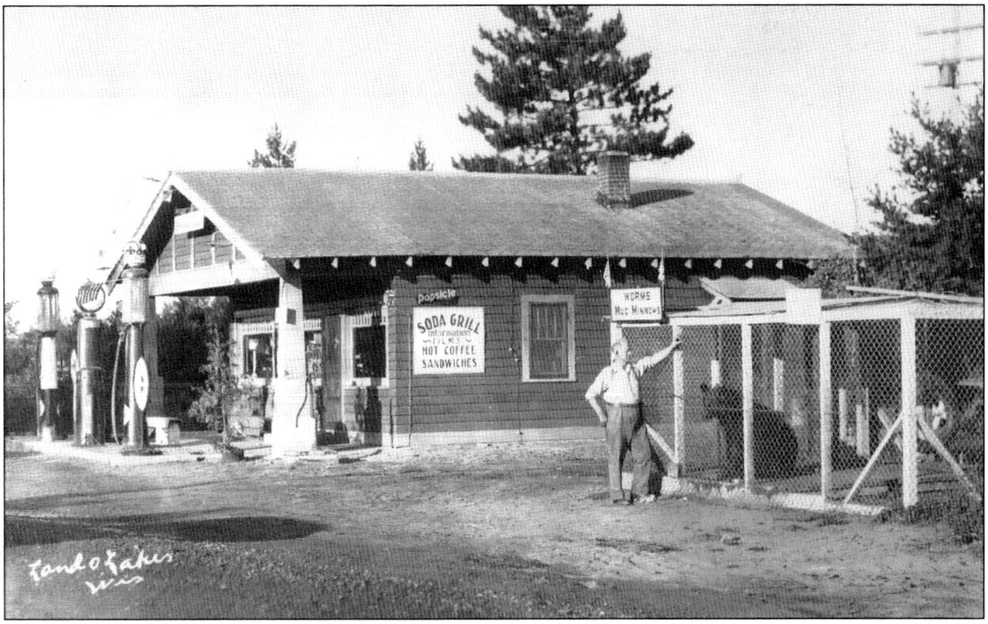

This photograph from the early 1930s shows the original bear cage at the Black Bear soda fountain, store, and gas station (formerly Conradsen's Store) on the northwest corner of Highways 45 and B. William Moenning (pictured) and his wife, Ida, ran the station for several years. For a dime, customers could feed the bears a pop-bottle of sugar water, dispensed via a chute into their cage. The bears would drink from the bottle, holding it with their front paws.

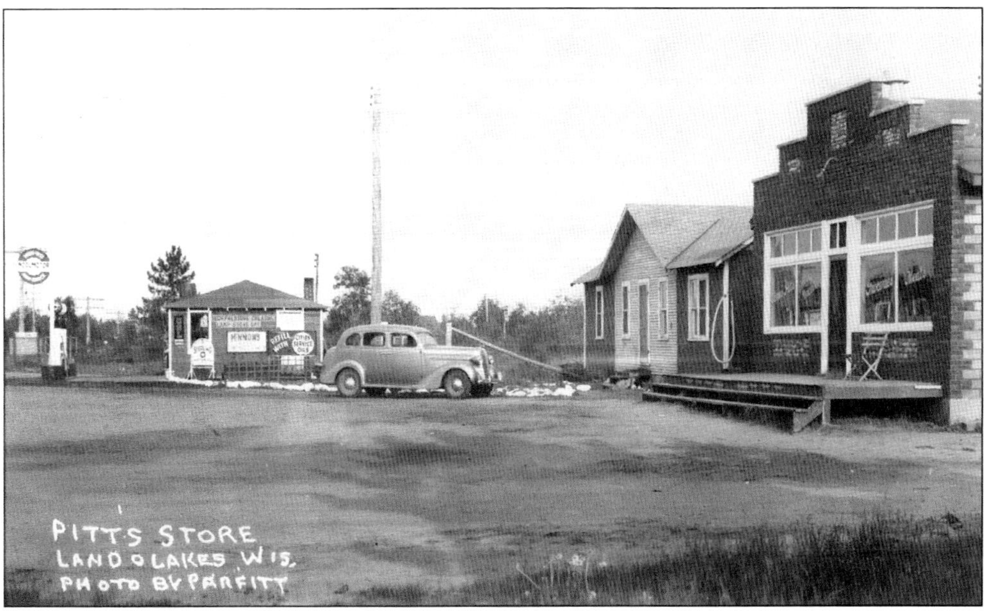

In the early 1930s, Pitts Grocery Store was at the heart of the Land O' Lakes business district along with LaChance's Store and Saloon, Dickman's Garage, the Hi Hat Club, and the Tackle Box.

Land O' Lakes Wisconsin Directory of Residents - 1938

Adams, Florence ... Land O'Lakes, teacher, State Line School
Adkins, Francis (Eloise) ... Land O'Lakes, laborer
Adkins, Roscoe (Ida) ... Land O'Lakes, laborer
Adkins, Virgil (Mae) ... Land O'Lakes, laborer
Aldrich, Claude (Mildred) ... Land O'Lakes, plasterer, own business
Allard, Peter (widower) ... Land O'Lakes, laborer
Babcock, Fred I ... Land O'Lakes, minister, Community Church
Baker, Burdette B (Leona) ... Land O'Lakes, bookkeeper, Kneeth Bros
Bawman, Chas (Cynthia) ... Land O'Lakes, cabins
Bent, Austin (Mary) ... Land O'Lakes, machinist, own business
Bent, Lawrence ... Land O'Lakes, guide, Camp Tenderfoot C Lundberg
Bent, Ronald (Mildred) ... Land O'Lakes, caretaker,
Mamie Lake R W McKinnon
Bingenheimer, Raymond ... Land O'Lakes, guide and caretaker,
Bloomquist Harold ... Land O'Lakes, laborer
Bloomquist, John E (Elizabeth) ... Land O'Lakes, laborer
Bloomquist, John Sr (widower) ... Land O'Lakes, laborer
Bloomquist, Theodore (Hilma) ... Land O'Lakes, laborer
Bruss, Harold ... Land O' Lakes, mechanic, Land O'Lakes Motor Co Dickman Bros
Buchanan, Louis L (widower) ... Land O'Lakes, map maker, own business
Butler, Emil ... Land O'Lakes, laborer, Kneeth Bros
Caniff, Jacob A (Emma) ... Land O'Lakes, carpenter
Carlson, Ernest E (Marie) ... Land O'Lakes, farmer
Carper, James D (Florence) ... Land O'Lakes, bldg carpenter
Caudill, Henry (Maudie) ... Land O'Lakes, gun repairer, self employed
Caudill, Lillian ... Land O'Lakes
Caudill, Ray ... Land O'Lakes
Cestkowski, Frank (Dorothy) ... Land O'Lakes, butcher and
depot helper, C & N W Depot H A Wilde
Chart, Cara ... Land O'Lakes, bookeeper, Land O'Lakes, Motor Co Dickman Bros
Chart, Stanley (Bernice) ... Land O'Lakes, caretaker, Black Oak Lake R A Woodshull
Christensen, Chris ... Land O'Lakes, carpenter, Carper & Turnquist
Christensen, Oswald ... Land O'Lakes, mechanic, Land O'Lakes, Motor Co
Dickman Bros
Coate, Reynold ... Land O'Lakes, caretaker, Tenderfoot Lake G Rohr
Coe, Joe ... Land O'Lakes, caretaker, Forest Lake G Faulber
Conradsen, August (Marie) ... Land O'Lakes, cabins
Cooper, Herbert W (Adella) ... Land O'Lakes, retired
Croaker, Harvey ... Land O'Lakes, laborer, Black Oak Resort G St Clair

In 1938, the population of Land O' Lakes was approximately 200 people. This is the first page from the 1938 town directory of residents.

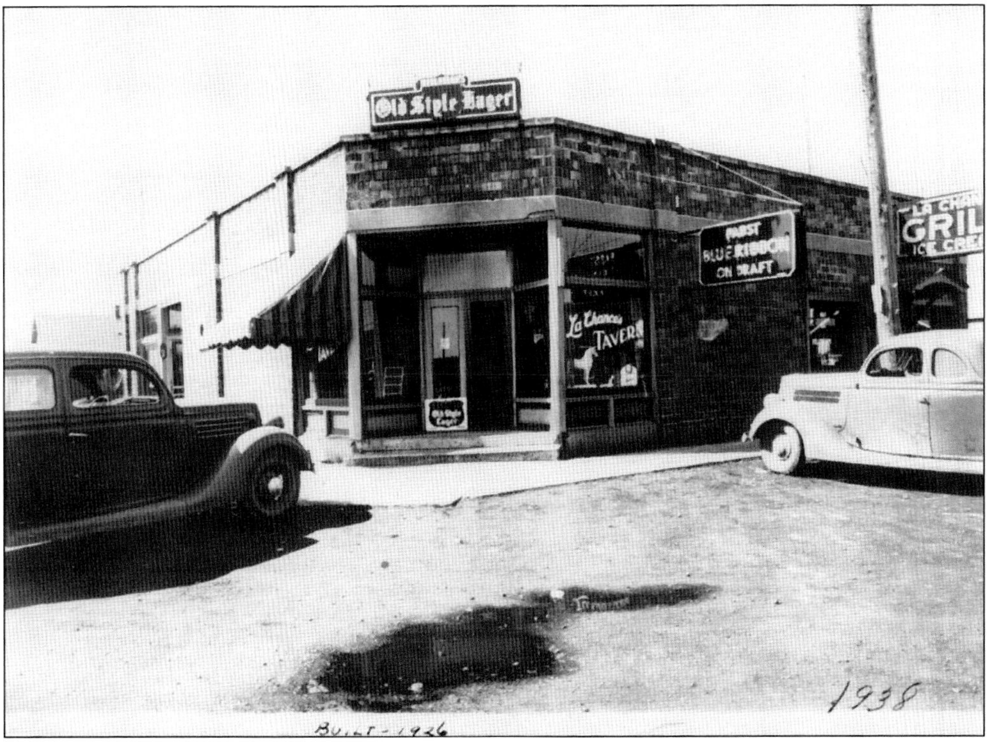

After the original LaChance Store burned in 1926, Peter's son Oliver rebuilt the facility and added a tavern, grill, and ice cream parlor. (Courtesy of the Jack LaChance Family Archives.)

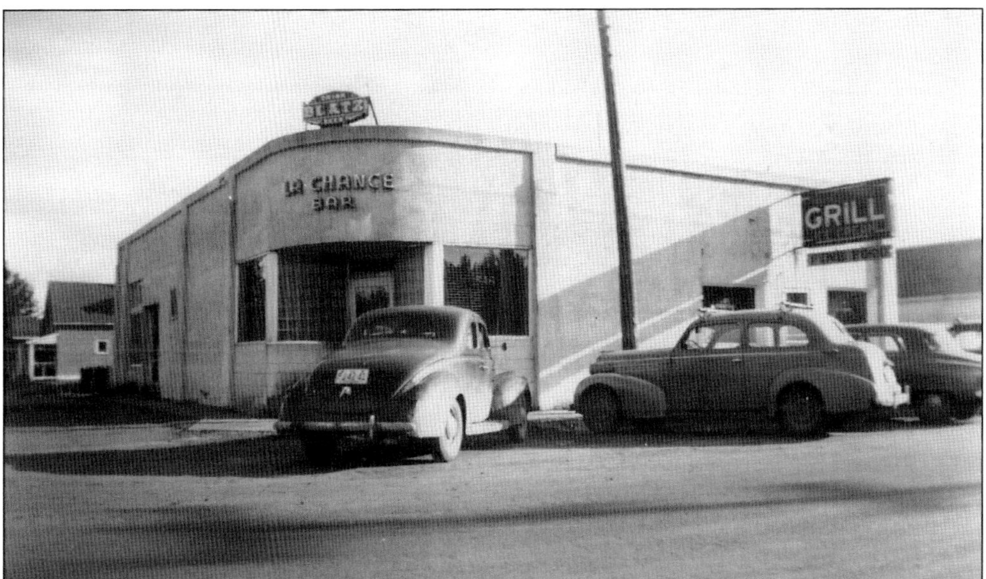

Oliver LaChance and his wife, Lulu (Dussault), remodeled the popular LaChance Bar and Ice Cream Parlor in the 1940s. Oliver's father, Peter LaChance, was one of the first settlers of State Line, arriving in 1894, and operated a store on this same site.

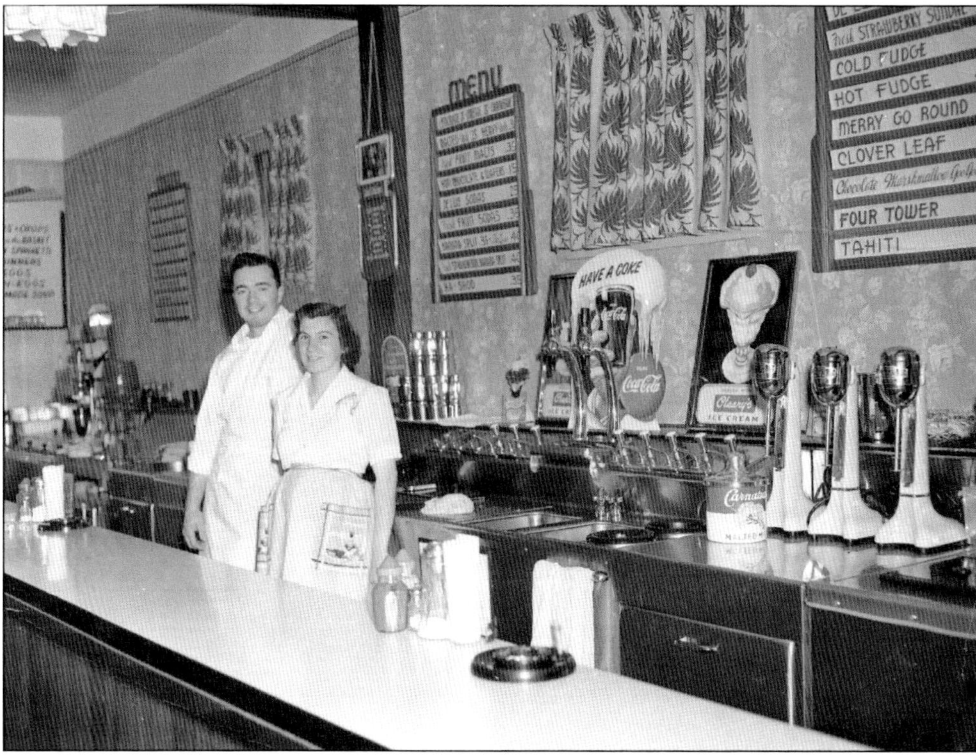

Jack LaChance Sr. and his wife, Ruth, stand behind the ice cream counter of the LaChance Ice Cream Parlor in 1949. Jack and Ruth were the third generation of the LaChance family to operate a business at the same location of grandfather Peter's original store, built in 1895. (Courtesy of the Jack LaChance Family Archives.)

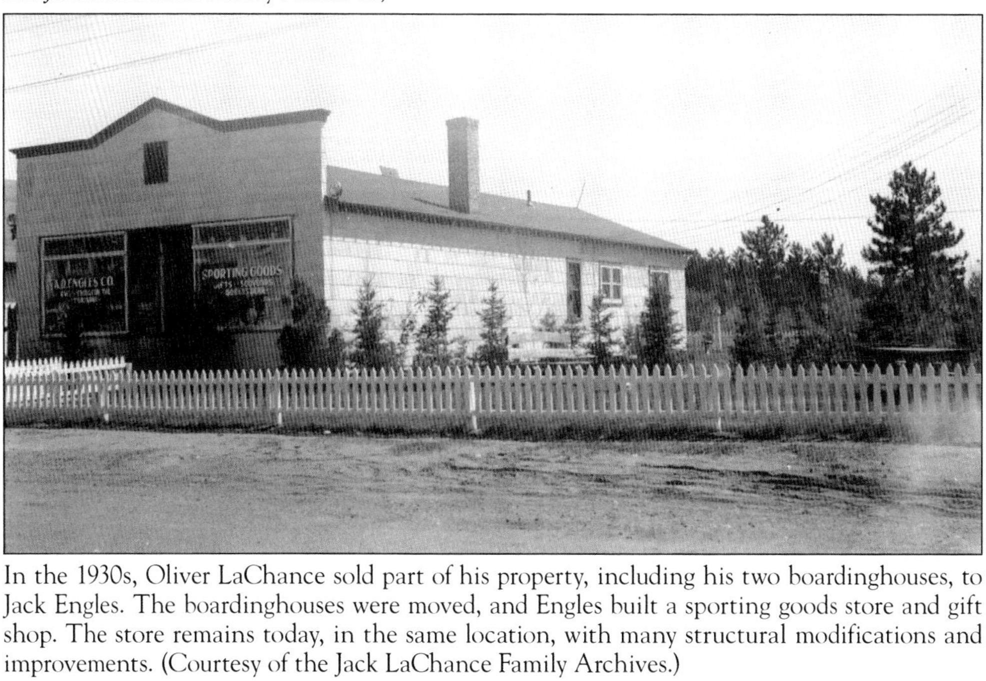

In the 1930s, Oliver LaChance sold part of his property, including his two boardinghouses, to Jack Engles. The boardinghouses were moved, and Engles built a sporting goods store and gift shop. The store remains today, in the same location, with many structural modifications and improvements. (Courtesy of the Jack LaChance Family Archives.)

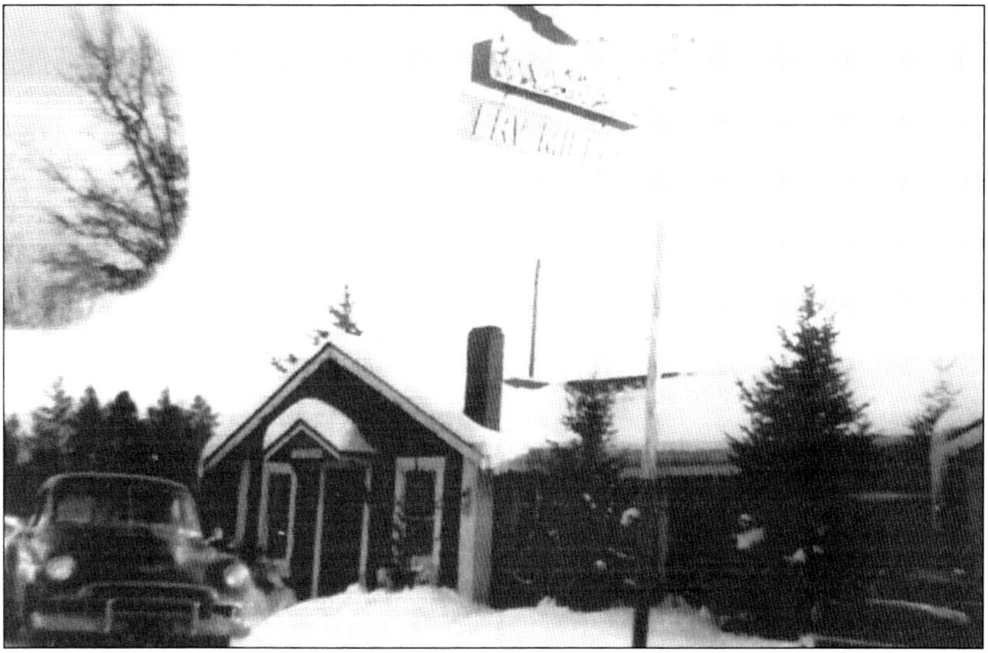

Erv Miller opened a bar and restaurant west of town along Highway B in the late 1930s. Later, it became the Wannigan Club. Today, it is the Bear Trap Inn.

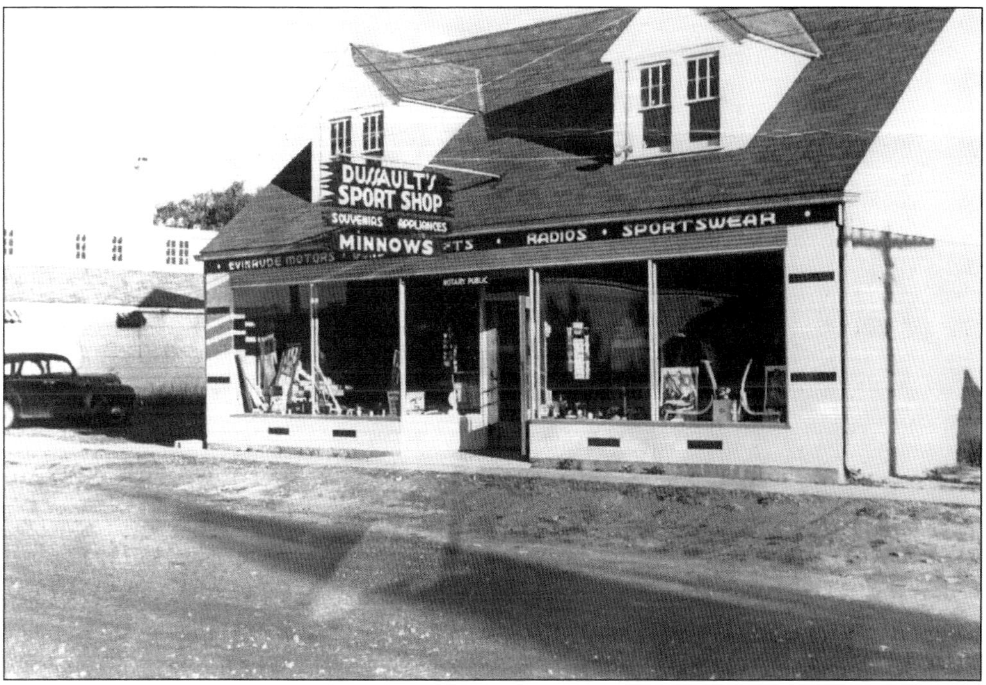

This 1946 photograph shows Lyle Dussault's Sport Shop. The building exists today.

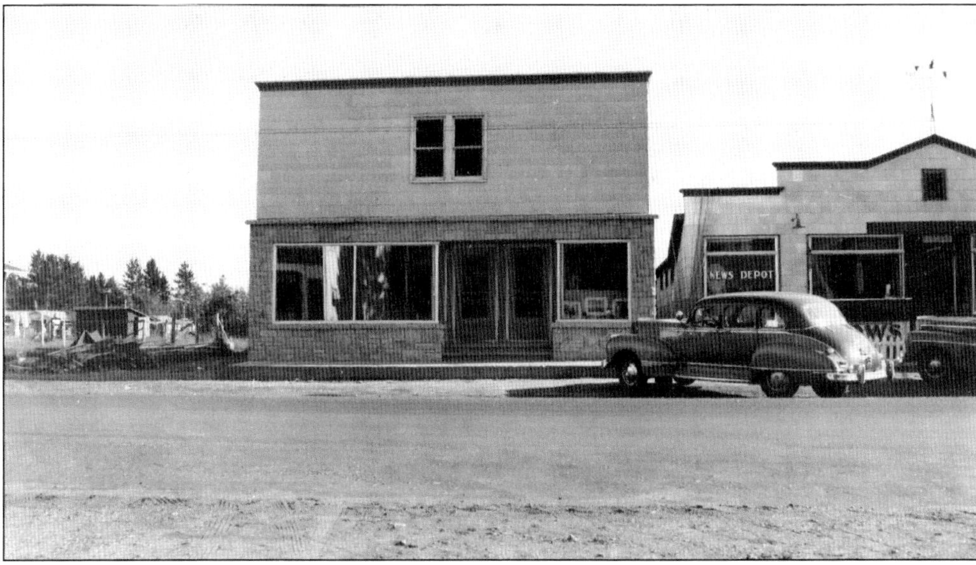

This building (currently the coin laundry) served as the Land O' Lakes Post Office from approximately 1940 to 1956. The structure to the right is A.D. Engle's Tackle Box. This photograph dates from around 1946. (Courtesy of Sally Dussualt Schlack.)

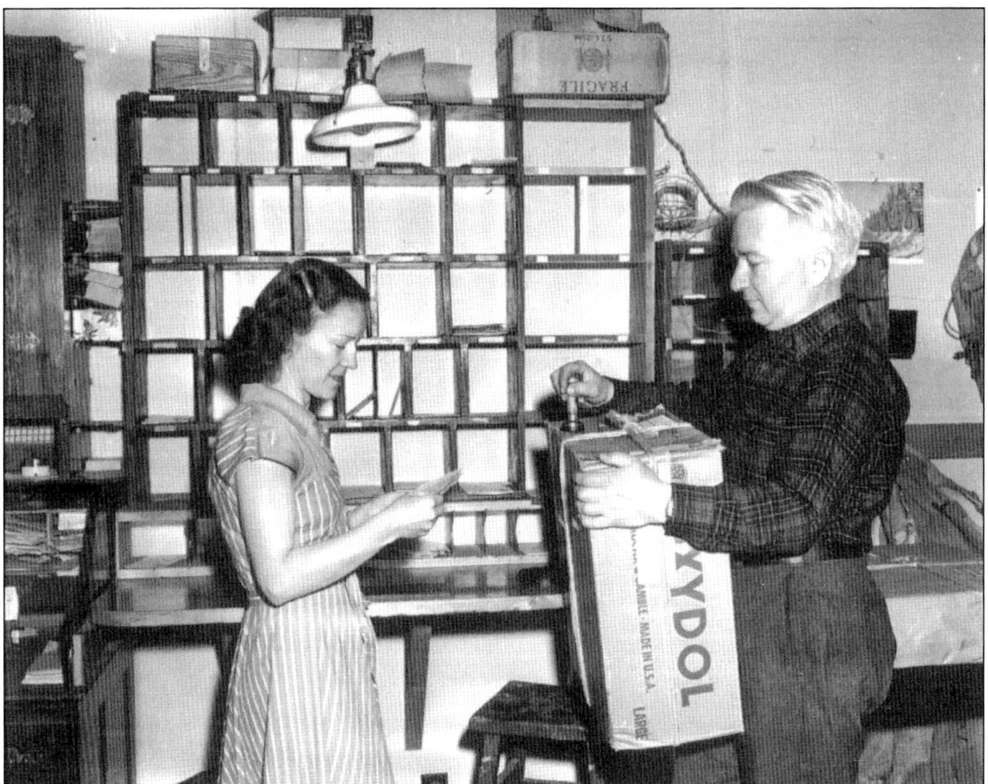

Elsie Dussault (left) was the first female postmistress of Land O' Lakes and served from 1940 to 1972. Pictured with her in this c. 1948 image is Clyde Dussault, town clerk. (Courtesy of Sally Dussault Schlack.)

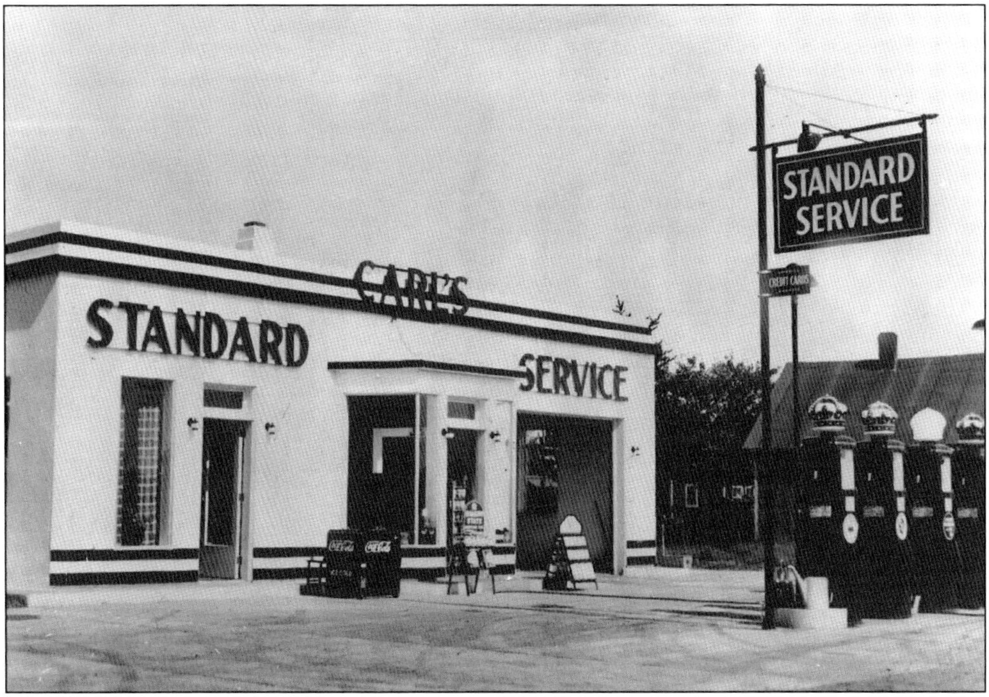

Built by the local Turnquist Brothers of Land O' Lakes in the 1930s, the Standard Service Station remained in operation for many years under various owners, including Les Gable and longtime town board member Henry Mitchell.

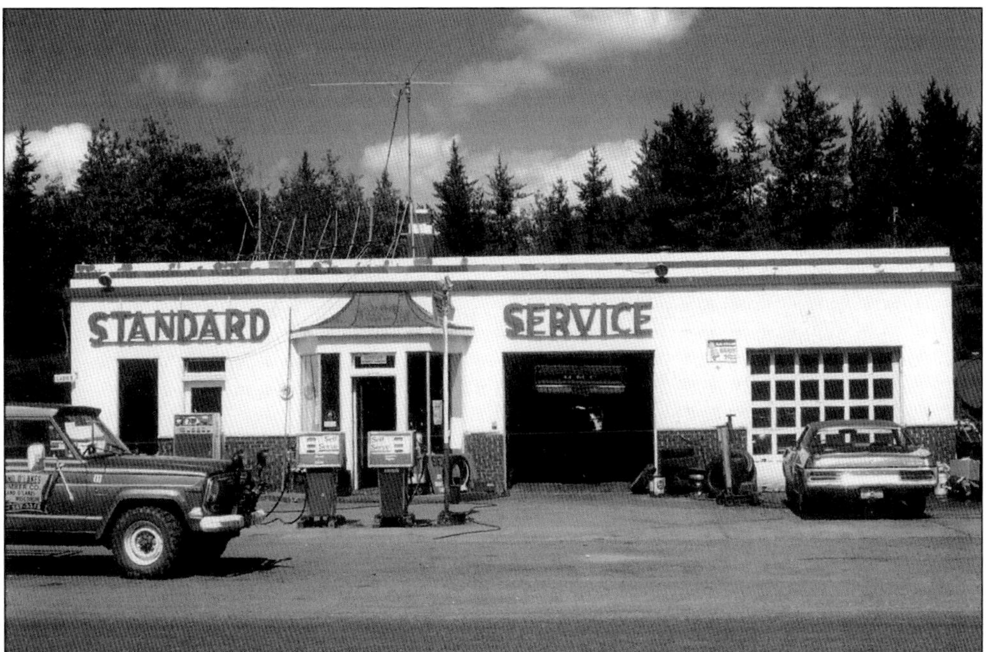

The same Standard station, seen here around 1976, closed in the 1990s and remained abandoned until it was razed in 2006. It was located downtown on the north side of Highway B, in what is now a vacant lot owned by Gasco.

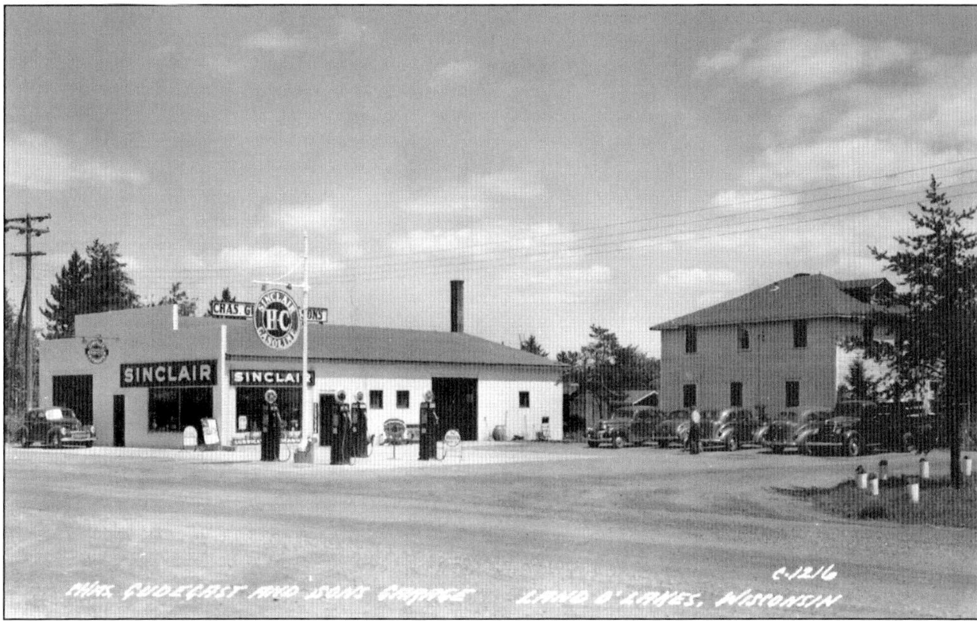

The Sinclair station was owned by Charles Gudegast & Sons in the early 1940s. This business, situated near the junction of Highway 45 and Crystal Lake Road, operated under several owners and sold various brands of fuel until the 1980s when it was demolished.

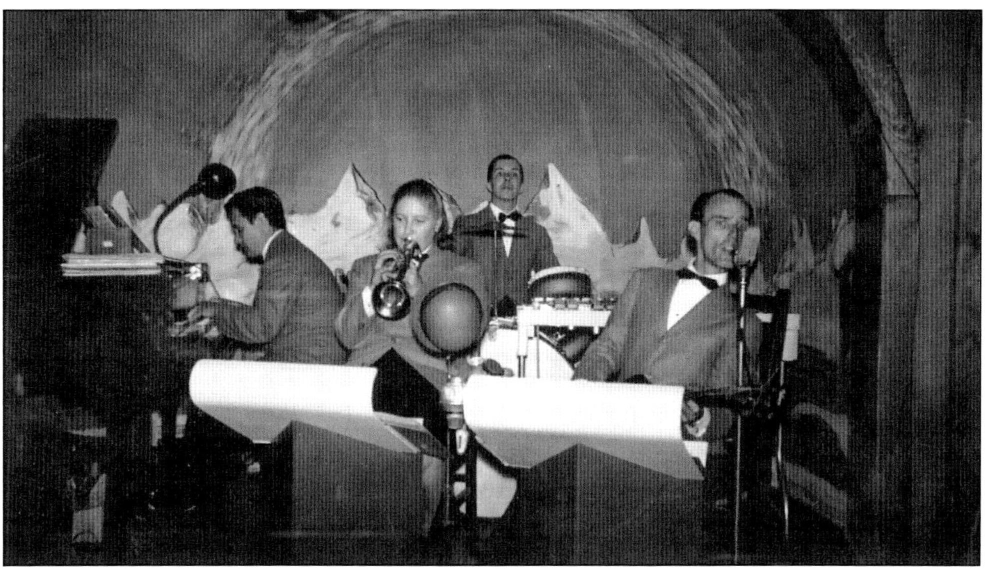

Weekends in Land O' Lakes meant drinks, dinner, and dancing to live music. Many establishments offered "big-city" bands, including this formally dressed group playing at the Tia Juana Restaurant and Night Club in the 1940s. (Courtesy of Sally Dussault Schlack.)

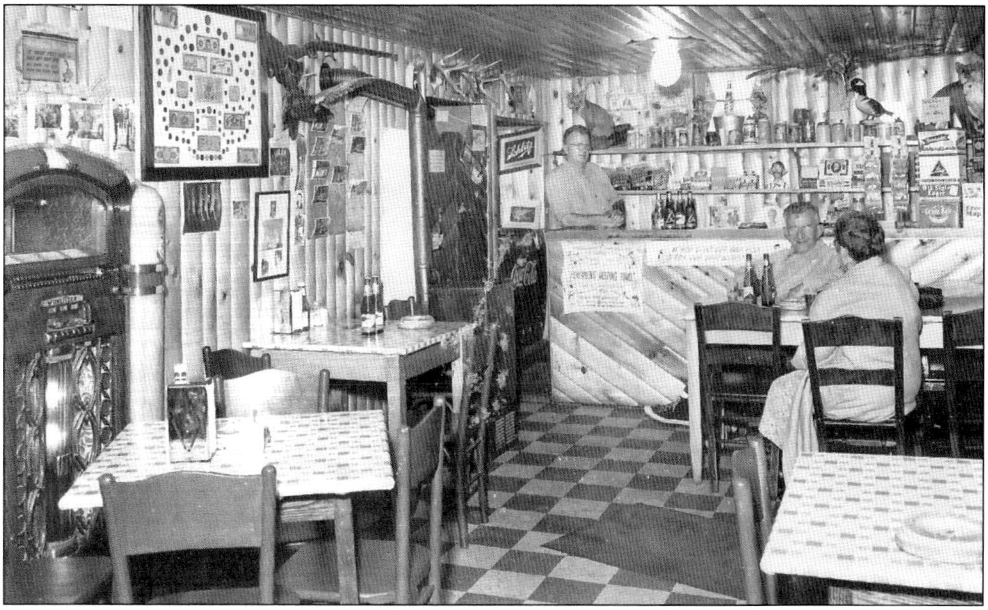

Stoeber's Cabins offered food and refreshments served in Bill's Fox Hole. The cabins and tavern were located on the west side of Highway 45, near the junction of Highway E. This photograph is from the early 1950s.

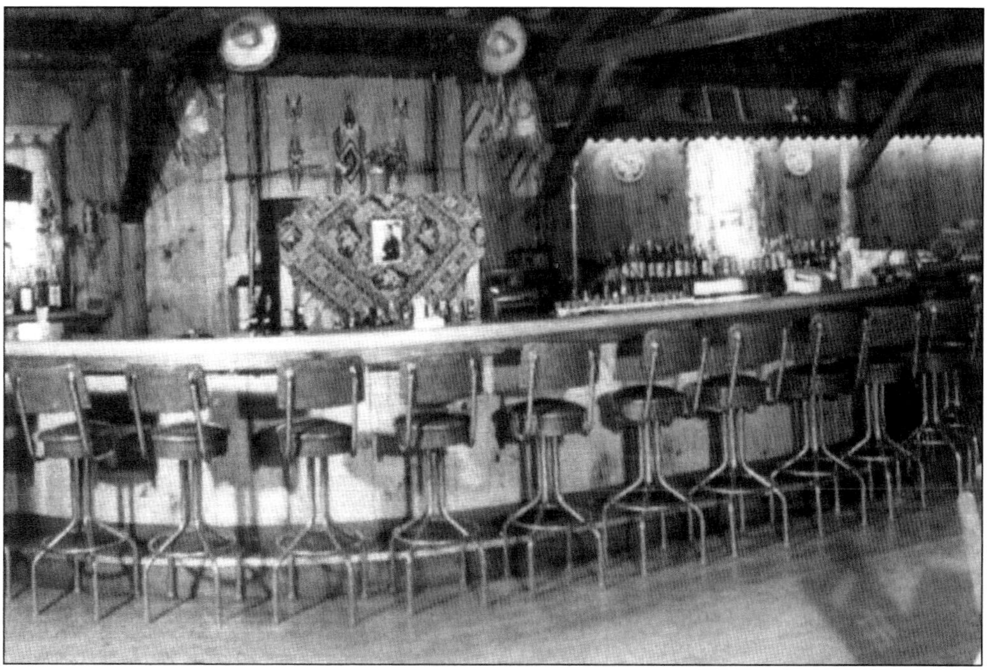

Julius "Dude" Dodge founded and built the Tia Juana nightclub in 1935. This photograph depicts the back bar, which was removed when the room was remodeled for dining in the early 1970s. A pianist entertained from a small stage (not pictured) at the far end of the bar. This image was taken around 1948, and the building exists today at the junction of Highways E and 45. (Courtesy of Rob Andersen.)

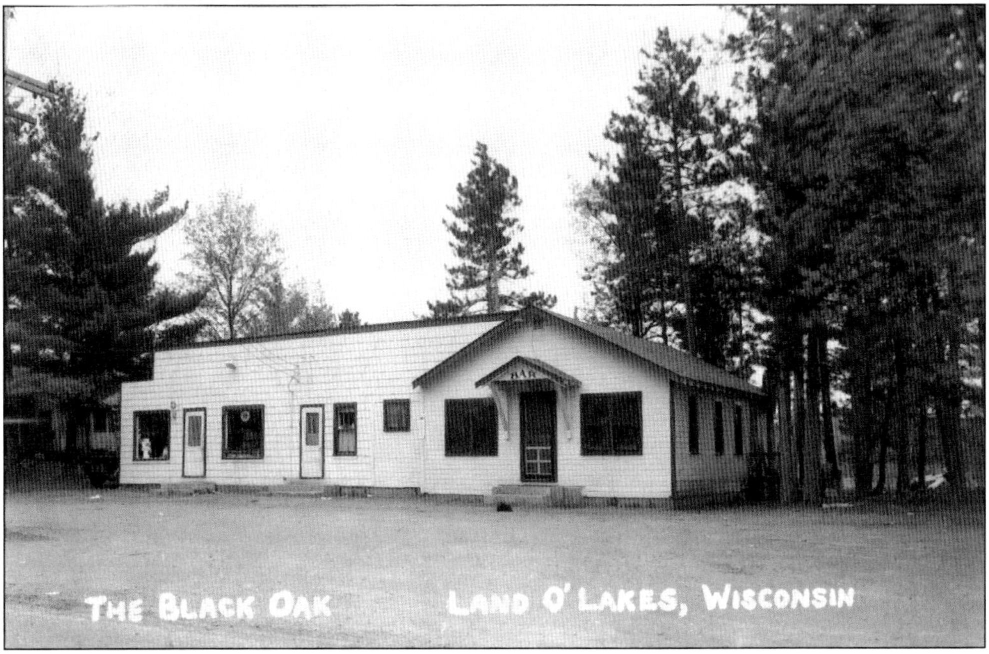

The original Black Oak Inn along Highway B had a small store, tavern, and a restaurant that served the famous Black Oak Burger. There was no refrigeration behind the bar, so ice cut from Black Oak Lake was used to chill the beer and also used for ice cubes. Gasoline pumps were added after this c. 1954 photograph was taken. (Courtesy of Mike Stopczynski.)

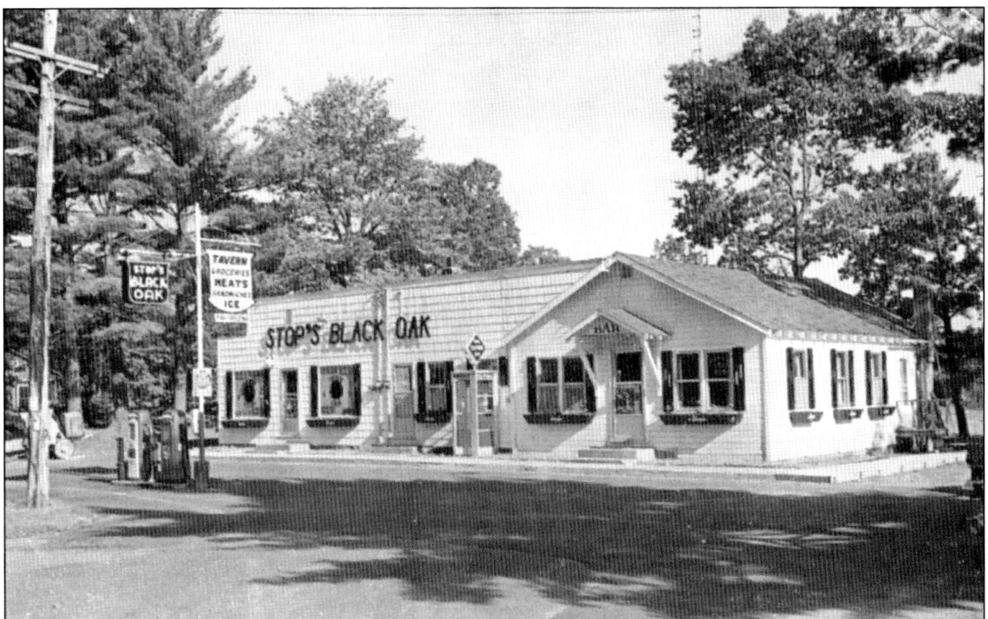

In 1959, Angie and Al Stopczynski bought the Black Oak Inn, seen here around 1962. In addition to improving the facility cosmetically, they added refrigeration and replaced the four potbellied oil-burners with modern heating. The current Black Oak Inn was again renovated in the 1990s by Cheryl and Al "Buck" Janny. (Courtesy of Mike Stopczynski.)

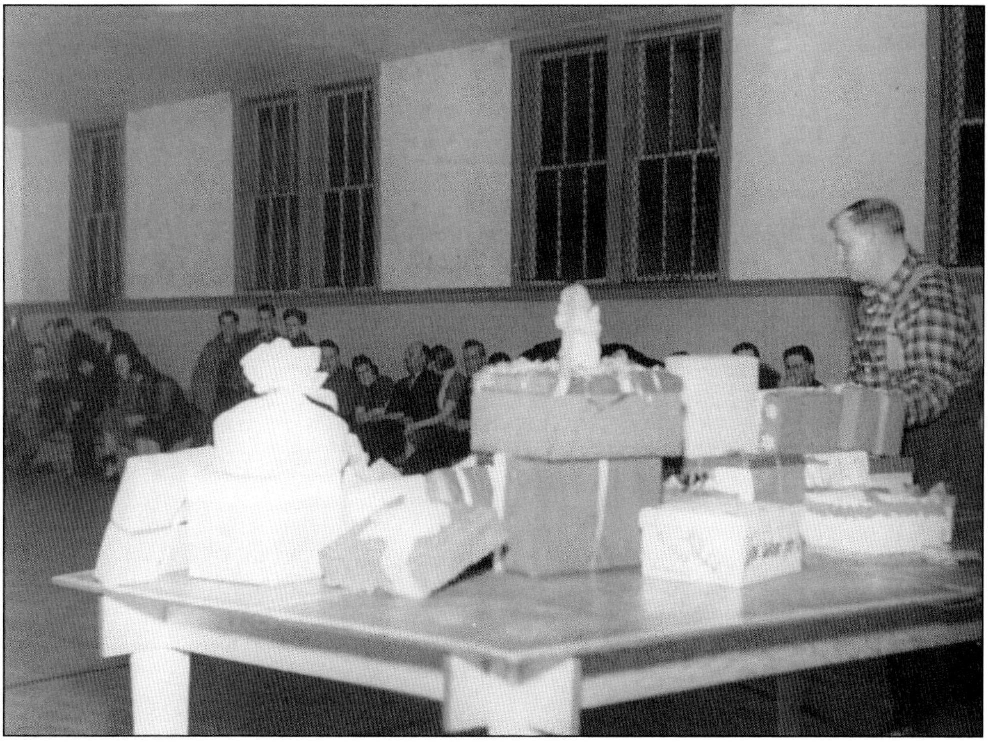

In 1940, tables in the gymnasium of the former town hall are lined with boxes of food, perhaps prepared by the eligible single women of Land O' Lakes. Each food box was auctioned, and the winner got to dine with the person who prepared it. A dance followed. (Courtesy of the Jack LaChance Family Archives.)

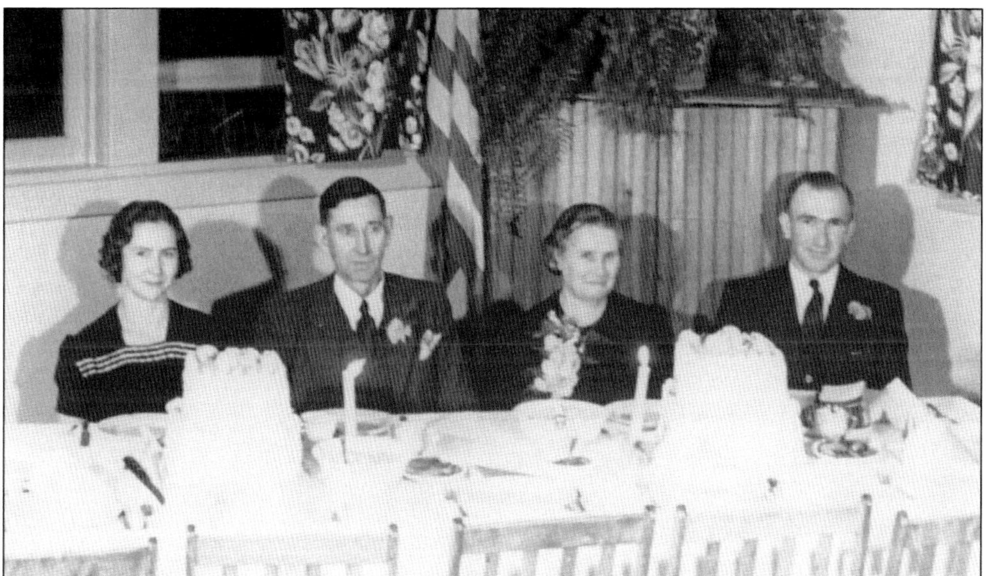

Frank and Polly Sparks (center) built and started the Black Oak Store along Highway B in the 1940s. Today, the building is the popular Black Oak Inn. (Courtesy of Sally Dussault Schlack.)

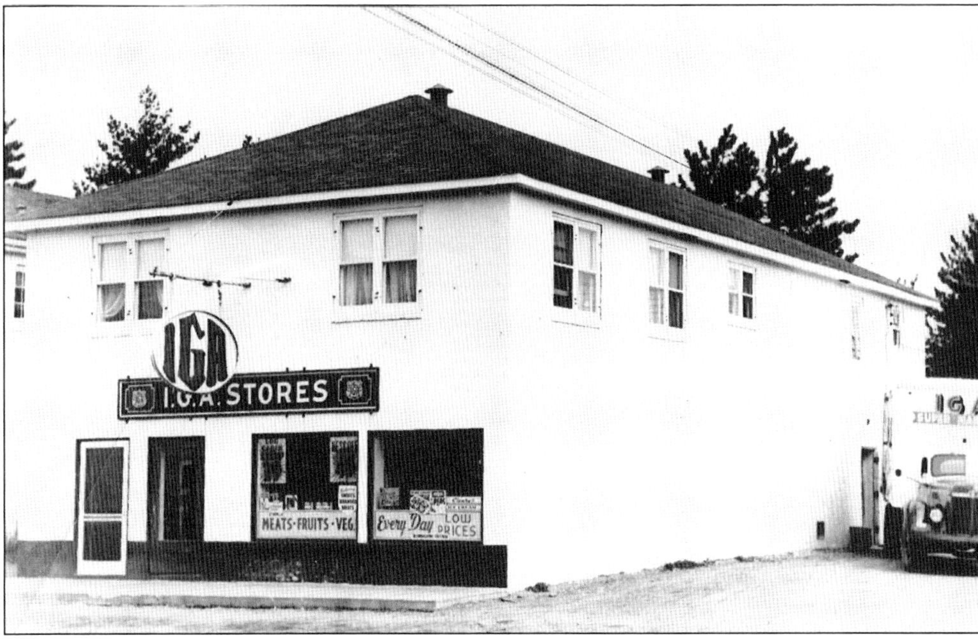

The IGA store was operated by Elvira and Mel Heise from approximately 1948 until 1952. This grocery store was located across the street from the current Schiltz Sport and Gift Shop and has since been sided with cedar and given a fieldstone foundation.

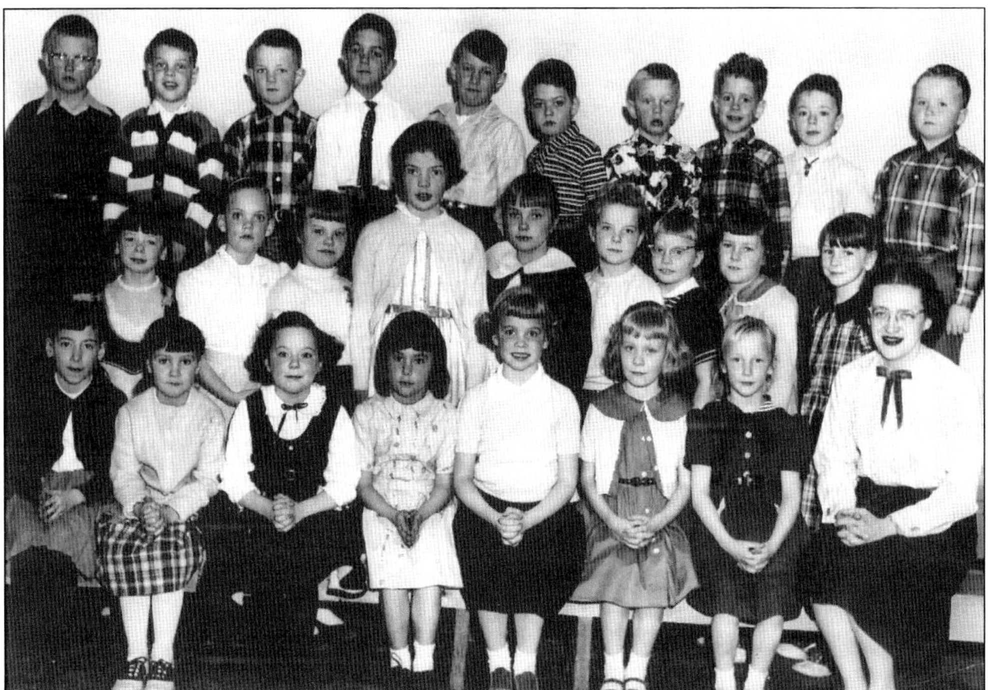

Anita L. Soquist taught at the Land O' Lakes School for 42 years, from 1948 to 1990. When this photograph was taken of her first- and second-grade class in 1959, her nine-month salary was $4,250. Soquist passed away June 15, 2005, at age 76.

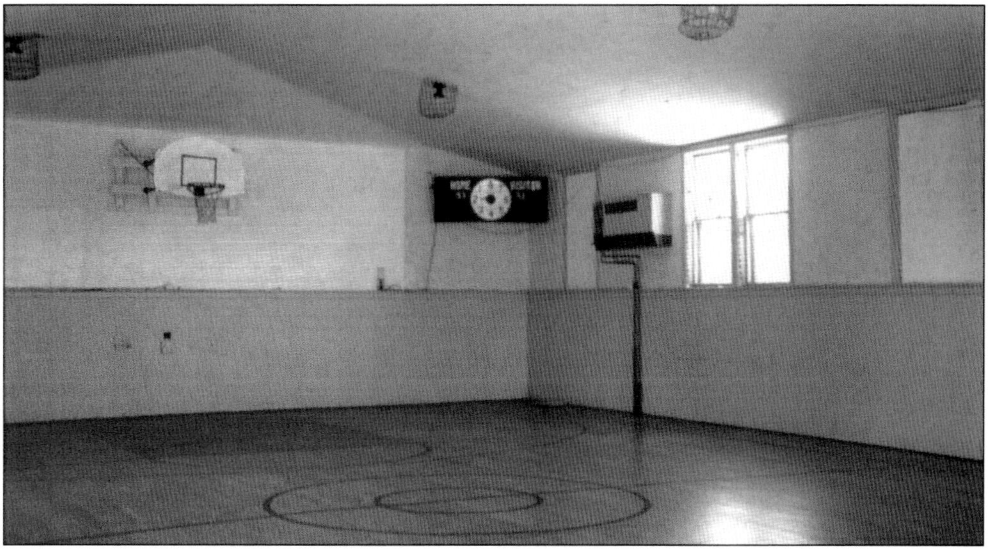

The gymnasium of the former Land O' Lakes Town Hall was used by the local grade school for gym class and also served as the home court of the Land O' Lakes School basketball team for over 50 years. It was also used for school Christmas plays and as a polling place during elections.

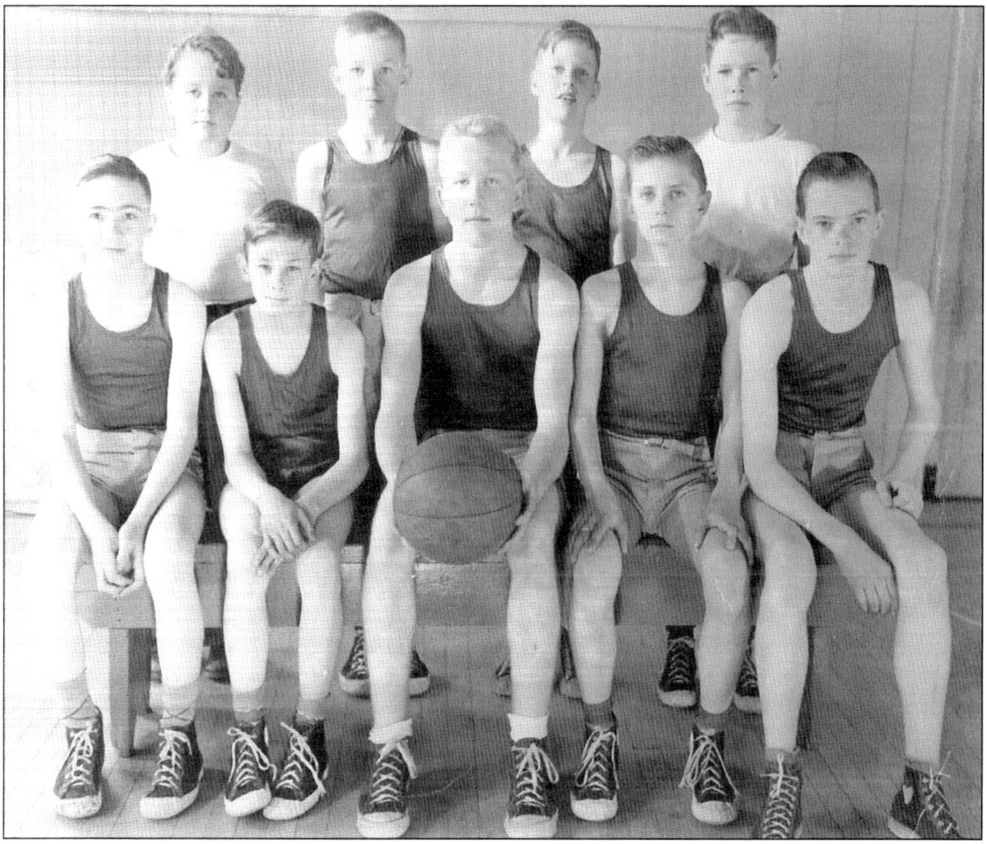

The 1950 seventh- and eighth-grade Land O' Lakes basketball team sits for the team photograph in the gym at town hall (formerly known as the Community House.)

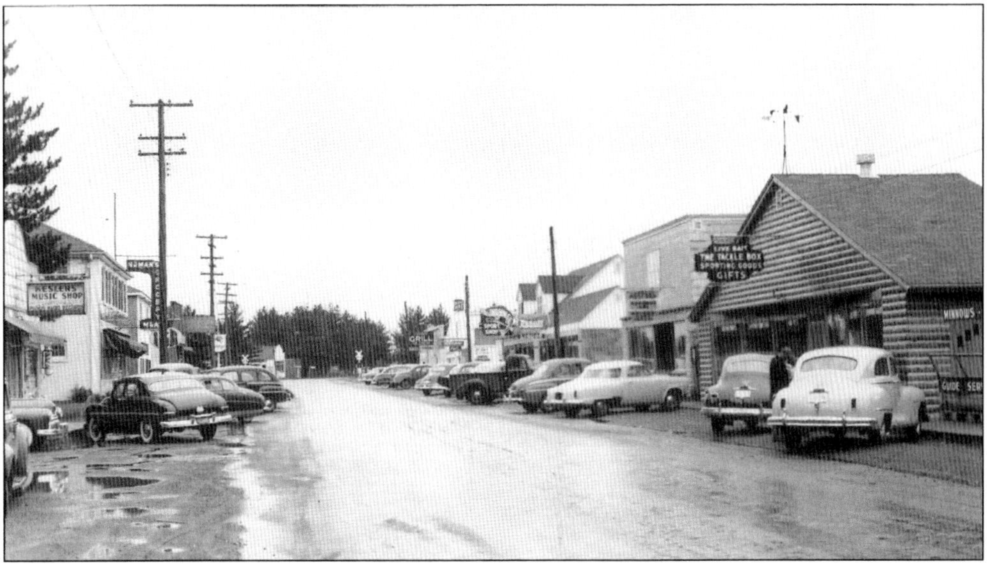

This c. 1950 view shows downtown Land O' Lakes looking east from the approximate location of today's post office. Kessler's Music Shop and Neiman's Grocery are on the left, and the Tackle Box and former post office (currently a coin laundry) are on the right.

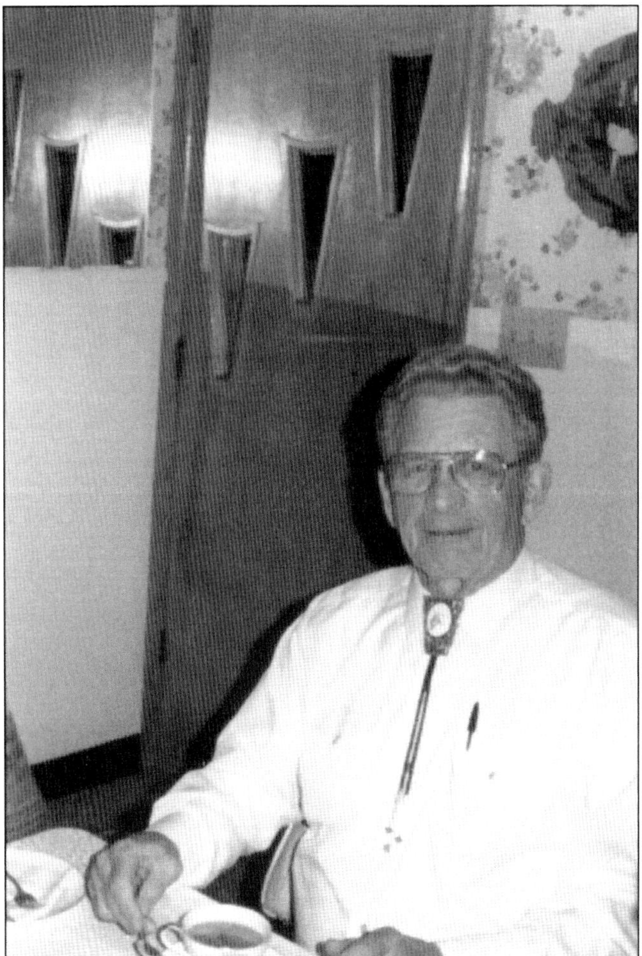

Everett "Doc" Eickhoff opened the first clinic in Land O' Lakes in 1948 and served the medical needs of the community for nearly 50 years. During World War II, he was a senior surgeon of the 3rd Marine Division and won a Bronze Star for service to his country during the battle for Iwo Jima, immortalized by the famous photograph of Marines raising the flag on Mount Suribachi. During this historic 36-day battle, the Americans suffered 26,000 casualties (killed or wounded), but their victory unquestionably hastened the end of the war. (Courtesy of Tom Reed.)

Violet "Vi" Becker, pictured with her husband, Wally, was the first woman to be elected as a town chairperson in the state of Wisconsin. Serving throughout 1960s, she started the Fish & Game Club and arranged for the construction of the second airport runway. Born in State Line in 1918 to Scandinavian parents, the last line of her handwritten memoirs read, "I had a wonderful life." (Courtesy of Carol Becker.)

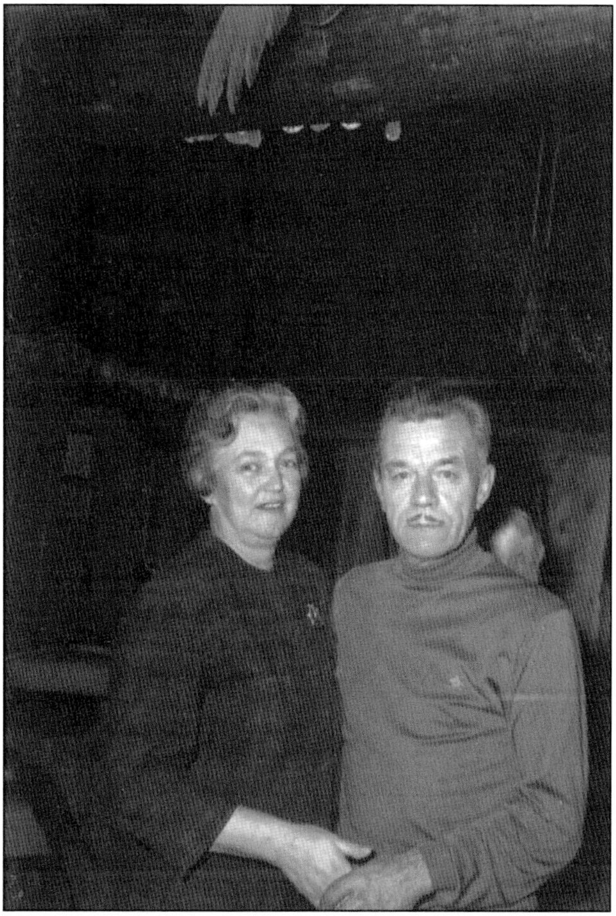

Vi and Wally Becker owned and operated the Wanigan Club (currently the Bear Trap Inn) for over a decade starting in the 1950s. As with most restaurants of the time, live music was provided, and Everett Engerson was the featured musician, playing piano, organ, guitar, violin, and other instruments. This photograph shows the interior of the Wanigan when the main entrance was the north side door. (Courtesy of Carol Becker.)

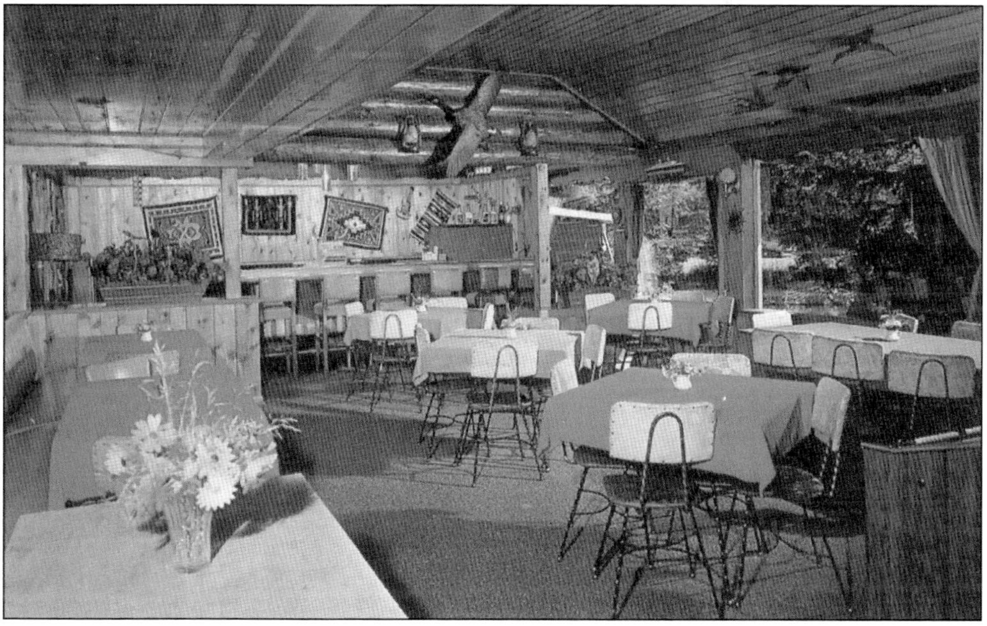

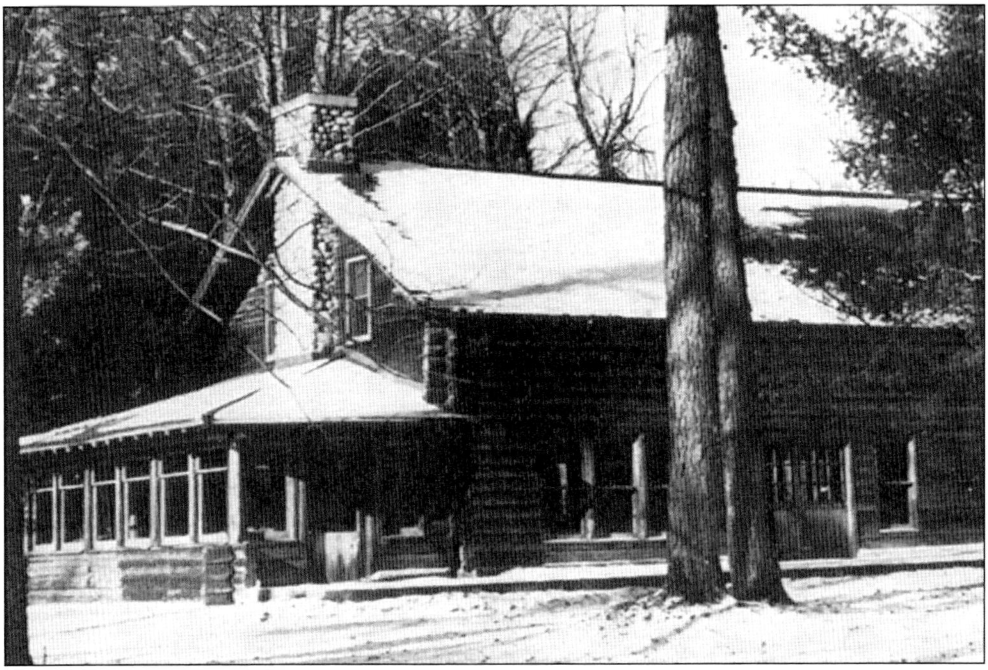

In 1895, lumberman A.D. Johnson purchased 80 acres of land along the southeast shore of Clark Lake. In 1930, he built a lodge for his personal use and a guesthouse (pictured). When the US Forest Service acquired the property in 1966, the Biddle House was envisioned as the welcome center for the new Sylvania wilderness tract. In 1971, however, the home was deemed "incompatible" with the Sylvania wilderness management plan, sold at auction for $1,611, and moved to Ironwood.

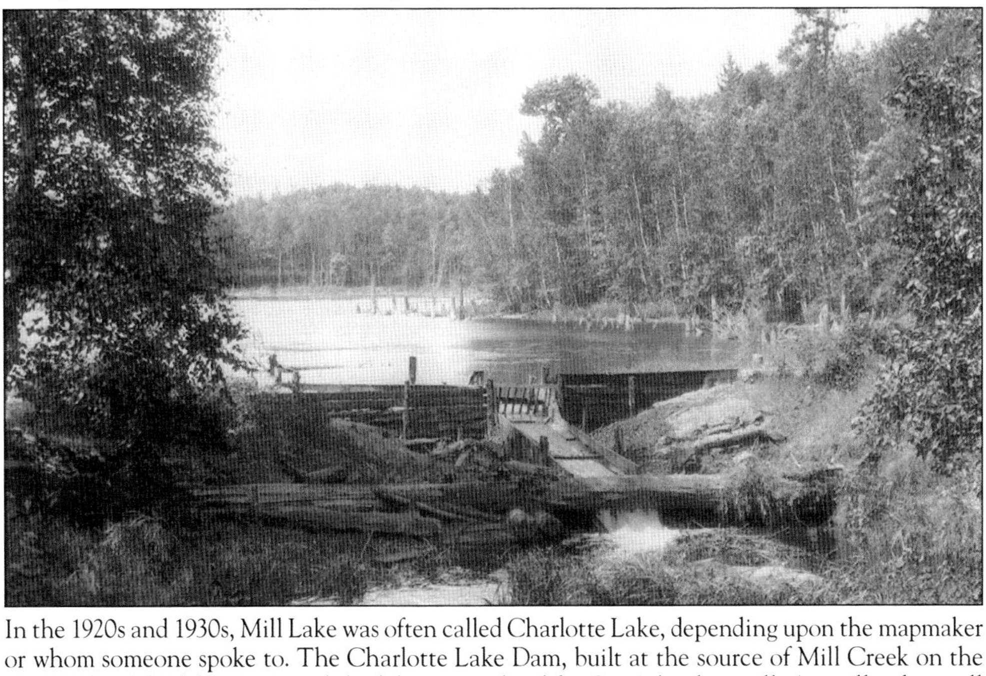

In the 1920s and 1930s, Mill Lake was often called Charlotte Lake, depending upon the mapmaker or whom someone spoke to. The Charlotte Lake Dam, built at the source of Mill Creek on the south side of the lake, increased the lake's water level for Otto's lumber mill. A smaller dam still exists today, visible from Highway B.

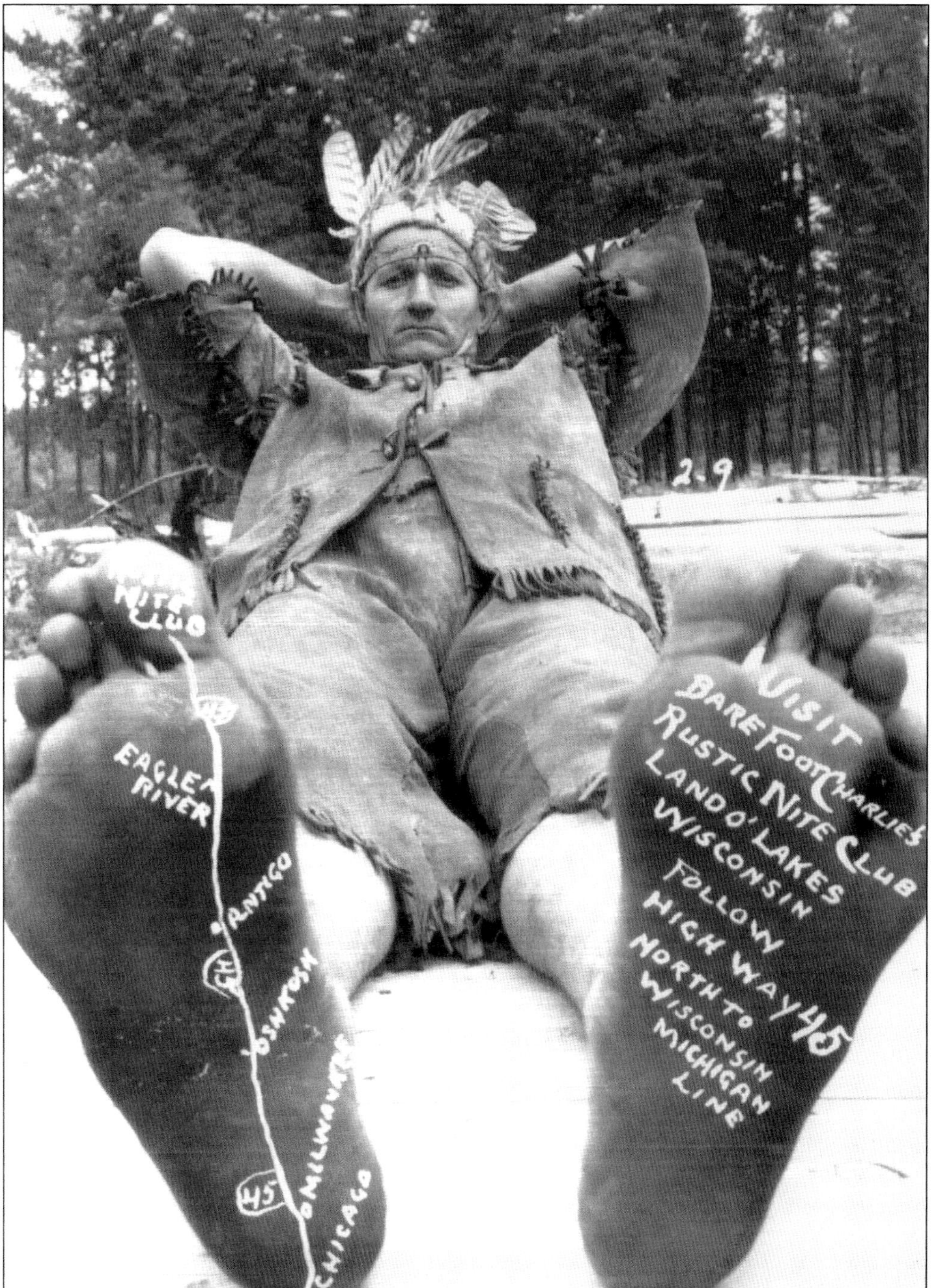

Part businessman, part craftsman, part lumberjack, and part entertainer, Barefoot Charlie gained a reputation for his bare feet, dressing in frontiersman or Indian garb and posing for hundreds of publicity photographs. In reality, Charlie was a loner and few knew him well. With little formal schooling, Charlie taught himself to read and write. He died October 29, 1970, at the Eagle River Memorial Hospital at age 79.

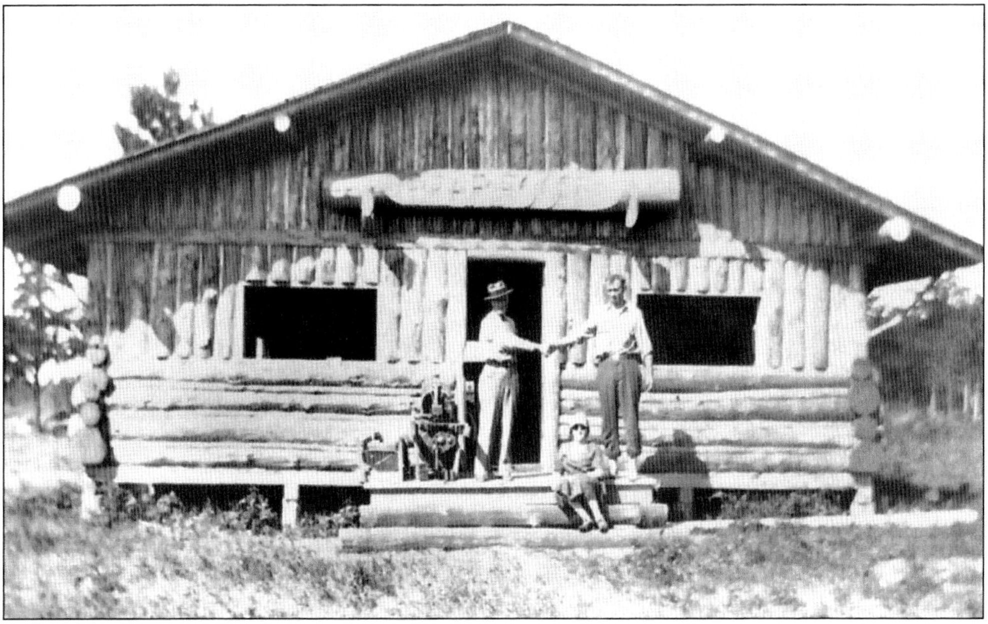

Charlie Haase, "Barefoot Charlie" (right) shakes hands with an unidentified man in this earliest known photograph of the original Bearfoot's Tavern. Even though Haase is pictured with bare feet, the carved sign above the door reads "*Bear*foot."

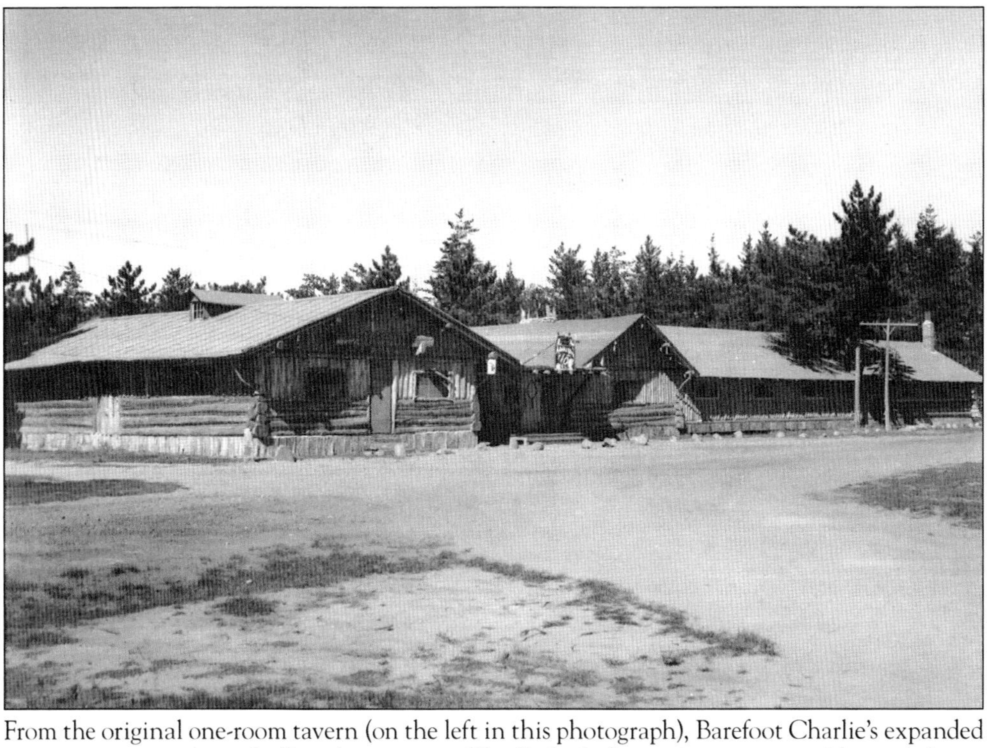

From the original one-room tavern (on the left in this photograph), Barefoot Charlie's expanded into a restaurant, dance hall, and a museum. Charlie built the entire structure with rough-hewn logs from the surrounding forests. It was located on the west side of Highway 45, just north of the Wisconsin River.

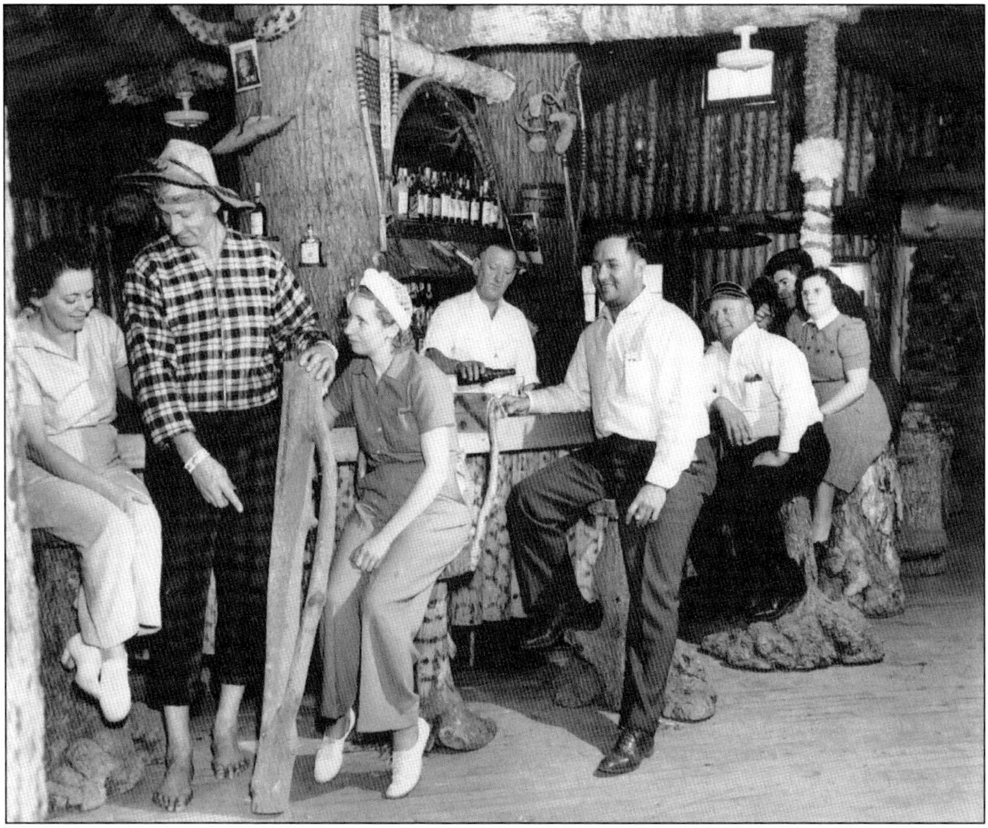

Barefoot Charlie chats with admiring customers seated on bar stools made from tree stumps. On a frigid night in January 1988, the famous attraction and landmark burned to the ground due to an overheated furnace stove. Thereafter, many claim that Land O' Lakes was never the same.

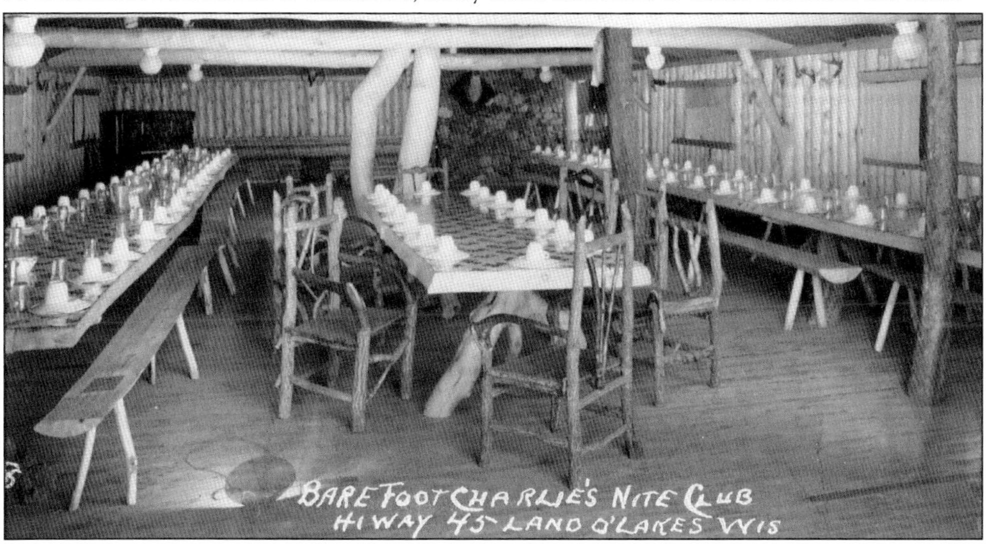

The dining room in Barefoot Charlie's could easily accommodate over 100 people. On Saturday nights, this room was often used as a dance floor, with the band playing from the stage seen at the back of this photograph. (Courtesy of Cindy Pekrul.)

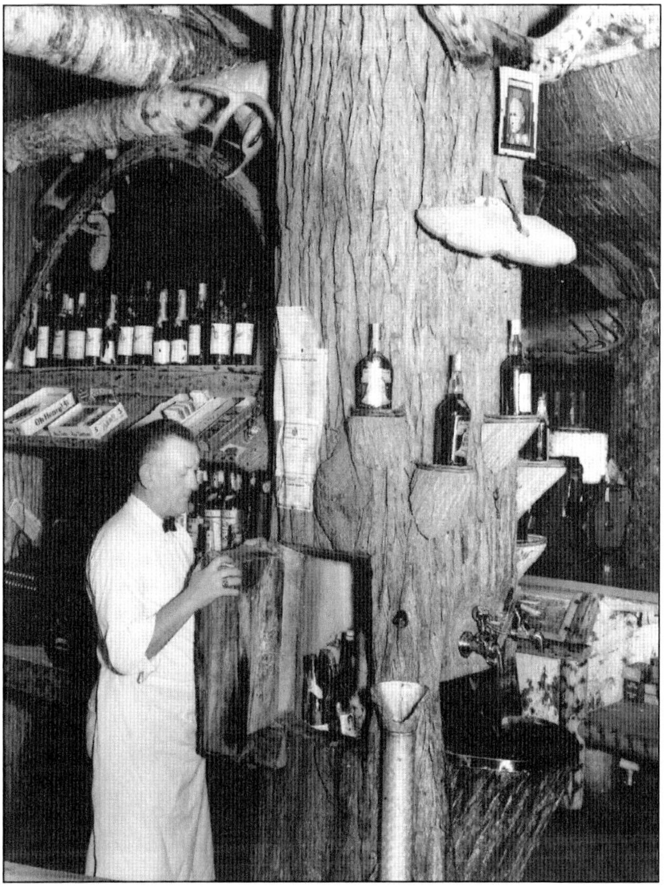

"A museum of wood" is how many described Barefoot Charlie's bar and nightclub. Wood oddities were incorporated into everything, including shelves, sinks, storage, bar stools, tables and chairs. Here, the bartender opens an icebox, and although no sap flows from the tree, the taps to the right furnish beer on demand.

Much of the wood oddities found in Barefoot Charlie's were made by Charlie himself, who tied saplings into the shapes he desired. When the young trees matured, Charlie cut them and added them to the structure.

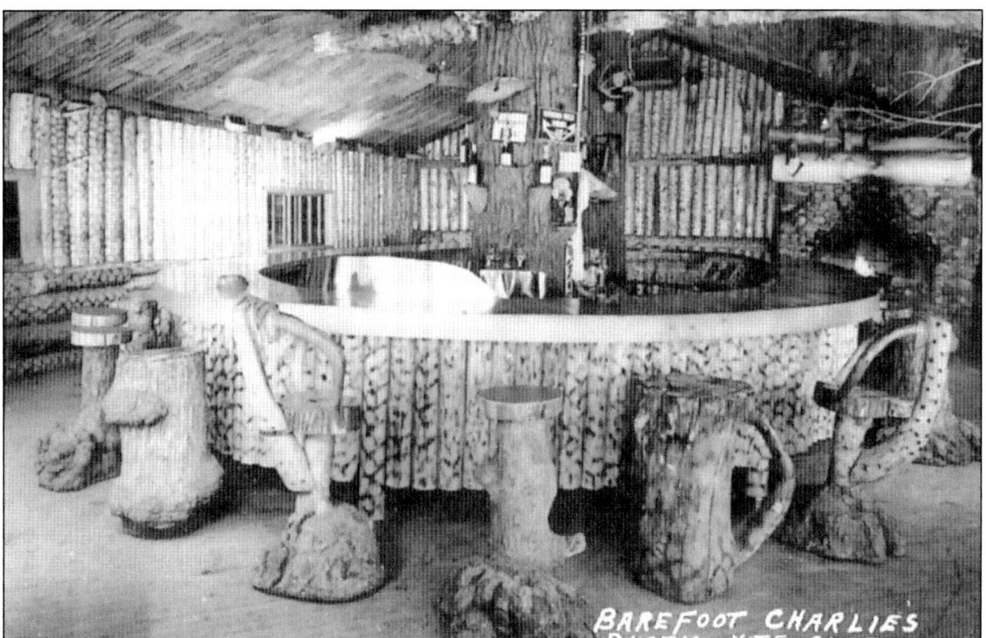

Barefoot Charlie built his tavern and restaurant around several large pine trees that required occasional watering. Regarding his bare feet, he once said, "When I was a boy, people used to think I went barefoot because I was poor. Lots of them gave me shoes and that was fine because I always managed to sell them and get myself some pocket money."

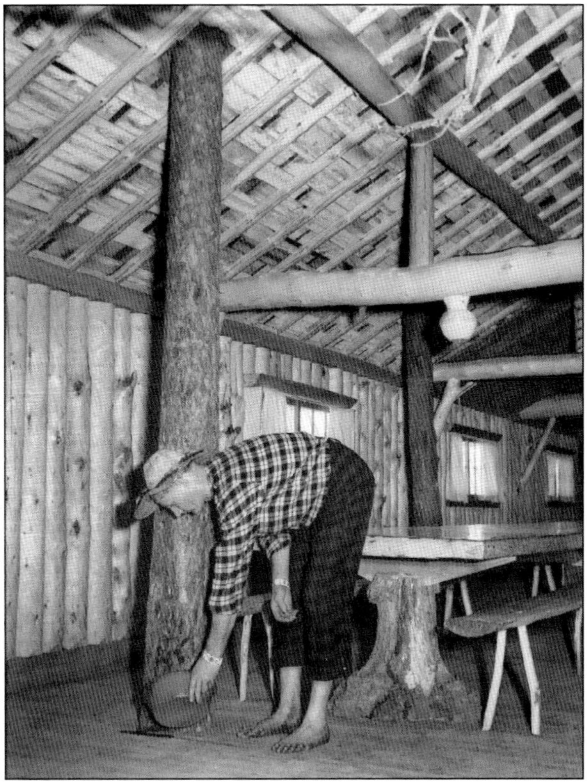

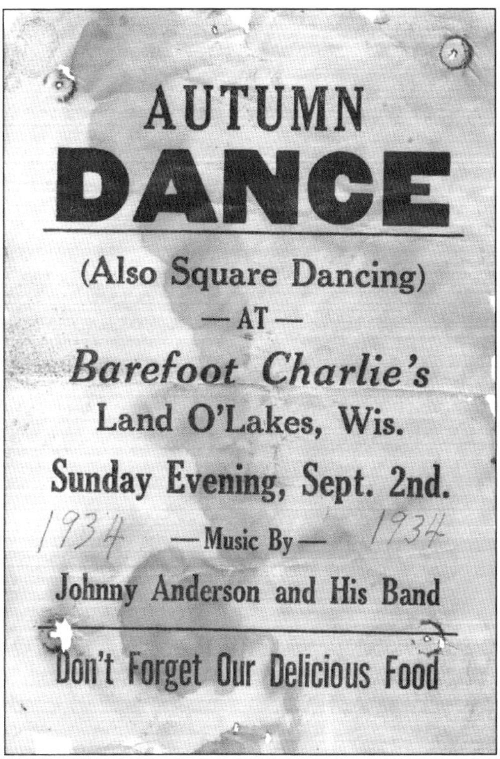

AUTUMN
DANCE
(Also Square Dancing)
— AT —
Barefoot Charlie's
Land O'Lakes, Wis.
Sunday Evening, Sept. 2nd.
1934 — Music By — 1934
Johnny Anderson and His Band
Don't Forget Our Delicious Food

Live music and dancing was the primary form of entertainment in the 1930s, and Barefoot Charlie's was one of the hottest spots in town. Dances were crowded, attracting people from Eagle River and Watersmeet. Back then, there were no televisions or computers, few telephones, and radio reception in the north woods was nil. Dances were prime entertainment.

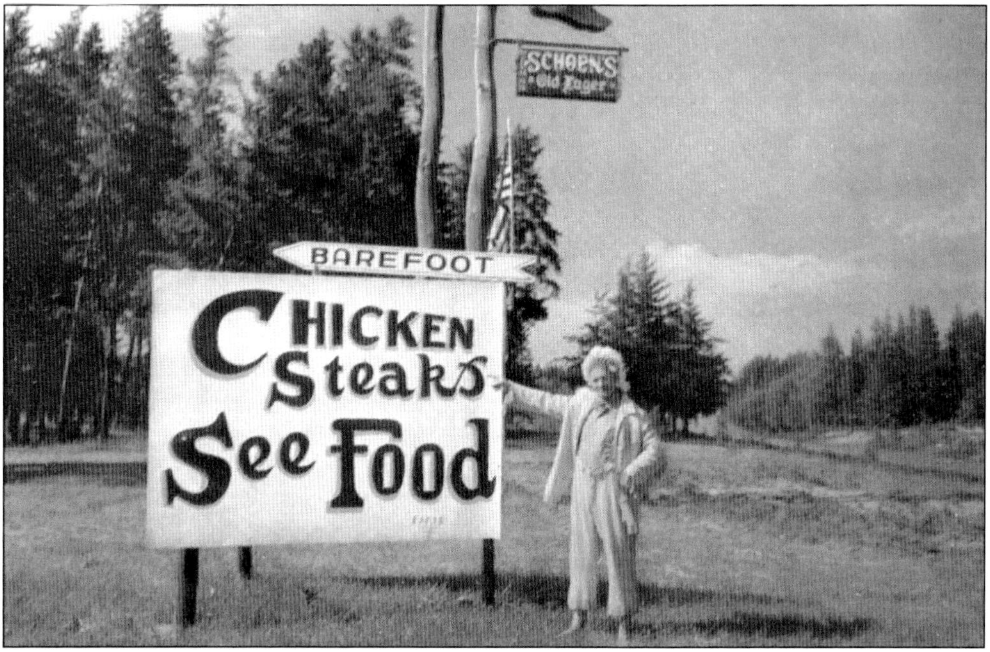

Charlie Haase (Barefoot Charlie) came to Land O' Lakes from the town of Alvin in Forest County, 20 miles to the southeast. He brought his two sons and two daughters, who attended the Donaldson School. Before building his tavern, Charlie earned money by constructing simple cabin accommodations and renting them.

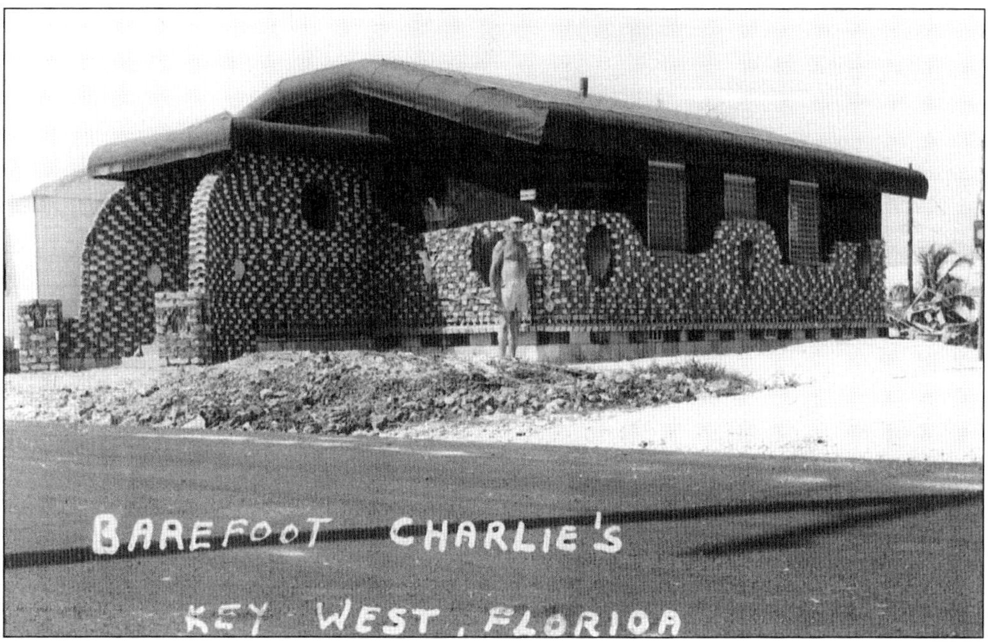

Despite the popularity of his tavern and restaurant, Barefoot Charlie disliked north woods winters. His home in Key West, Florida, was built in unique Charlie Haase style, with turtle shells and seashells added for decoration.

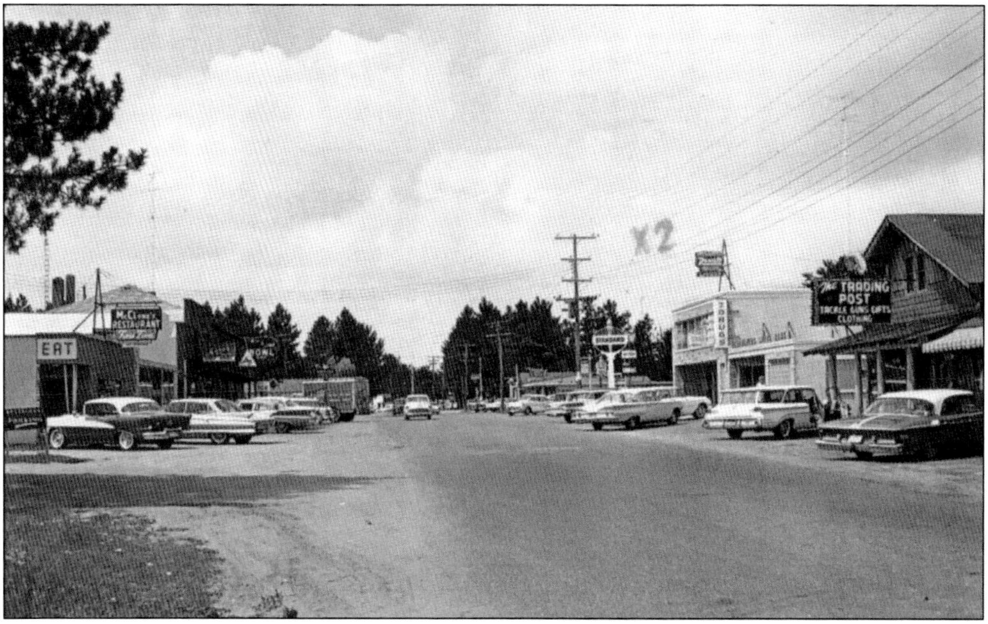

In 1964, Highway B had no painted centerline, and the parking areas next to the shops and restaurants were gravel. This photograph presents a west view. (Courtesy of Cindy Pekrul.)

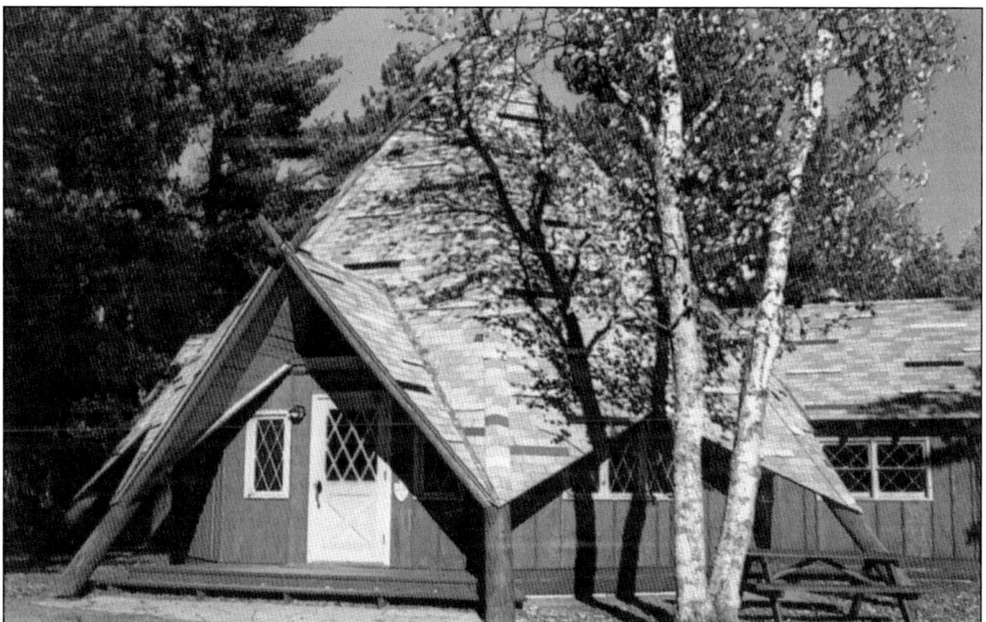

The original teepee portion of the Red Man Inn was built by Nig DeMers in the 1950s and served hamburgers, hot dogs, and sodas. In the 1970s, an addition was built next to the teepee, and the restaurant became a supper club.

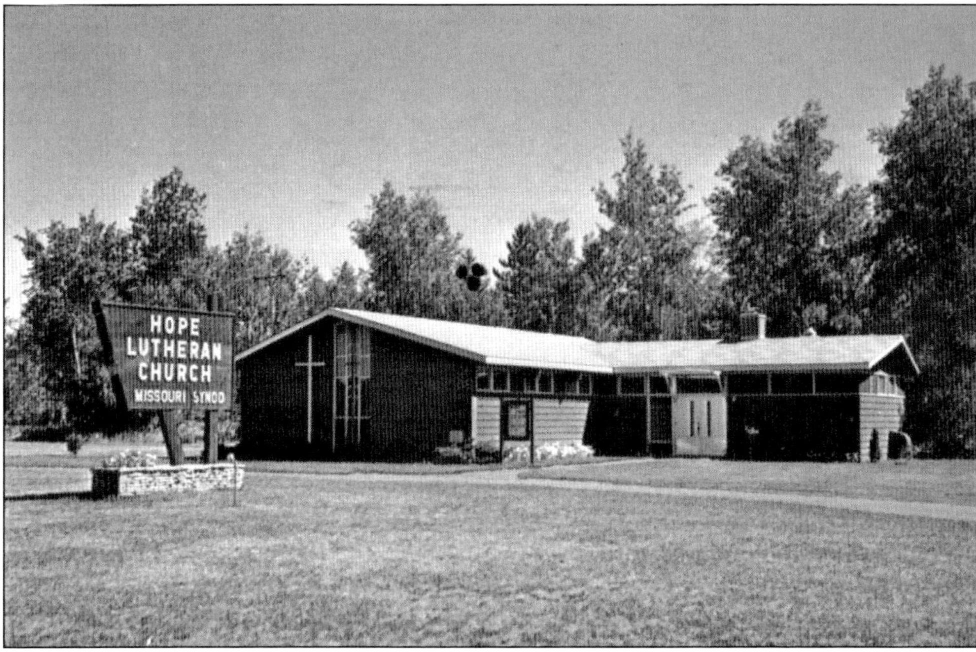

This photograph of the Hope Lutheran Church, located just north of the junction of Highways 45 and B, was taken shortly after it opened in the 1950s. Over the years, a steeple spire, flagpole, and south building extension were added.

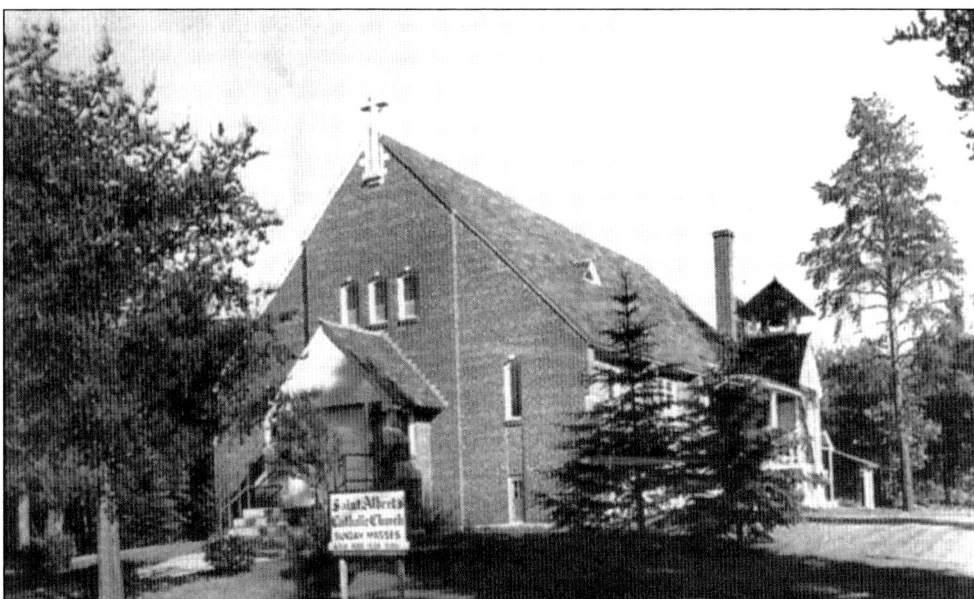

Before the St. Albert's Catholic Church was built, Catholics in Land O' Lakes belonged to the parish of Eagle River. In the summer, a visiting priest would say Mass in the community building. This photograph shows the church after its completion in 1949. An addition to the north side was made in 1959.

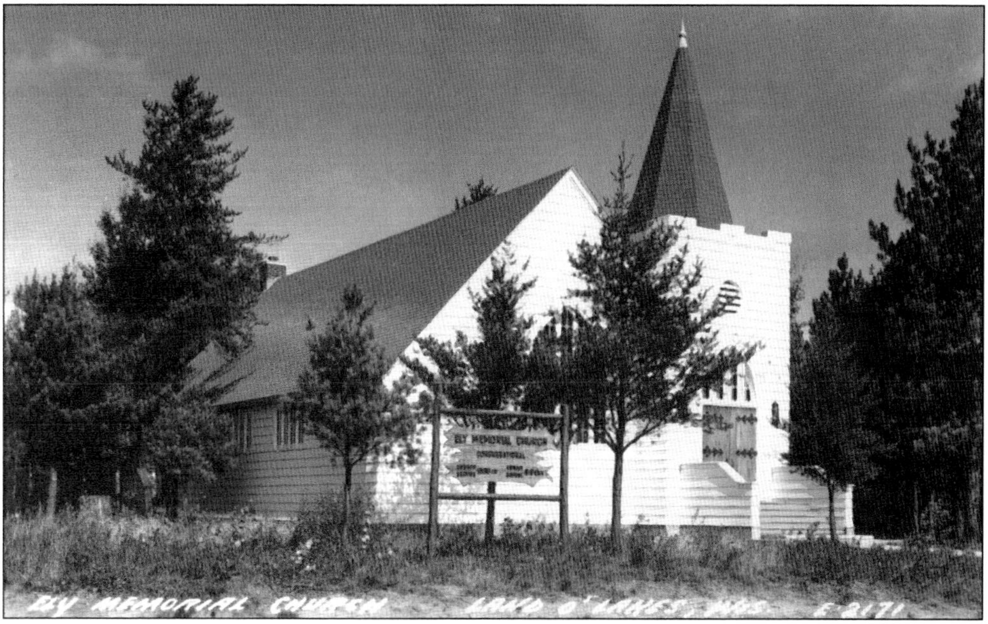

The first services of the Ely Memorial Church were held monthly in the Donaldson School from 1907 to 1920 and then in the Community House from 1928 until the congregation built its own church, pictured here, in 1939. The funds for the building were donated by Deborah and Frank Ferry. The current church was rebuilt after the original building burned in 2003.

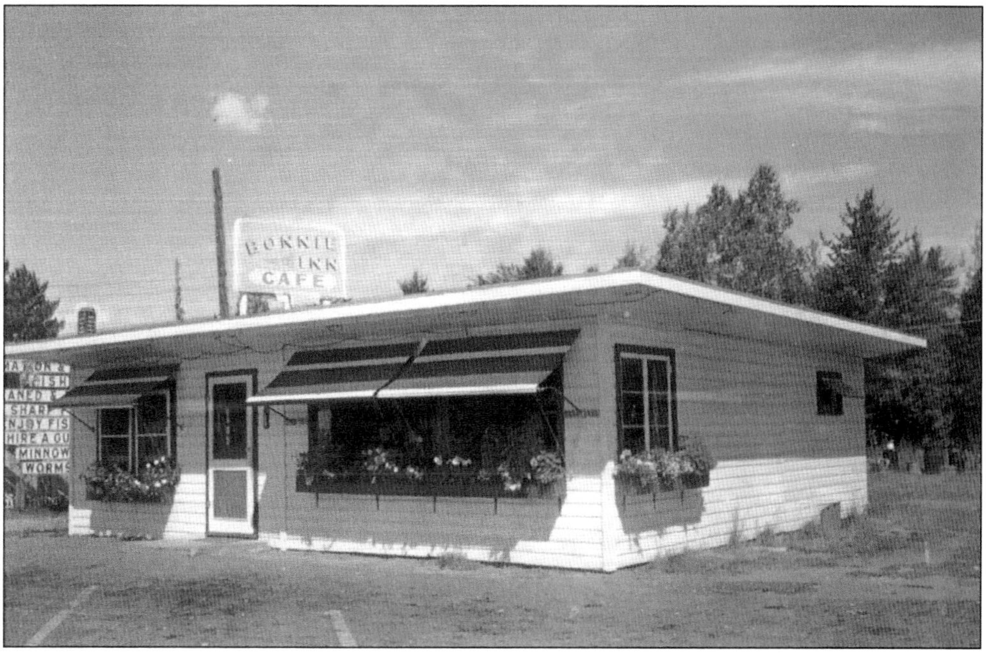

The Bonnie Inn Café was operated by fishing guide Abe Eberly's wife and was located just to the east of Eberly's Sporting Goods store. After the café was sold in the 1970s, it was expanded and re-sided. The building remains today, north of the junction of Oak Street and Highway B, and formerly housed Caudill Plumbing. The original café occupies the northwest corner of the facility. (Postcard courtesy of Cindy Pekrul.)

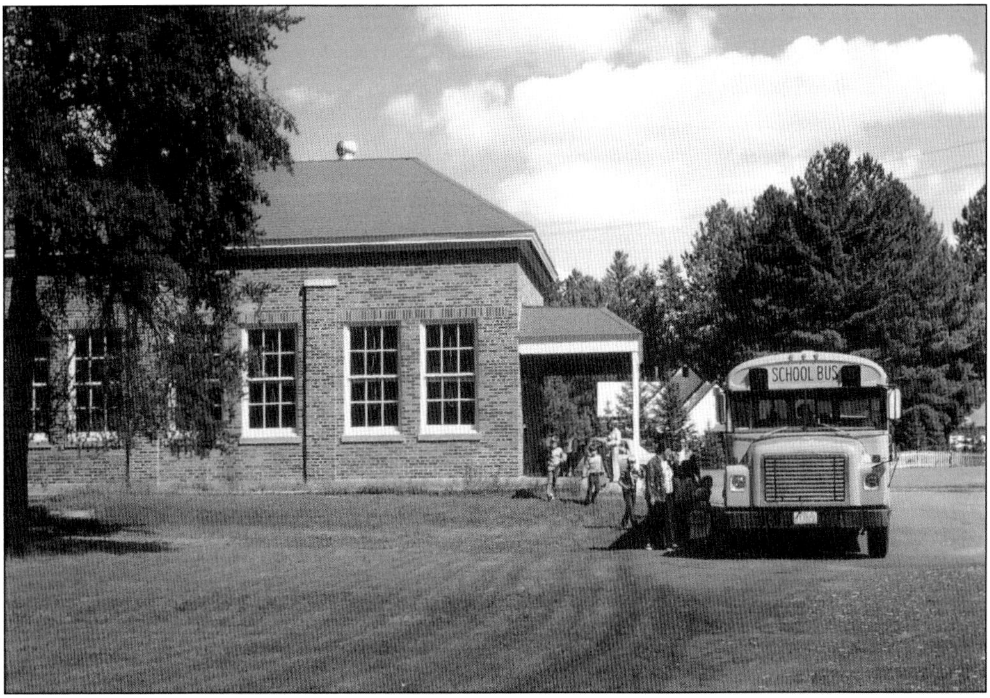

Dedicated on January 23, 1932, the new Land O' Lakes Elementary School was built on property donated by Deborah and Frank Ferry and served students and teachers for over 60 years. Newspaper accounts of the former school's opening stated that it was a "one-story structure with three standard classrooms, office, and library." An addition was made in 1950. This photograph shows students boarding the bus in 1976. The building is now the town hall.

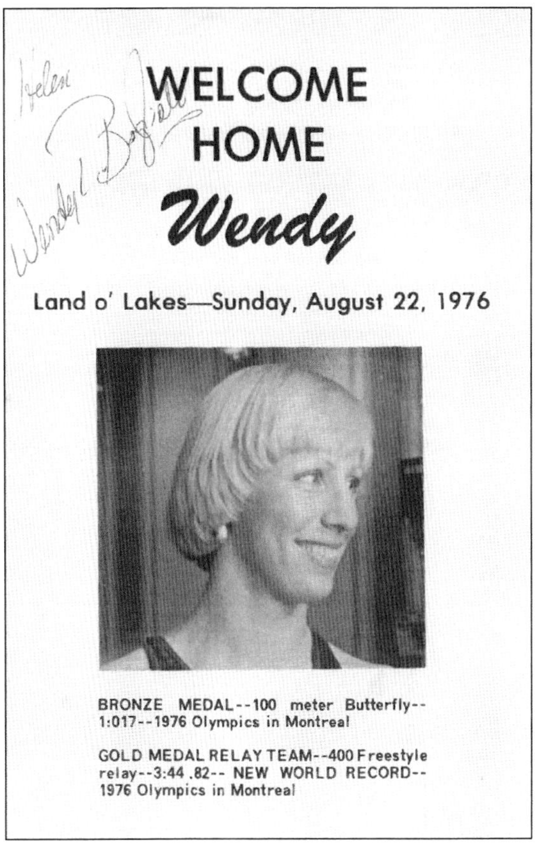

WELCOME HOME

Wendy

Land o' Lakes—Sunday, August 22, 1976

BRONZE MEDAL--100 meter Butterfly--1:017--1976 Olympics in Montreal

GOLD MEDAL RELAY TEAM--400 Freestyle relay--3:44 .82-- NEW WORLD RECORD--1976 Olympics in Montreal

At the 1976 Summer Olympics, local resident Wendy (Lansbach) Boglioli won the bronze medal in the 100-meter butterfly and a gold medal as part of the 400-meter freestyle relay team. She was a member of the Gateway swim team and often trained in the Gateway pool. This photograph shows the cover of the program for her post-Olympics "welcome home" celebration, held at the Tia Juana Club at the junction of Highways 45 and E.

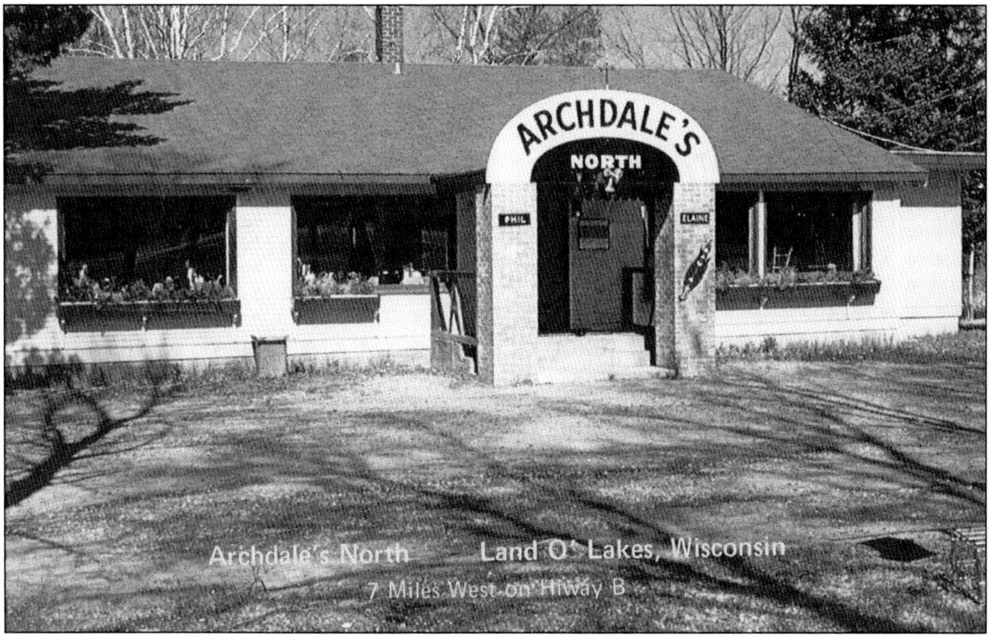

Archdale's Merrill Inn was another popular restaurant that burned in 1988. Noted for its "flaming dinners," it was located on the south side of Highway B, in what is now the empty lot across from the Forest Lake Country Store. Built by Kingstad family, the eatery was also known as Kingstad's, Archdale's (when owned by the Archdale family), and Cab's (when owned by the Fassbender family.)

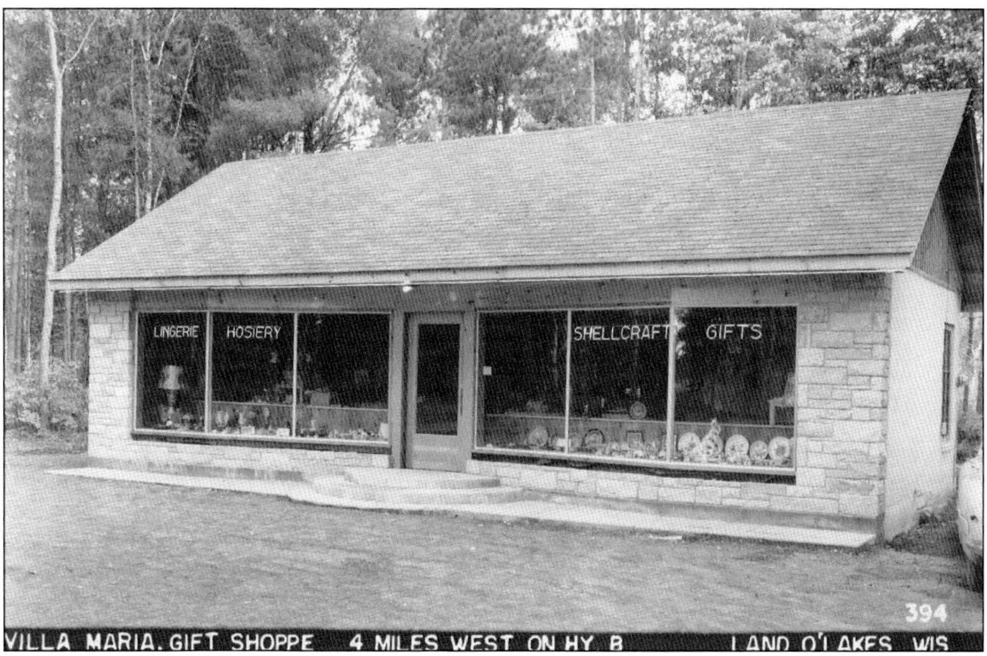

Marie and Fred Kinsler built the Villa Marie gift shop in the 1960s. Located on the north side of Highway B, the business had two other owners before it burned in the late 1970s. (Courtesy of Cindy Pekrul.)

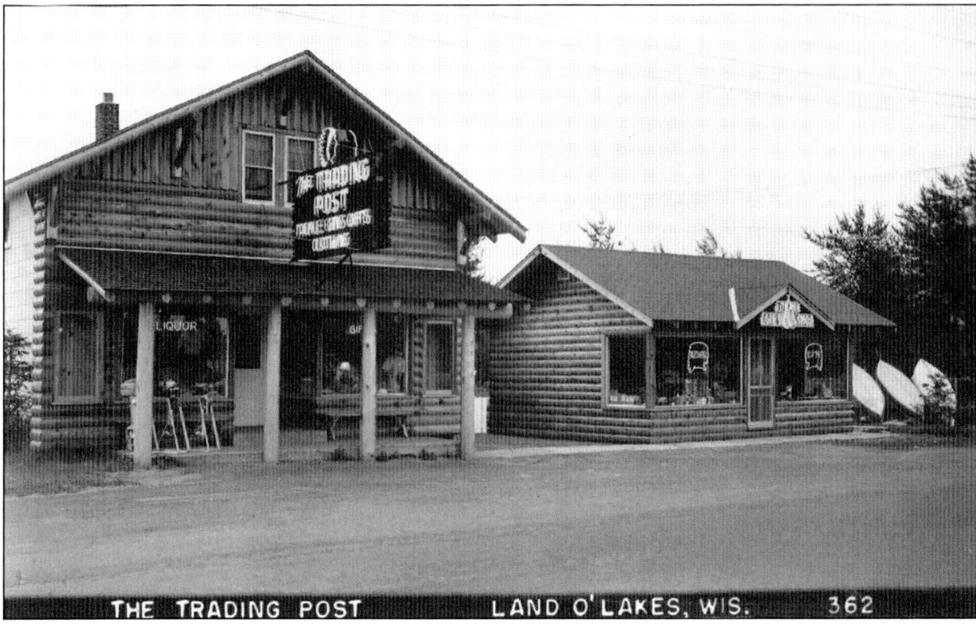

The Trading Post was established in 1945 by Gene and Cele Best. Eventually, the two separate buildings were joined together by a central section. In 1964, the business was taken over and renamed the Trading Post International, Inc., by Cele Best's nephew Harold Nehring and his wife, Barbara, who added another store, Trading Post Antiques, just west of the Trading Post buildings. The Nehrings currently operate both businesses.

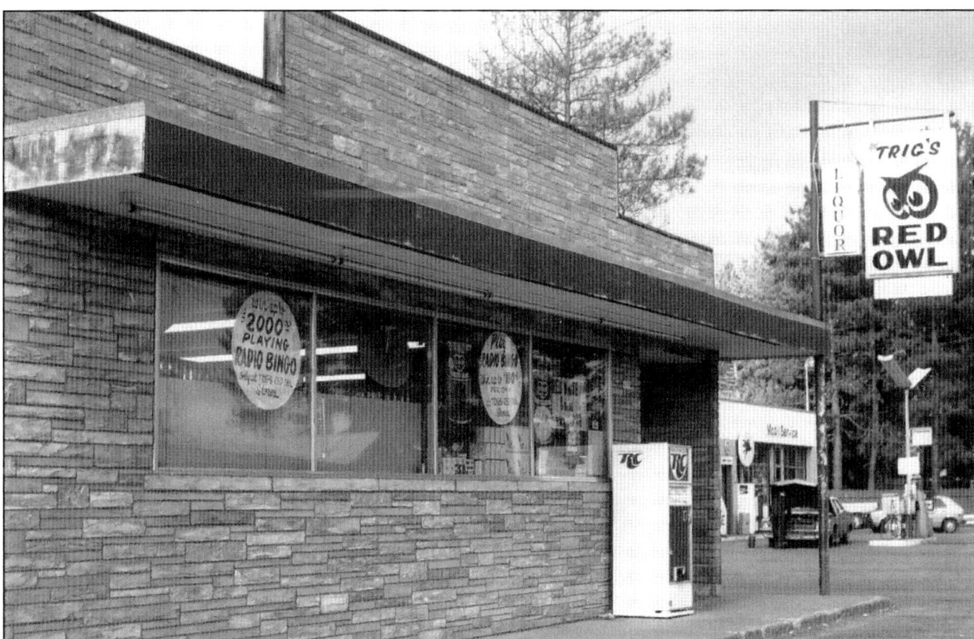

From the 1950s until the late 1970s, anyone going to the grocery store in the north woods was probably going to the Red Owl.

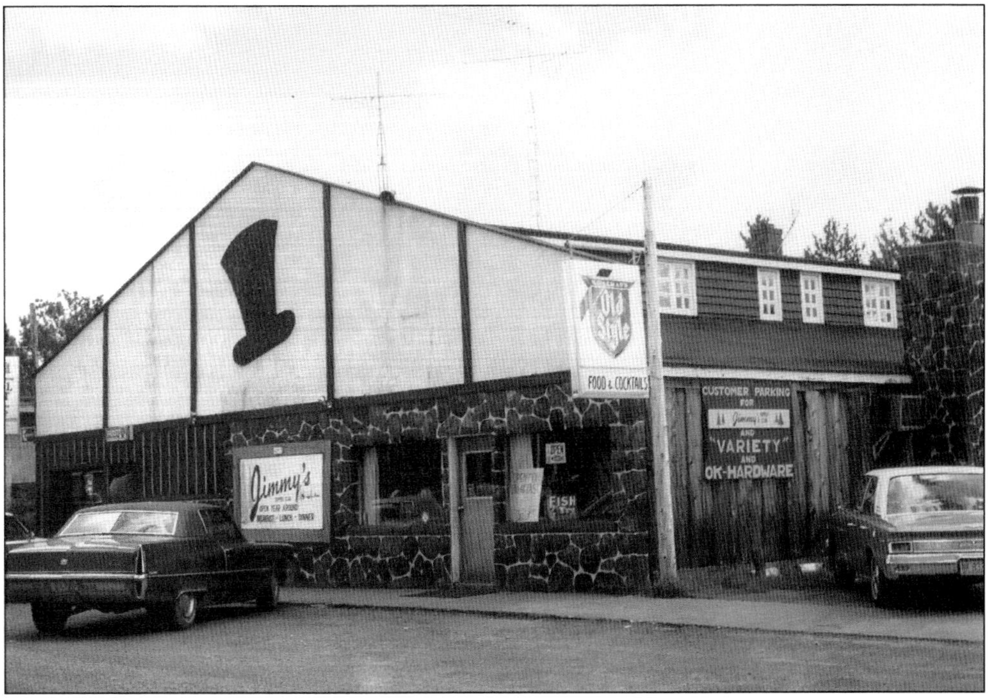

The Hi Hat Club was a popular downtown supper club operated for many years by the first person born in State Line, Cora (Dickman) Harris, and her husband, Chet. When this photograph was taken in 1976, it was known as Jimmy's. It burned on January 11, 1988, due to an unknown cause.

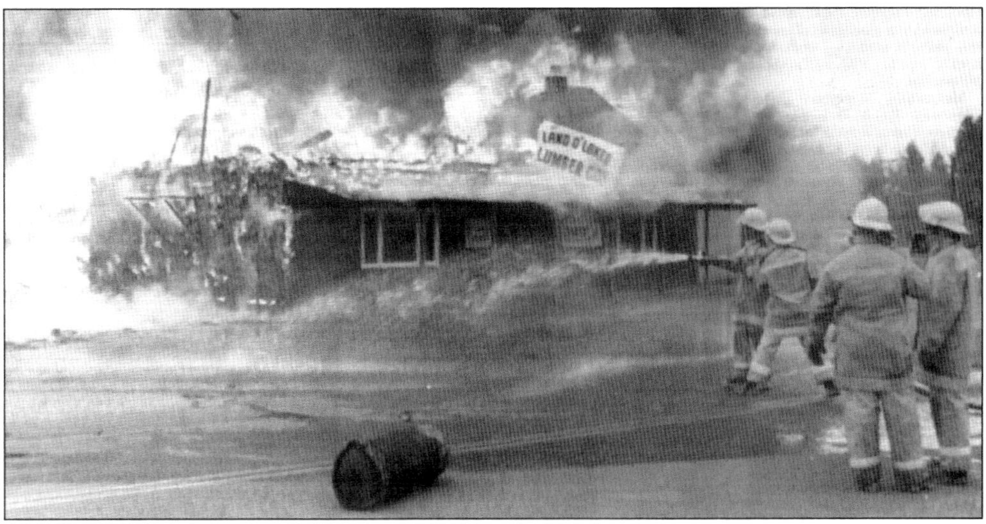

Also, in 1988, the downtown Land O' Lakes Lumber Company was destroyed by fire. It took nearly seven hours and 50 firemen to extinguish the blaze, which shot flames more than 100 feet into the air. Arson was the suspected cause. The facility was never rebuilt, and the open space is now the site of the Land O' Lakes farmer's market.

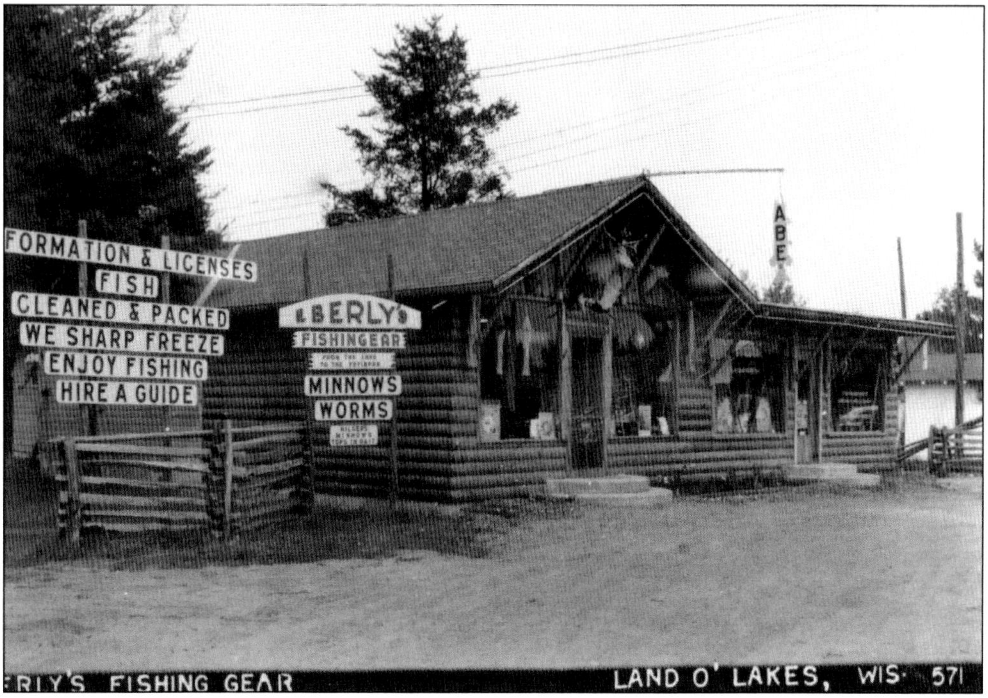

Longtime Land O' Lakes resident and renowned fishing guide Abe Eberly built and operated a sporting goods store until his death in the late 1970s. The building, on the north side of Highway B across from the current Citgo Station, was later renovated and most recently served as a real estate office.

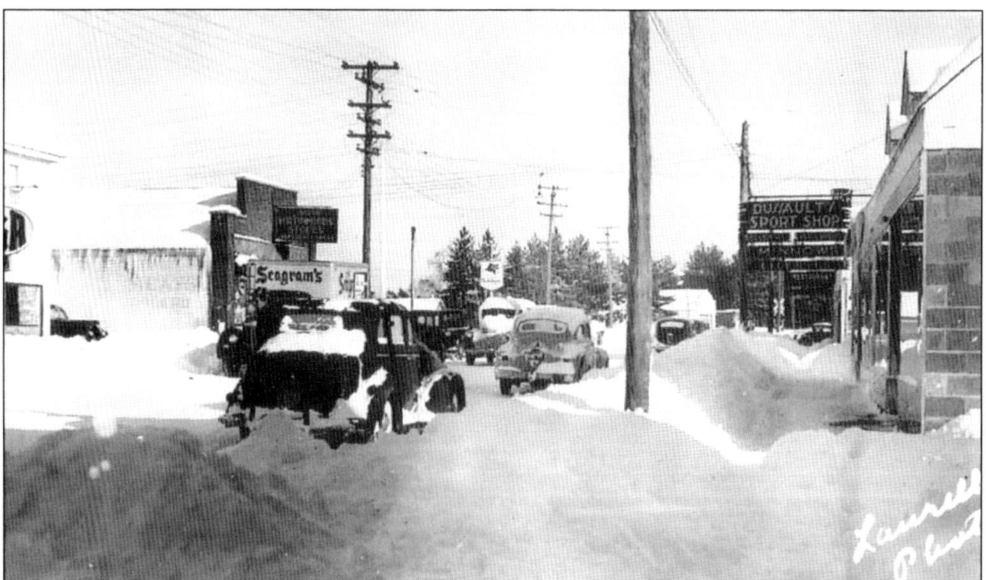

Lake Superior, the world's second largest lake, rests just 43 miles north of Land O' Lakes. Cold northerly winds from Canada, flowing over the warmer water of Lake Superior, create heavy snowfalls in Land O' Lakes, historically averaging around 100 inches or more. This photograph was taken in the winter of 1948.

Three

Wagon Trails, Railroads, Roads, and Airports

Bringing Settlers, Vacationers, and Celebrities

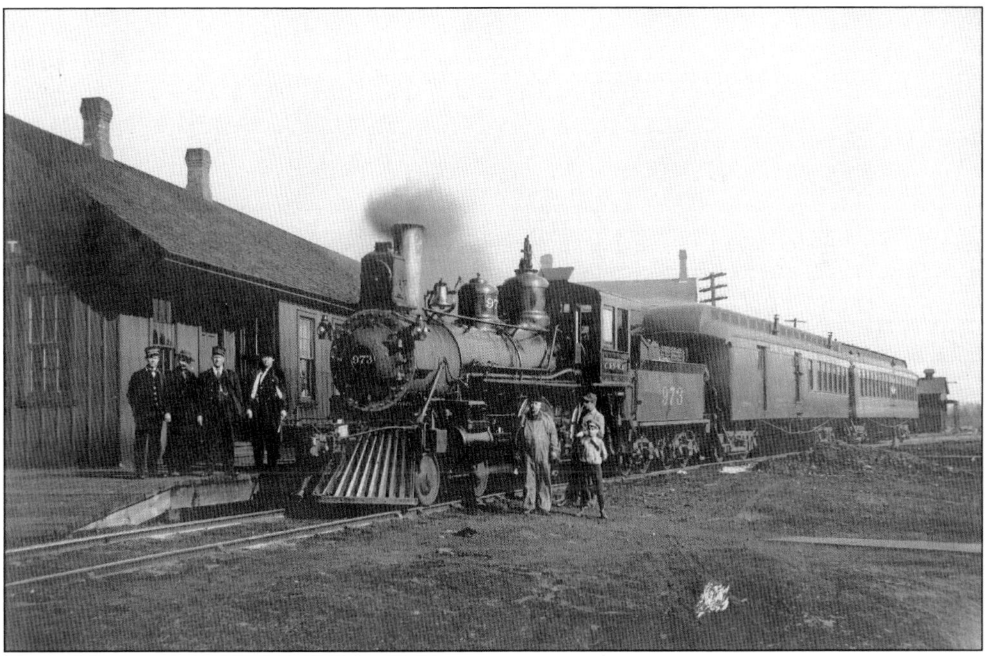

After leaving Conover, "Old 973" stopped at Rummels (near the current intersection of Rummels Road and Highway 45), State Line (now Land O' Lakes), and then Watersmeet. This photograph was taken at the Watersmeet Railroad Depot, where the train turned around for the trip back south. An early passenger recalled, "The coach was stuffy and packed with lumberjacks, deer hunters and whatnot, all smelling equally bad or anyway the car did."

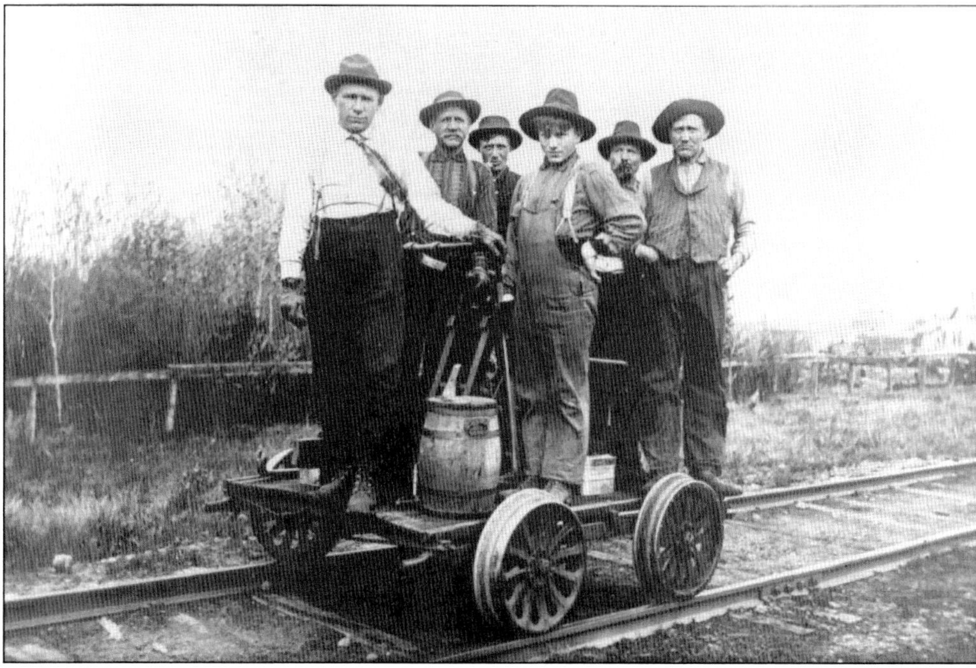

Since railroads were the lifeblood for fledgling northern Wisconsin communities, the tracks needed to be regularly inspected and repaired. This section crew, photographed in 1905, maintained between 6 and 10 miles of track near State Line.

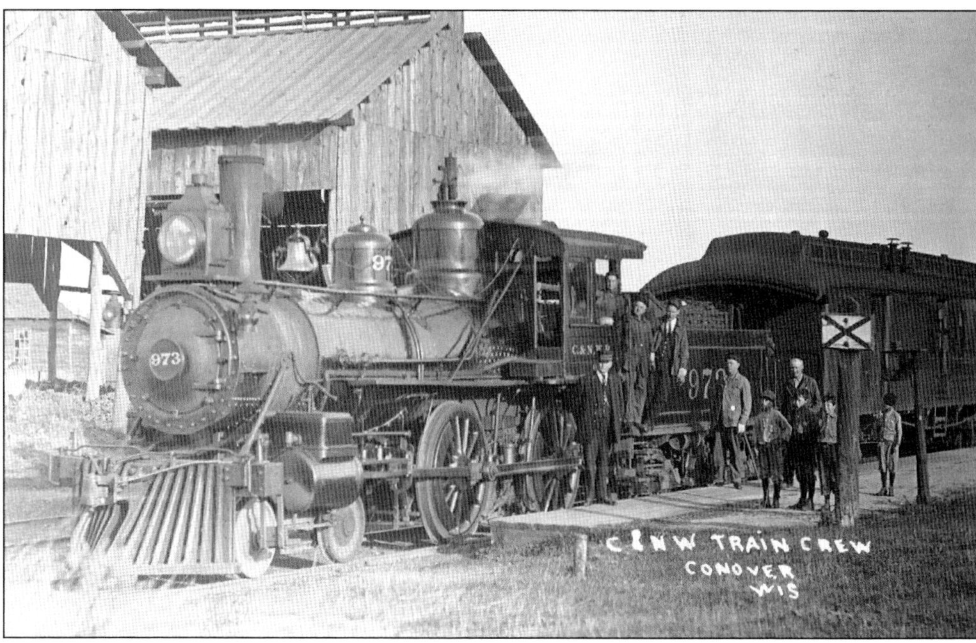

The coal-fired steam engine "Old 973" served Land O' Lakes for much of the early 1900s. The conductor, a Mr. Durkee, stands below the unidentified engineer at the Conover depot.

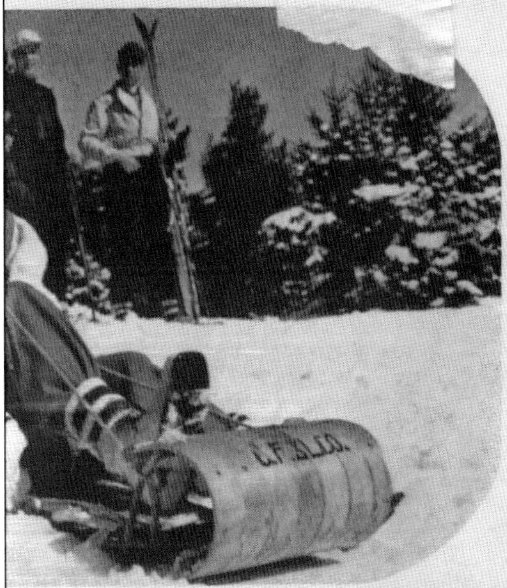

LAND O' LAKES, WISCONSIN

Season: December 21 to March 31

$15.25 and up from CHICAGO **$12.30 and up from MILWAUKEE**

One of the attractive winter sports centers in the north country. Here you have a wide choice of winter out-of-door sports topped off by skiing. The skiing area is about one mile from the hotel with transportation furnished, with ski runs that will thrill the novice and test the skill of the experienced. Haas Hill where the winter sports are centered has a 500-foot rope ski tow. And, too, a fast toboggan run that gives added zest to your outing. At the Inn skating, and many other recreational endeavors can be indulged in with plenty of indoor diversions for the evenings.

KING'S GATEWAY HOTEL—A modern new Inn, completed in 1938 with comfortably appointed rooms and a dining room that cannot be surpassed in the serving of delectable foods—graciously served amid pleasant surroundings.

"SKI-TIME" Week-End Trip Costs Per Person

(Leave Friday night and return Monday morning. Also leave on Saturday night and return Tuesday morning.)

From	2 in Lower Berth	1 in Upper Berth	1 in Lower Berth	2 in Compt.	2 in Draw. Room	3 in Draw. Room	In Coaches
	In Standard Pullman Sleeping Cars						
Chicago, Ill.	$17.90	$19.25	$20.55	$22.60	$24.70	$21.55	$15.25
Milwaukee, Wis.	14.95	16.30	17.60	19.65	21.75	18.60	12.30

Above prices include transfers between depot and hotel, and

Lodgings—2 to a room without bath (50c extra per night for single room; $1.00 each 2 to a room with bath; $1.50 for single room with bath.)

Additional Days—For those desiring to leave earlier and stay longer add $2.50 per person for each additional day—2 to a room without bath. See above extra costs for superior lodging accommodations.

No meals on trains or at destination included.

C. & N. W. Ry. Train Schedules

GOING:		RETURNING:	
Lv. Chicago	6.00 pm Friday	Lv. Land O' Lakes	7.15 pm Sunday
Lv. Milwaukee	8.15 pm "	Lv. Monico (a)	
Ar. Land O' Lakes	7.20 am Saturday	Ar. Milwaukee (a)	4.40 am Monday
		Ar. Chicago	7.15 am "

a—Milwaukee pas ... ilwaukee sleeping car at Monico at 9.10 pm.
Car may be occupied ... 1.

In 1939, the Chicago and Northwestern Railway added Land O' Lakes to its "Winter Weekend Tour" packages. Passengers left Milwaukee or Chicago on Friday evening and arrived at Land O' Lakes Saturday morning. Horse-drawn sleighs took them from the depot to the Gateway Lodge ski chalet and returned them to the depot on Sunday night for the 7:15 p.m. departure back to the big cities.

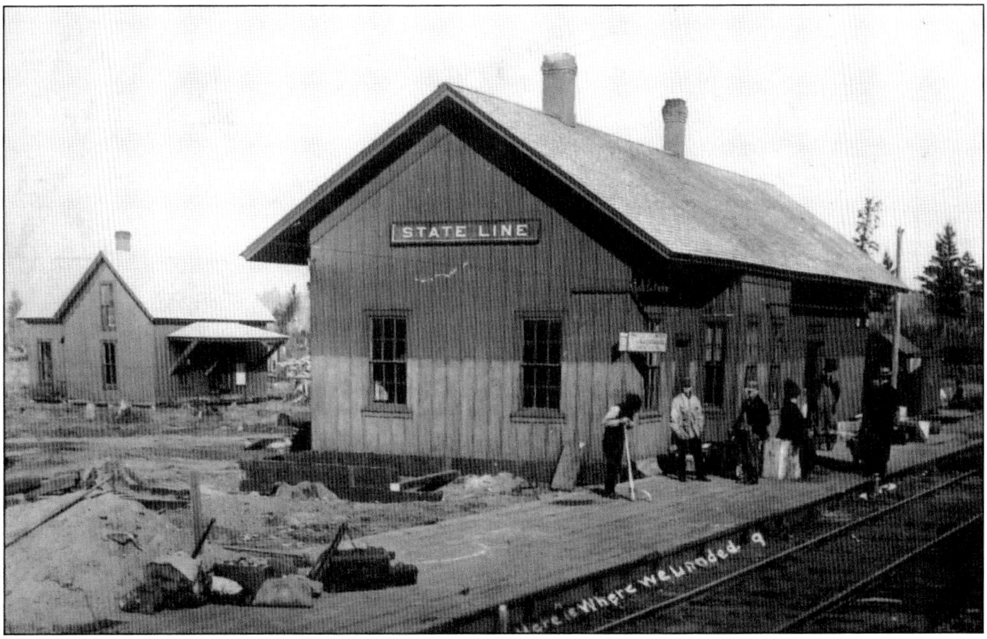

The State Line Railroad depot was the hub of arrival for lumbermen, vacationers, fishermen, hunters, land speculators, and men looking for work. Early conditions were basic, with most homes and resorts relying on food gathered from gardens or hunted with shotguns and rifles. The pictured depot burned to the ground in 1928, and a new facility was built shortly thereafter. When this photograph was taken in 1920, the population of State Line was 75.

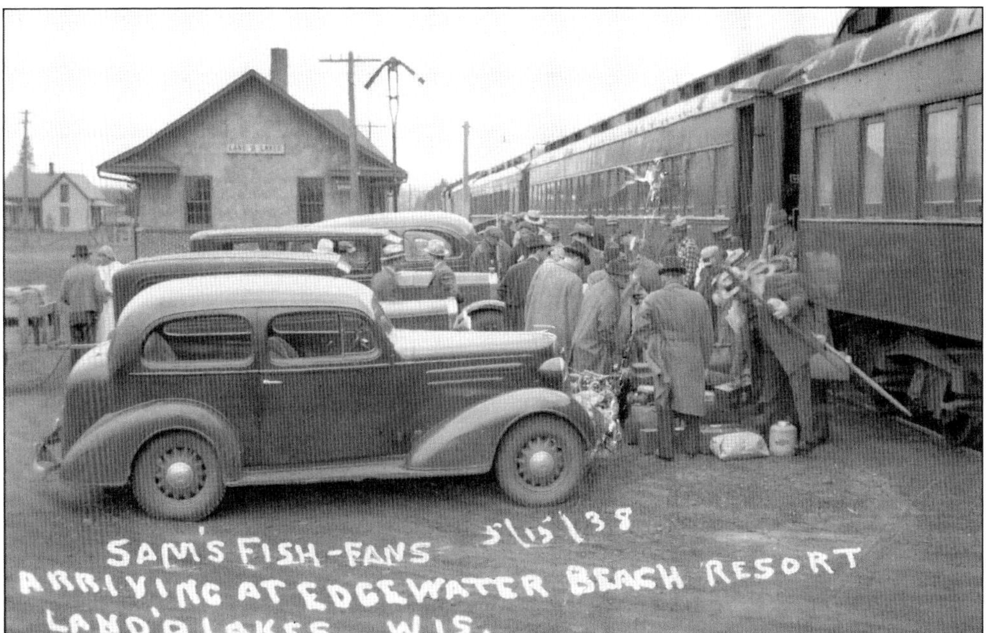

City men of the 1930s prided themselves on dressing smartly, even if they were arriving for a north woods hunting or fishing vacation. This group of fishermen disembarked from the morning train in May 1938 en route to the Edgewater Beach Resort on Lac Vieux Desert.

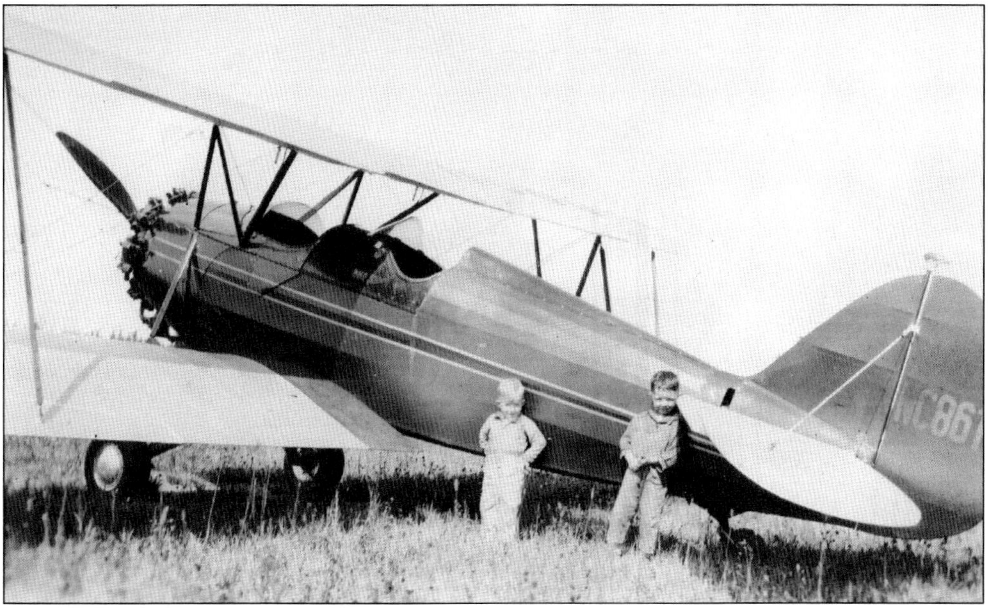

This Boeing Stearman aircraft landed at the Black Oak Airport in 1931. Located on the southeast side of Black Oak Lake, the Black Oak airfield had a primary east to west runway and a shorter strip running north-south. Pilots also used a more primitive field closer to town, which eventually became the King's Gateway Airport in 1939. (Photograph courtesy of Jack LaChance Family Archives.)

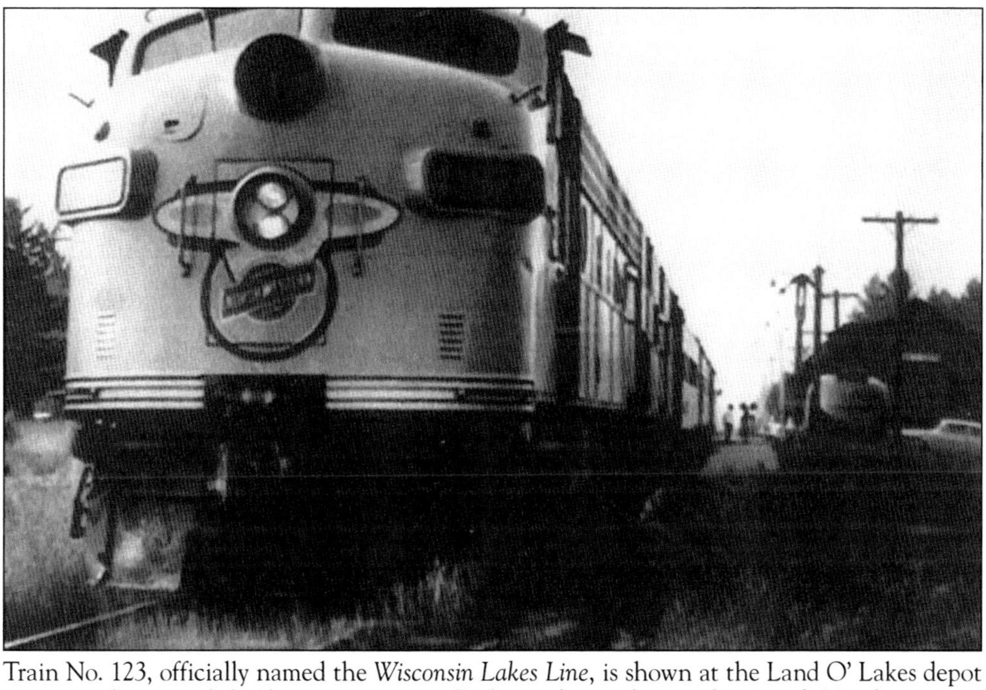

Train No. 123, officially named the *Wisconsin Lakes Line*, is shown at the Land O' Lakes depot in 1960. This train left Chicago at 7:30 on Friday nights and arrived in Land O' Lakes at 7:20 a.m. Saturday. Then it departed for Watersmeet, where the crew laid over until Sunday afternoon when it returned to Land O' Lakes for the 6:00 p.m. run back to Chicago. The *Wisconsin Lakes Line* was nicknamed "The Fisherman's Special" by railroad employees.

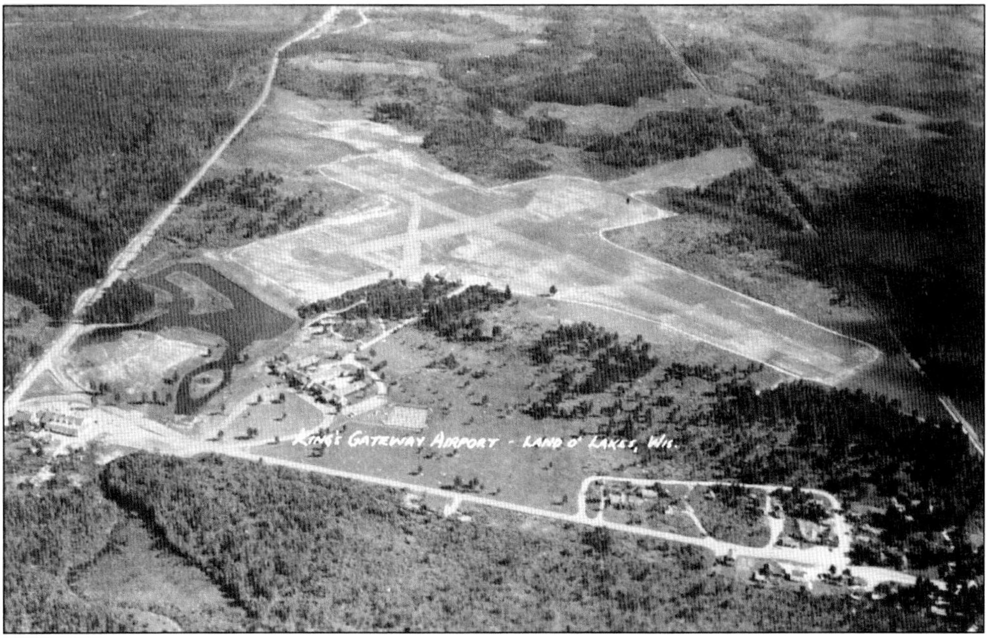

This southerly view depicts the Gateway Inn (left), lodge (center), town (lower right), and the King's Gateway Airport. In the fall of 1953, the main airport runway was extended by 500 feet and paved, allowing North Central Airline to reinstate seasonal service using its larger DC-3 aircraft.

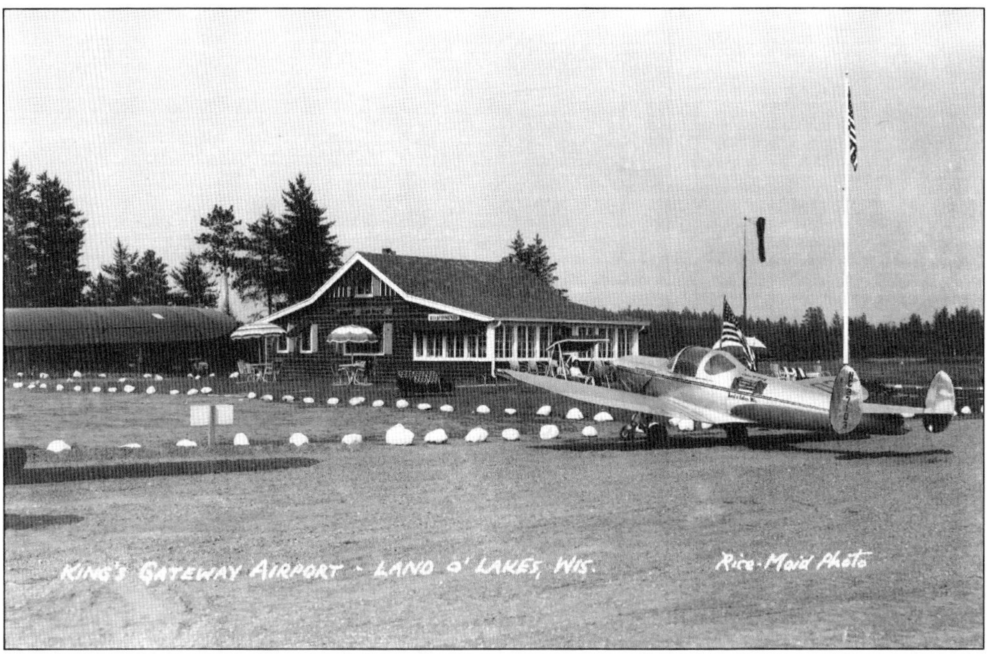

The King's Land O' Lakes airport was owned and operated by the King's Gateway Corporation until it was donated to the town in 1954 by King's widow, Sug (short for Sugar). The original airport building, pictured here, was then moved to the north side of Highway B to serve as the golf course clubhouse, where it remains today.

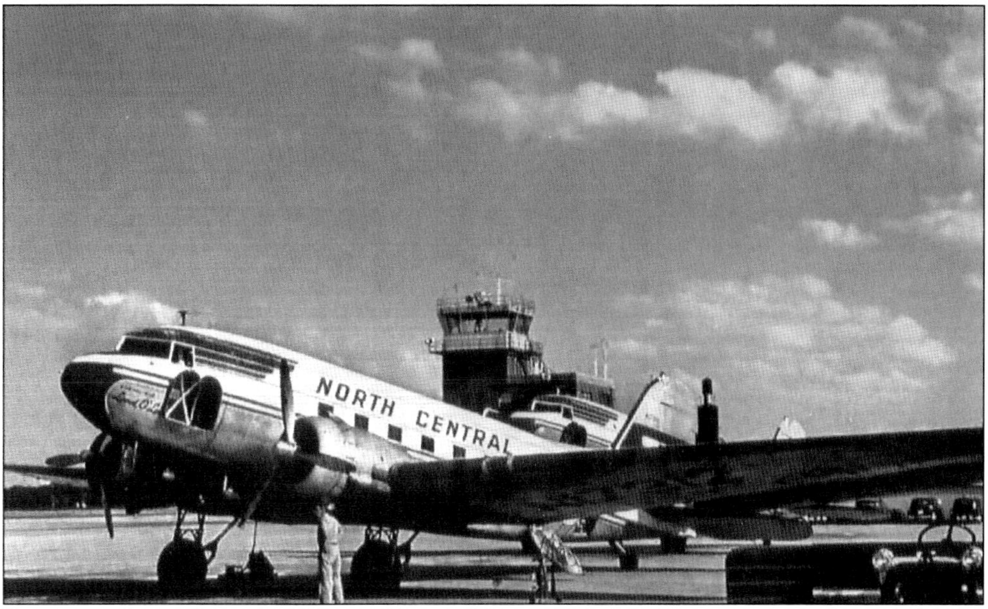

This North Central Airlines DC-3 was named *Land O' Lakes*. Although difficult to see in this photograph, the name is painted on the nose, to the left of the open cargo door. Registered as N17312, it was first delivered to Trans World Airlines (TWA) in 1937, impressed into service during World War II, then acquired by North Central Airlines in 1952. It spent its final years under private ownership in Puerto Rico and was scrapped in 1980.

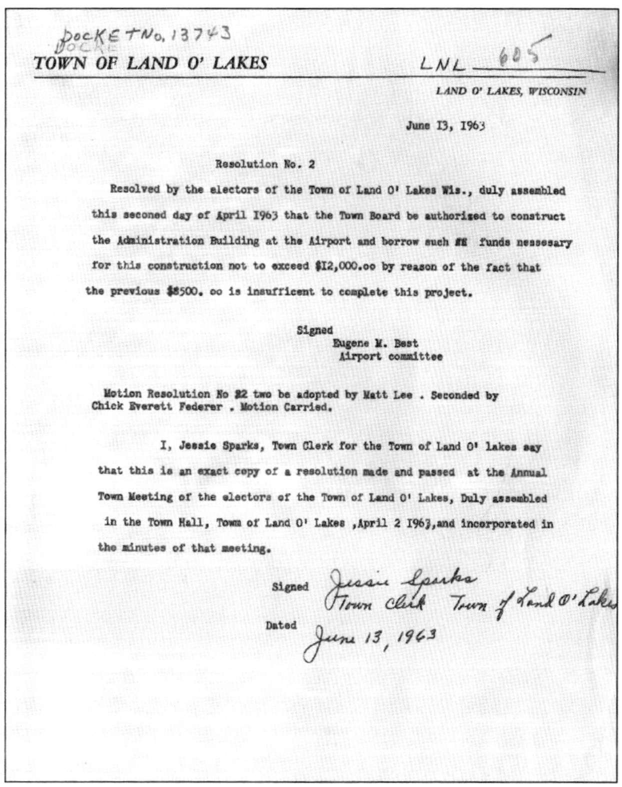

DOCKET No. 13743

TOWN OF LAND O' LAKES LNL 605

LAND O' LAKES, WISCONSIN

June 13, 1963

Resolution No. 2

Resolved by the electors of the Town of Land O' Lakes Wis., duly assembled this seconed day of April 1963 that the Town Board be authorized to construct the Administration Building at the Airport and borrow such ## funds nessesary for this construction not to exceed $12,000.oo by reason of the fact that the previous $8500. oo is insufficent to complete this project.

Signed
Eugene M. Best
Airport committee

Motion Resolution No #2 two be adopted by Matt Lee . Seconded by Chick Everett Federer . Motion Carried.

I, Jessie Sparks, Town Clerk for the Town of Land O' lakes say that this is an exact copy of a resolution made and passed at the Annual Town Meeting of the electors of the Town of Land O' Lakes, Duly assembled in the Town Hall, Town of Land O' Lakes ,April 2 1963,and incorporated in the minutes of that meeting.

Signed Jessie Sparks
Town Clerk Town of Land O' Lakes

Dated June 13, 1963

When the original airport terminal was moved to the golf course, it was replaced with a small shack. That facility proved unsuitable for processing North Central Airlines passengers, so in 1963 the town board voted to construct a new administration building. That building remains today. North Central ceased service to Land O' Lakes in 1965, as the airport runways could not be lengthened to accommodate the airline's new fleet of Convair 440 turboprop aircraft.

Now on the Route of the Northliners!

LAND O' LAKES

. . . in the World's Muskie Cen

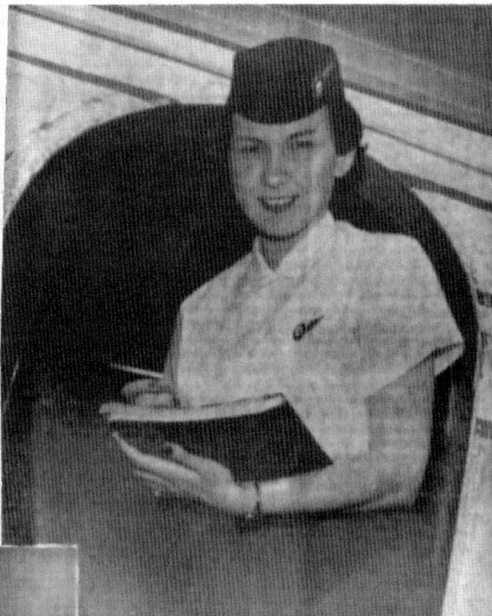

Your new municipal airport and re-inauguration of airline service again brings the famous Headwaters Country within commuter distance of Chicago, Milwaukee, Madison, Oshkosh, Beloit and Janesville, Green Bay, Wausau, Stevens Point and many other cities in Wisconsin and surrounding states.

Now -- with daily airline service -- your summer visitors will be able to come up more often and spend more time here, making this fabulous fishing and vacation center more attractive than ever before!

We are happy to announce that on June 1st, North Central Airlines will add a "Land o' Lakes Express Flight" -- non-stop service between Chicago-Milwaukee and Rhinelander-Land o' Lakes, bringing twice daily round-trip service to your community.

We congratulate you upon the dedication of your first municipal airport, resumption of airline service and your enterprise in developing the Headwaters Country into one of America's most popular vacation spots. It will be a pleasure to serve you and your summer visitors again and make our contribution to the progress of the Land o' Lakes area.

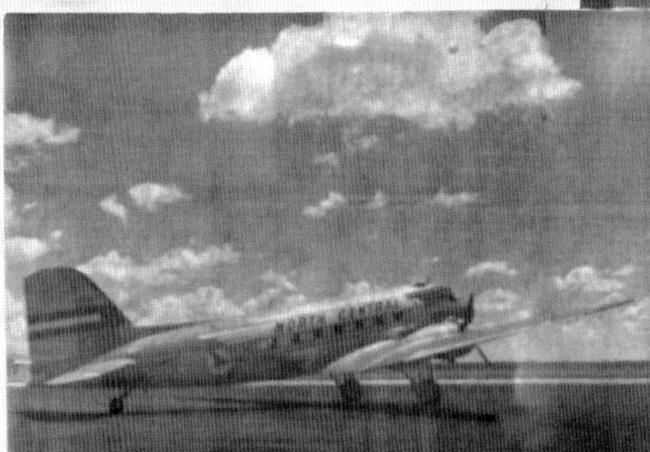

MAY FLIGHT SCHEDULE

To Chicago, Milwaukee, Madison, Oshkosh, Beloit-Janesville, Green Bay, Wausau, Stevens Point and other cities.

Leave 4:50 P. M.

Arrive from These Cities at 11:26 A. M.

JUNE FLIGHT SCHEDULE

Leave Land o' Lakes

Southbound

2:15 P. M.

4:54 P. M.

Northbound

11:19 A. M.

To Duluth--Superior--Hibbing

NORTH CENTRAL AIRLINES

Serving North Dakota - Minnesota - Wisconsin - Michigan - Illinois

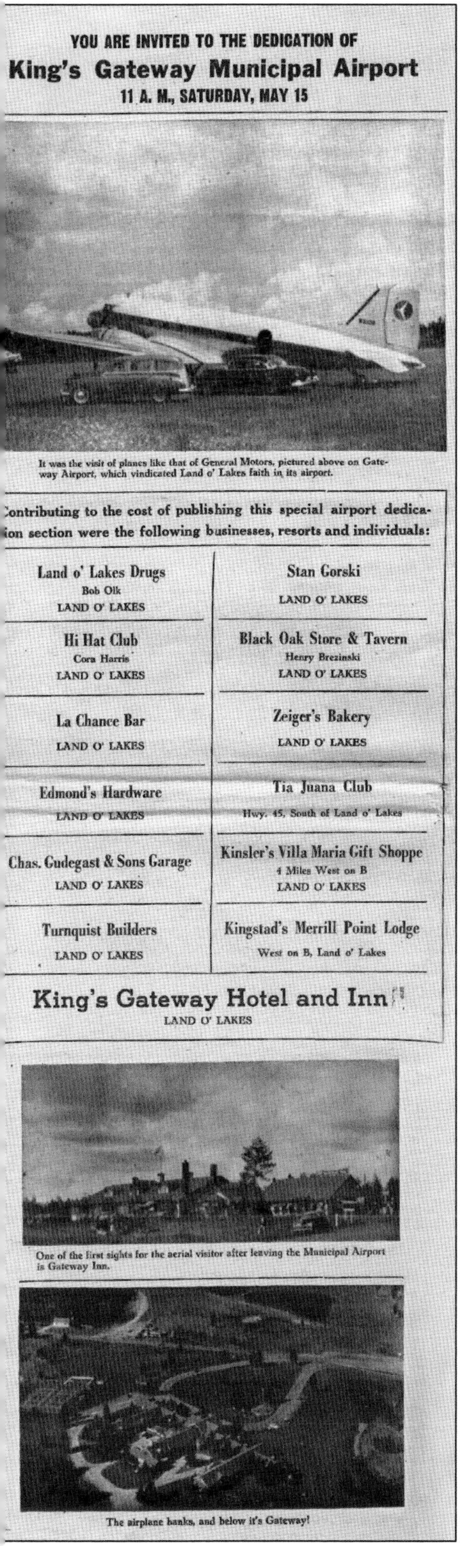

YOU ARE INVITED TO THE DEDICATION OF

King's Gateway Municipal Airport

11 A. M., SATURDAY, MAY 15

It was the visit of planes like that of General Motors, pictured above on Gateway Airport, which vindicated Land o' Lakes faith in its airport.

Contributing to the cost of publishing this special airport dedication section were the following businesses, resorts and individuals:

Land o' Lakes Drugs Bob Olk LAND O' LAKES	Stan Gorski LAND O' LAKES
Hi Hat Club Cora Harris LAND O' LAKES	Black Oak Store & Tavern Henry Brezinski LAND O' LAKES
La Chance Bar LAND O' LAKES	Zeiger's Bakery LAND O' LAKES
Edmond's Hardware LAND O' LAKES	Tia Juana Club Hwy. 45, South of Land o' Lakes
Chas. Gudegast & Sons Garage LAND O' LAKES	Kinsler's Villa Maria Gift Shoppe 4 Miles West on B LAND O' LAKES
Turnquist Builders LAND O' LAKES	Kingstad's Merrill Point Lodge West on B, Land o' Lakes

King's Gateway Hotel and Inn

LAND O' LAKES

One of the first sights for the aerial visitor after leaving the Municipal Airport is Gateway Inn.

The airplane banks, and below it's Gateway!

In this two-page advertising spread, North Central Airlines announces its renewed seasonal service to Land O' Lakes. When North Central No. 573 from Chicago touched down on May 15, 1954, a celebration began, including a jet flyover, ribbon cutting, and a marching band. Attending were television crews, newspaper reporters, and a special appearance by Lester J. Maitland, the first man to fly over the Pacific Ocean to Honolulu. Land O' Lakes was again the smallest town in the country served by a commercial airline.

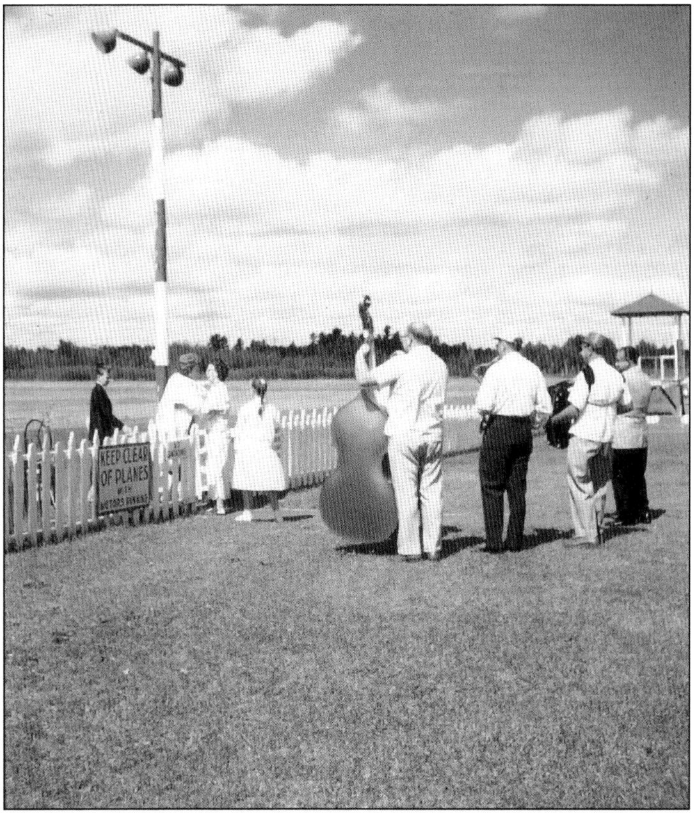

In this c. 1960 photograph, John King's widow, Sug, is greeted at the airport by her sister Oni Garber, wife of Gateway general manager John Garber. Also pictured is the "welcome home" band, which played every spring when Sug returned from California. Sug maintained control of the Gateway operations until 1961 when she sold to Walter Williamson. After John King's death in January 1952, Sug married actor and entertainer Charley Foy. They owned a home on Black Oak Lake. (Courtesy of Lee Bennett.)

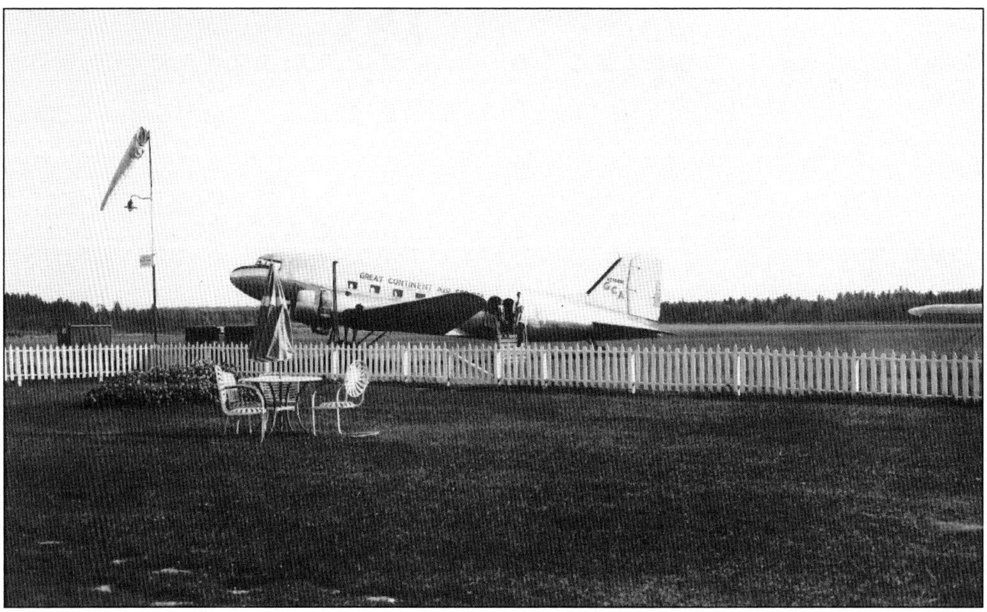

This DC-3, owned by Great Continental Air Service, was probably chartered to fly employees of Fisher Auto Body or Holly Carburetor into Land O' Lakes. In the 1950s, executives of both companies owned property and lodges in the area, including 14,000 acres in the present-day Sylvania Wilderness and Recreation Area.

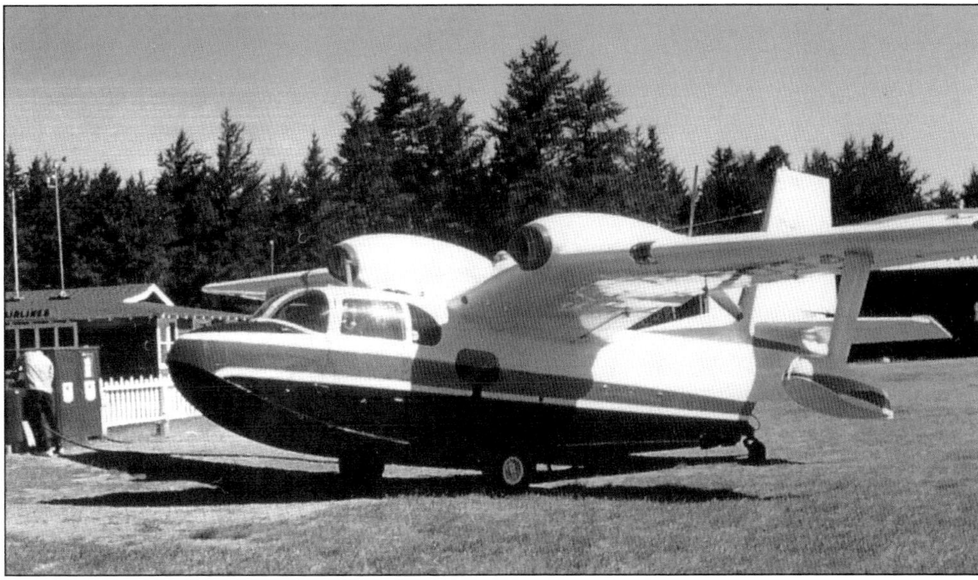

This photograph depicts the location of the old airport fueling station and also the North Central Airlines airport terminal building (far left) that was used between 1954 and 1964. At the request of North Central Airlines, this terminal facility was replaced by the present facility to allow for the better handling of passengers. (Courtesy of Lee Bennett.)

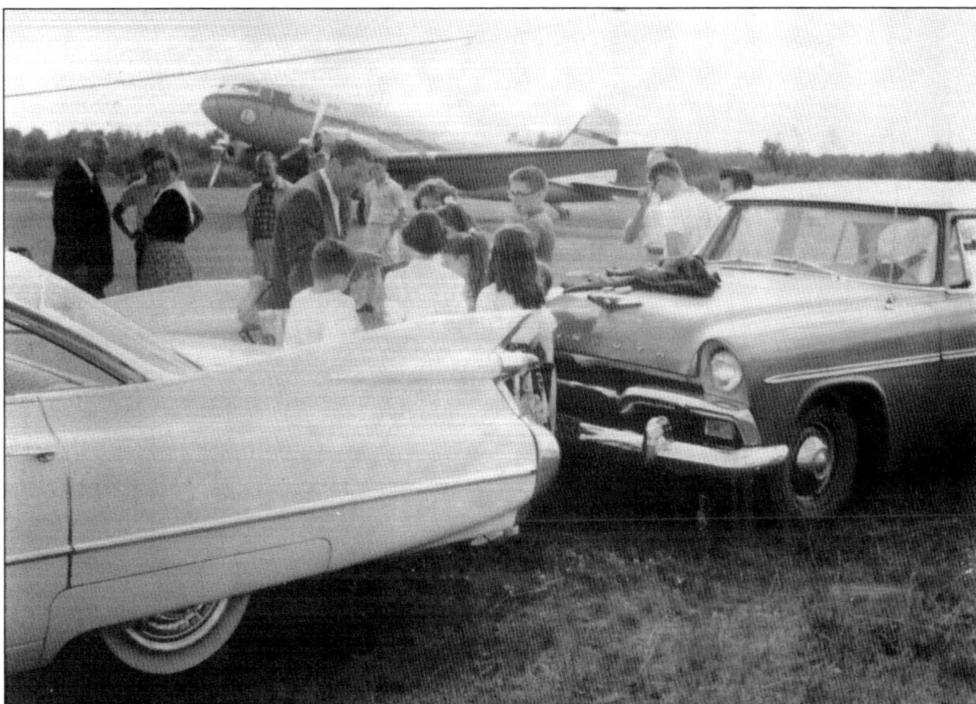

Lawrence Welk is greeted at the King's Land O' Lakes airport by the LaChance and Garber children in 1957. At the invitation of manager John Garber, Welk often vacationed at the Gateway, arriving by a North Central Airlines DC-3, pictured in the back. (Courtesy of the Jack LaChance Family Archives.)

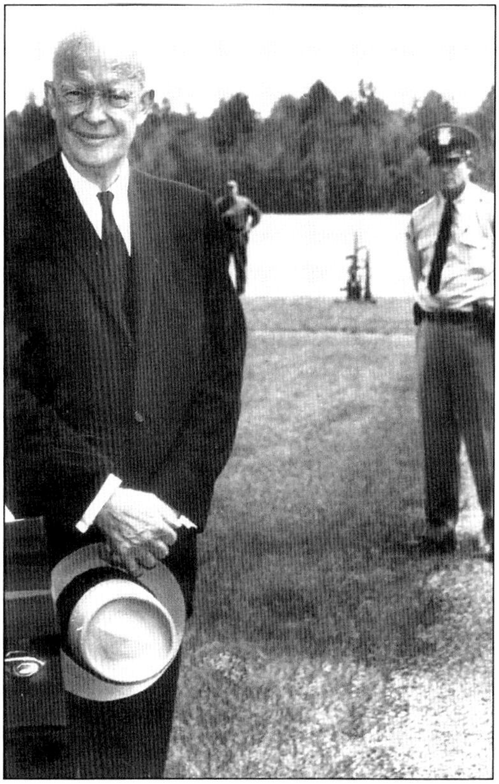

When former president Dwight Eisenhower arrived in Land O' Lakes, security was always high. This photograph of Ike was taken at the King's Land O' Lakes airport after his arrival in early 1960.

With a buck strapped to the engine hood of a Ford Model T, these men pose at the State Line railroad depot in the late 1920s. In the winter, the primary freight load taken south was ice, used in the Milwaukee and Chicago food industries and icehouses. These men could not have foreseen the popularity and recognition their town would have just 10 years later due to the opening of the Gateway Inn and Lodge.

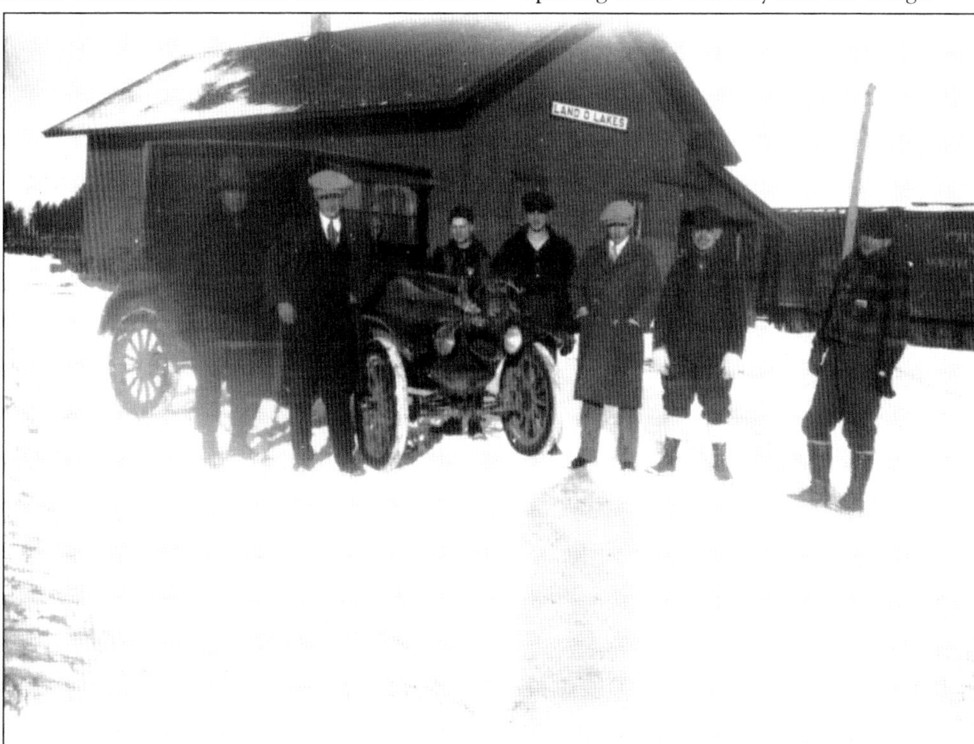

Four

The King's Gateway Inn and Lodge

Making Land O' Lakes a Premier Destination

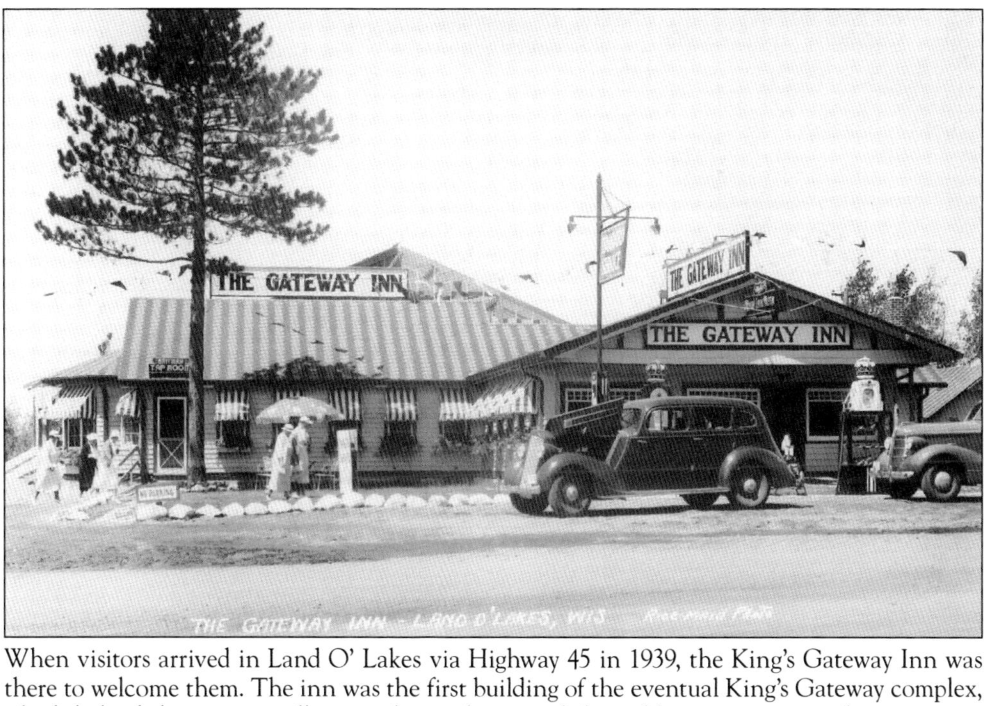

When visitors arrived in Land O' Lakes via Highway 45 in 1939, the King's Gateway Inn was there to welcome them. The inn was the first building of the eventual King's Gateway complex, which helped the town rapidly ascend into the most fashionable entertainment destination in the north woods. Originally a small store and gas station, the facility was remodeled by King, who also built a western addition, which is under construction in this photograph.

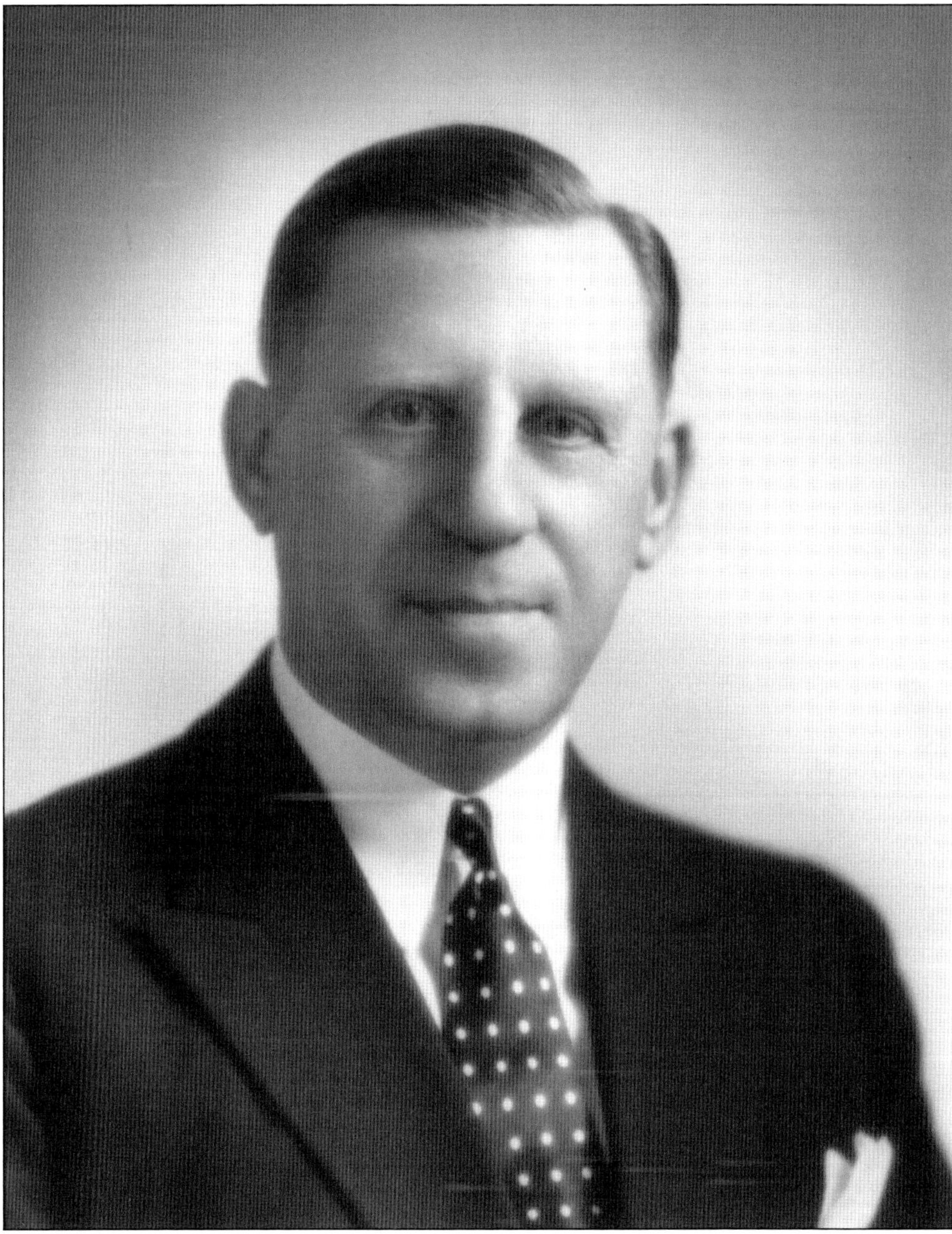

John H. King (born John H. Kunsky in 1875) was a radio and movie theater magnate from Detroit, Michigan, and founder of the King's Gateway Inn and Lodge. The son of an immigrant railroad worker, he worked his way through business school by shining shoes and selling newspapers. Recognizing the potential of the fledgling movie industry, King went on to build many of Detroit's grandest movie theaters. In 1936, at age 61, he stopped at Harrington's gas station, soda fountain, and hamburger stand. The owners told him it was for sale, and King bought it several weeks later.

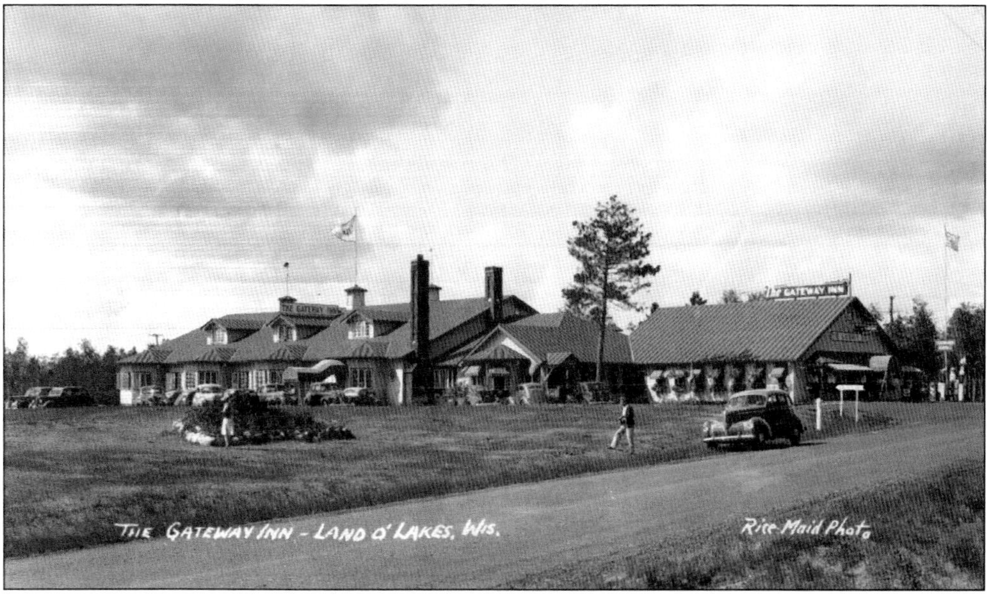

When the King's Gateway Inn opened in 1938, it retained the gas pumps from the store run by Harrington, from whom King bought the property. King renovated and expanded the store with the Tap Room bar and a small café. The new addition (at left) contained bowling alleys, a pool hall, a dining room, and the Red Deer cocktail lounge. The original portion of the inn (on the right) was razed in 1992 and replaced with a BP gas station.

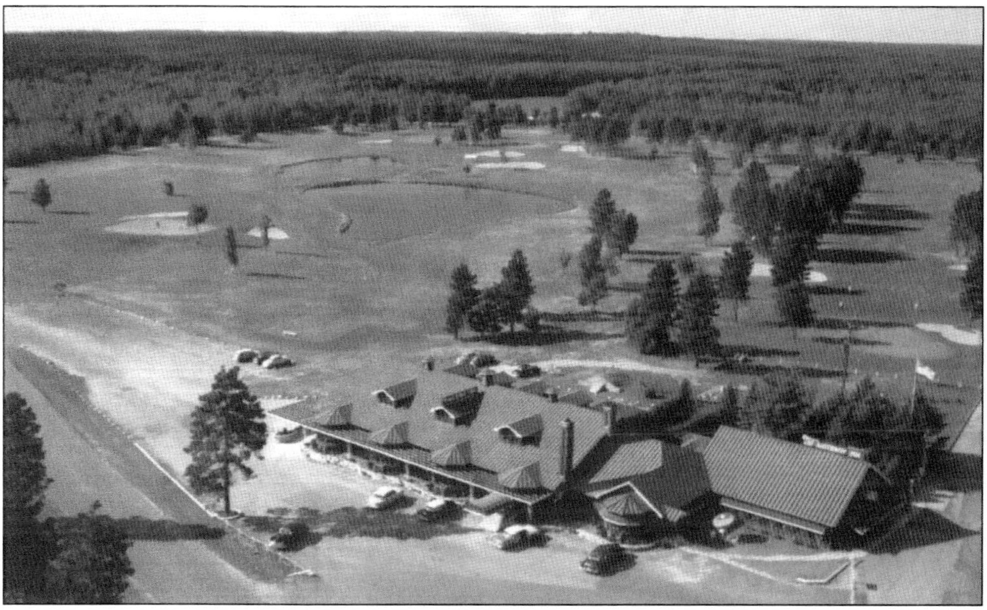

This photograph depicts a northwest view of the King's Gateway Inn toward the golf course on the north side of Highway B. When King decided to add the course, longtime resident Henry Mitchell recalled King approaching him and his friends in his distinctive long, black Cadillac with red wheels, rolling down the window, and saying, "Pick up your shovels, boys, and follow me. We're going to build a golf course!"

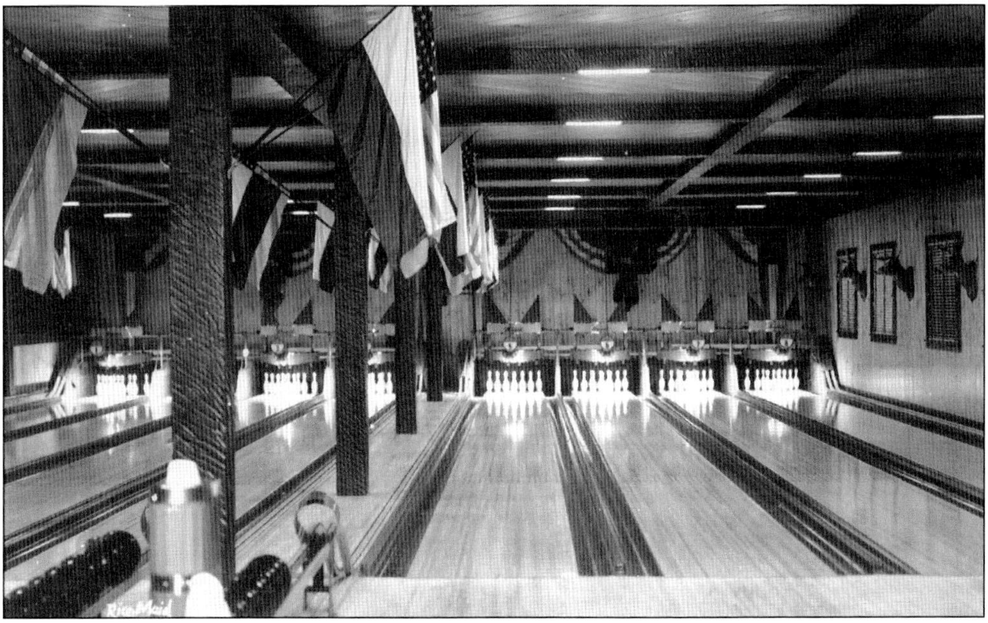

The first facility built by John H. King was the Gateway Inn, located on the north side of Highway B, across from the present-day Gateway Lodge. The inn offered lodging, gasoline, a restaurant, a bowling alley (above), and a pool hall (below). Before automation, pinsetters were often tipped with quarters rolled down the alley. Gambling, with slot machines, was allowed until it was outlawed in 1946.

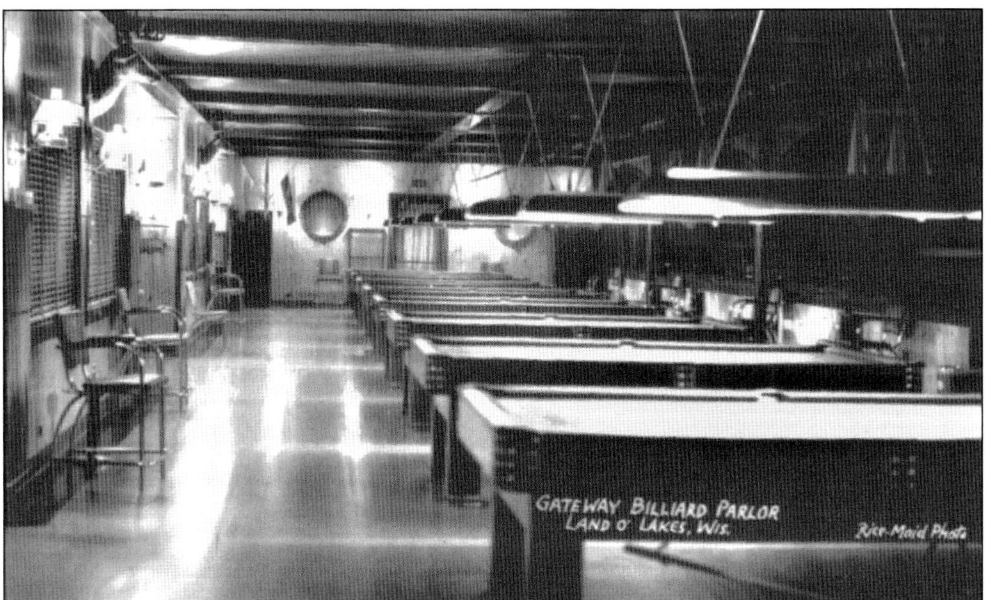

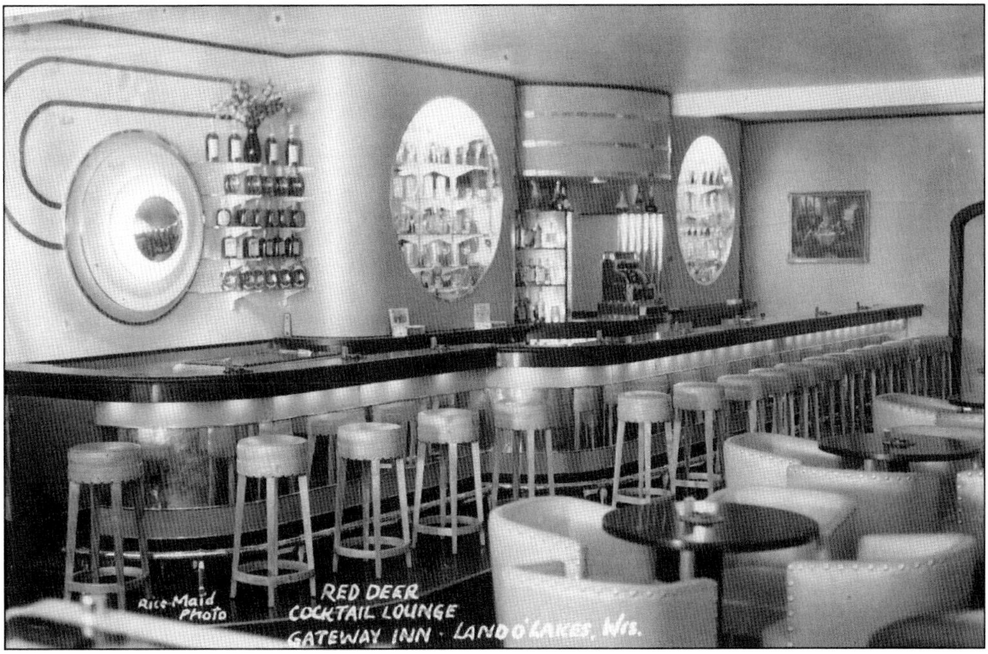

Considered the most fashionable bar in the north woods, the Red Deer Cocktail lounge (above) in the Gateway Inn was a popular cocktail and late-night venue. A large picture window on the north wall (below) overlooked a meticulously landscaped rock garden, which was lighted at night.

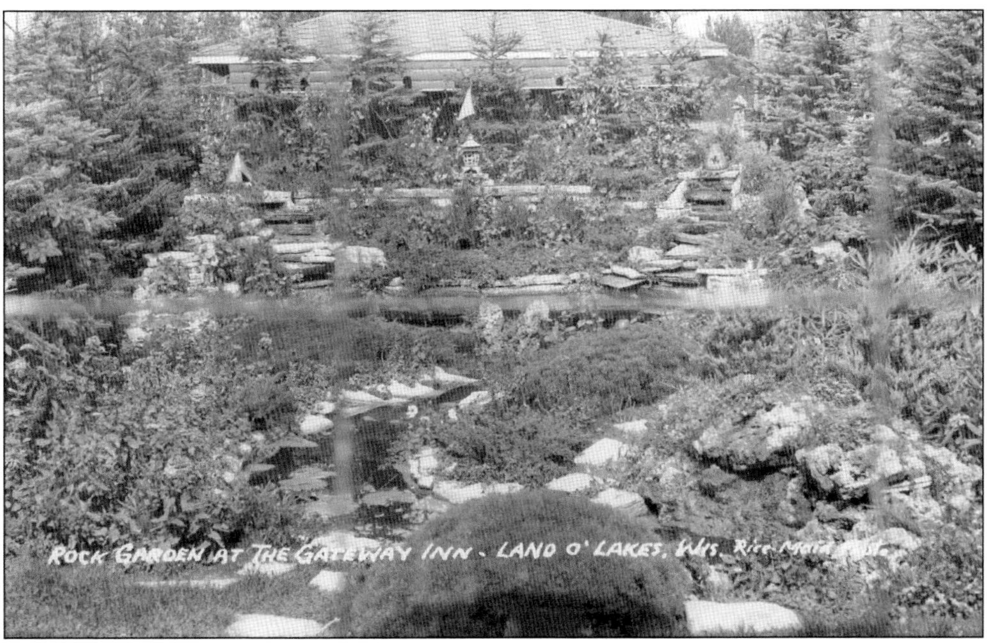

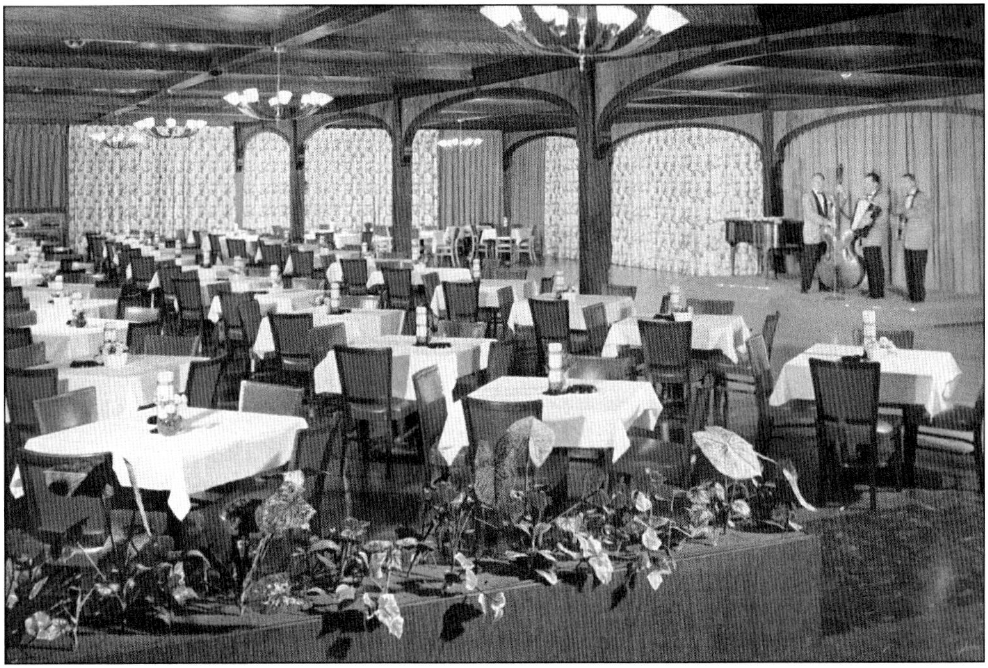

Seen here around 1956, the dining hall of the original Gateway Inn required semiformal attire. On weekends, music was provided by groups that John King personally hired. Being in the theater business, King was well connected in the entertainment world and arranged for appearances by Bob Hope, Lawrence Welk, and Mitzi Gaynor.

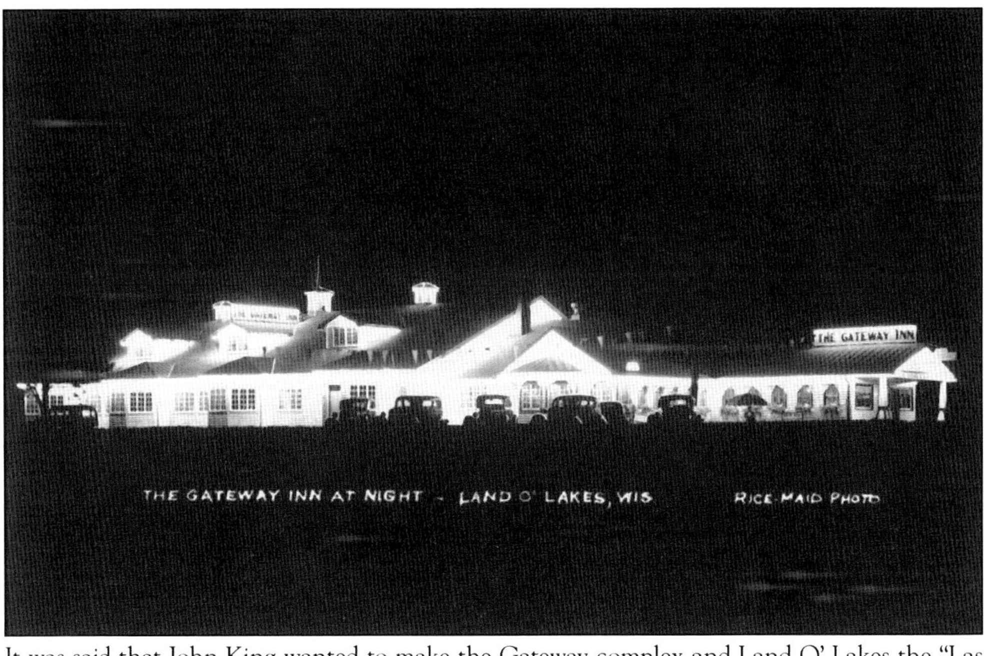

It was said that John King wanted to make the Gateway complex and Land O' Lakes the "Las Vegas of the north." Accordingly, the Gateway Inn was fully lighted every night. On a clear night, pilots could see it from 50 miles away, the only visible light in an otherwise pitch-black ground of forests and lakes.

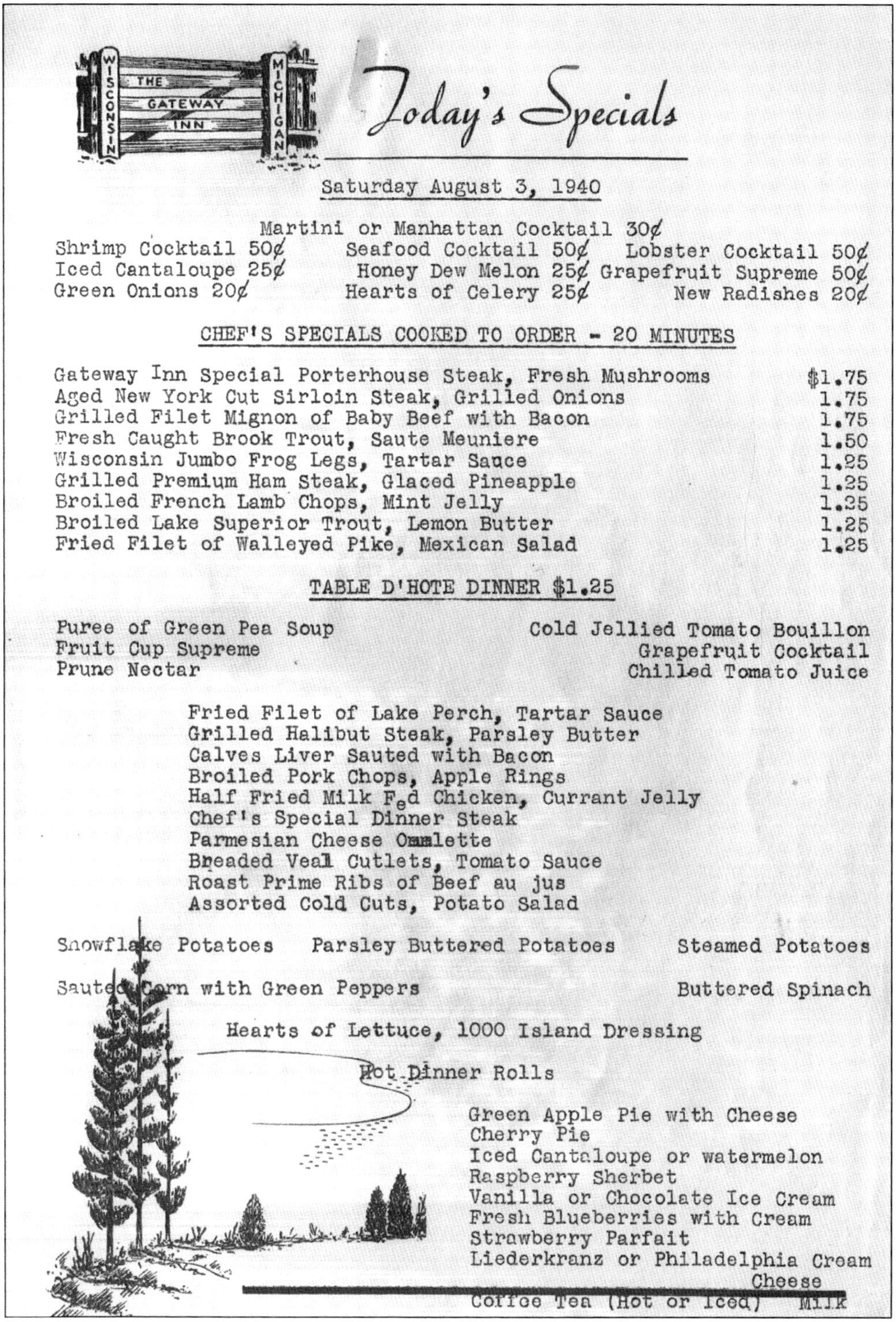

THE GATEWAY INN

WISCONSIN MICHIGAN

Today's Specials

Saturday August 3, 1940

Martini or Manhattan Cocktail 30¢

Shrimp Cocktail 50¢ Seafood Cocktail 50¢ Lobster Cocktail 50¢
Iced Cantaloupe 25¢ Honey Dew Melon 25¢ Grapefruit Supreme 50¢
Green Onions 20¢ Hearts of Celery 25¢ New Radishes 20¢

CHEF'S SPECIALS COOKED TO ORDER - 20 MINUTES

Gateway Inn Special Porterhouse Steak, Fresh Mushrooms $1.75
Aged New York Cut Sirloin Steak, Grilled Onions 1.75
Grilled Filet Mignon of Baby Beef with Bacon 1.75
Fresh Caught Brook Trout, Saute Meuniere 1.50
Wisconsin Jumbo Frog Legs, Tartar Sauce 1.25
Grilled Premium Ham Steak, Glaced Pineapple 1.25
Broiled French Lamb Chops, Mint Jelly 1.25
Broiled Lake Superior Trout, Lemon Butter 1.25
Fried Filet of Walleyed Pike, Mexican Salad 1.25

TABLE D'HOTE DINNER $1.25

Puree of Green Pea Soup — Cold Jellied Tomato Bouillon
Fruit Cup Supreme — Grapefruit Cocktail
Prune Nectar — Chilled Tomato Juice

Fried Filet of Lake Perch, Tartar Sauce
Grilled Halibut Steak, Parsley Butter
Calves Liver Sauted with Bacon
Broiled Pork Chops, Apple Rings
Half Fried Milk Fed Chicken, Currant Jelly
Chef's Special Dinner Steak
Parmesian Cheese Ommlette
Breaded Veal Cutlets, Tomato Sauce
Roast Prime Ribs of Beef au jus
Assorted Cold Cuts, Potato Salad

Snowflake Potatoes Parsley Buttered Potatoes Steamed Potatoes

Sauted Corn with Green Peppers Buttered Spinach

Hearts of Lettuce, 1000 Island Dressing

Hot Dinner Rolls

Green Apple Pie with Cheese
Cherry Pie
Iced Cantaloupe or watermelon
Raspberry Sherbet
Vanilla or Chocolate Ice Cream
Fresh Blueberries with Cream
Strawberry Parfait
Liederkranz or Philadelphia Cream Cheese

Coffee Tea (Hot or Iced) Milk

The Gateway Inn and Lodge were considered upscale and fashionable. John H. King, a man of sophisticated tastes, made sure the dinner offerings would be akin to meals found in Chicago, Milwaukee, or Detroit. This menu is from 1940.

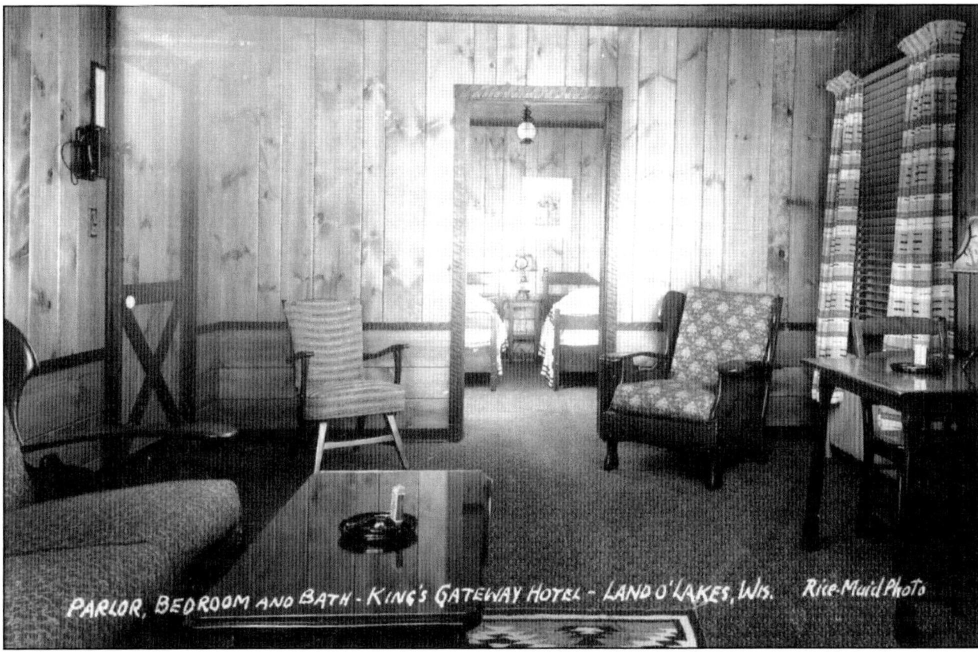

When the Gateway Lodge opened in 1939, it had 55 guest rooms, many with a parlor and bedroom. Private baths were a luxury, so most of the guests booked rooms with shared hallway facilities.

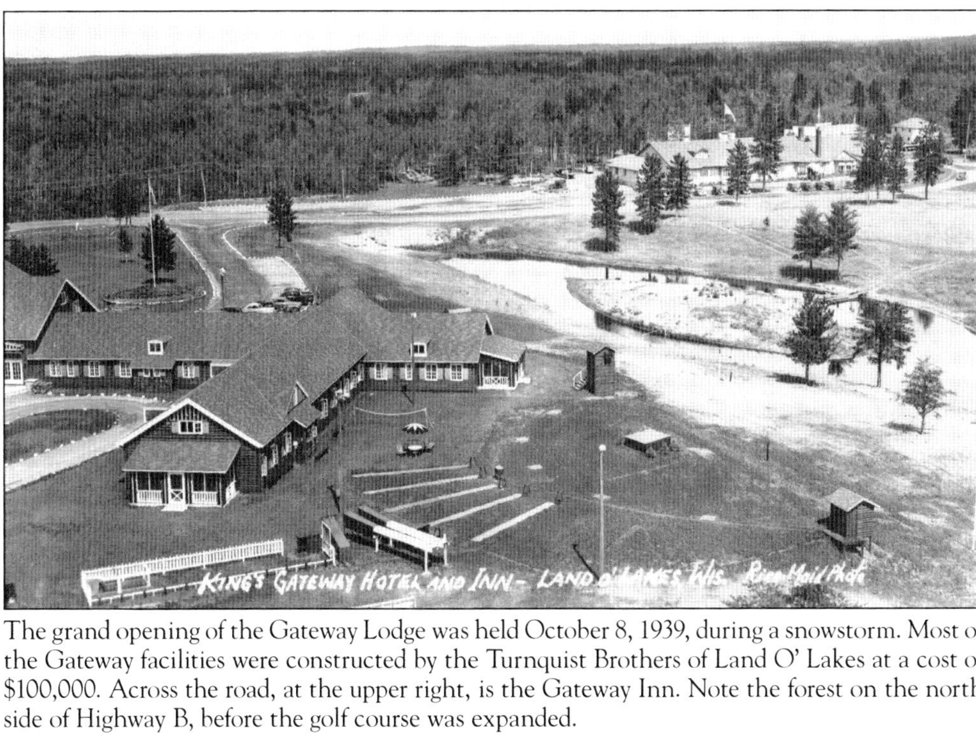

The grand opening of the Gateway Lodge was held October 8, 1939, during a snowstorm. Most of the Gateway facilities were constructed by the Turnquist Brothers of Land O' Lakes at a cost of $100,000. Across the road, at the upper right, is the Gateway Inn. Note the forest on the north side of Highway B, before the golf course was expanded.

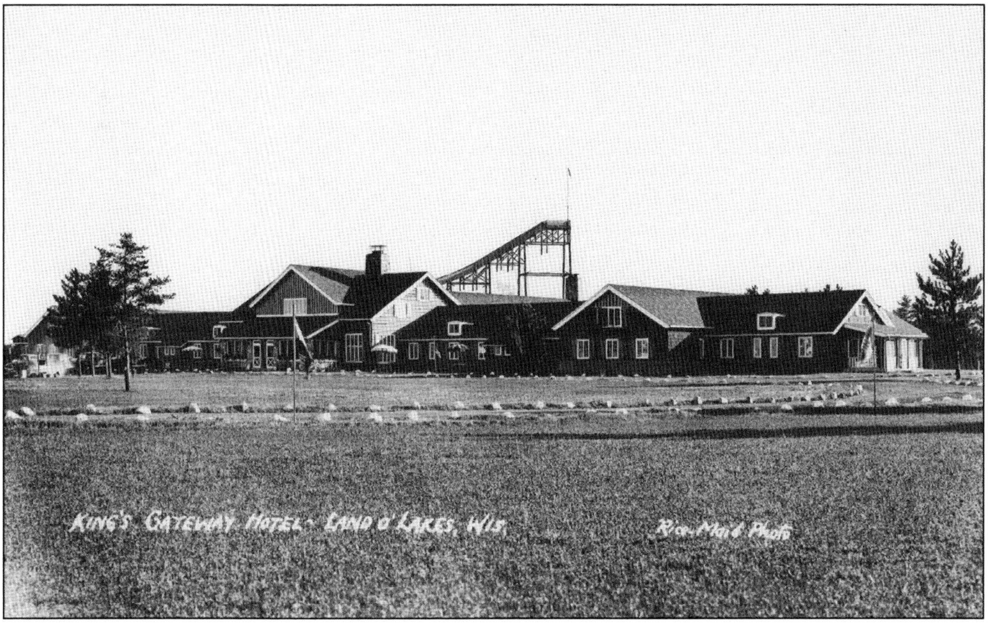

The original Gateway Lodge was a one-story building. (Second owner Walt Williamson added a second story in 1961). Finnish carpenters, paid 37¢ an hour, created the tools required to score the trademark furrows into the beams and wood trim. Local craftsman Felix Turnquist, age 24, handcrafted the cabinetry and interior woodwork. King originally wanted to build his dream resort in Watersmeet, but for political and financial reasons, he chose Land O' Lakes.

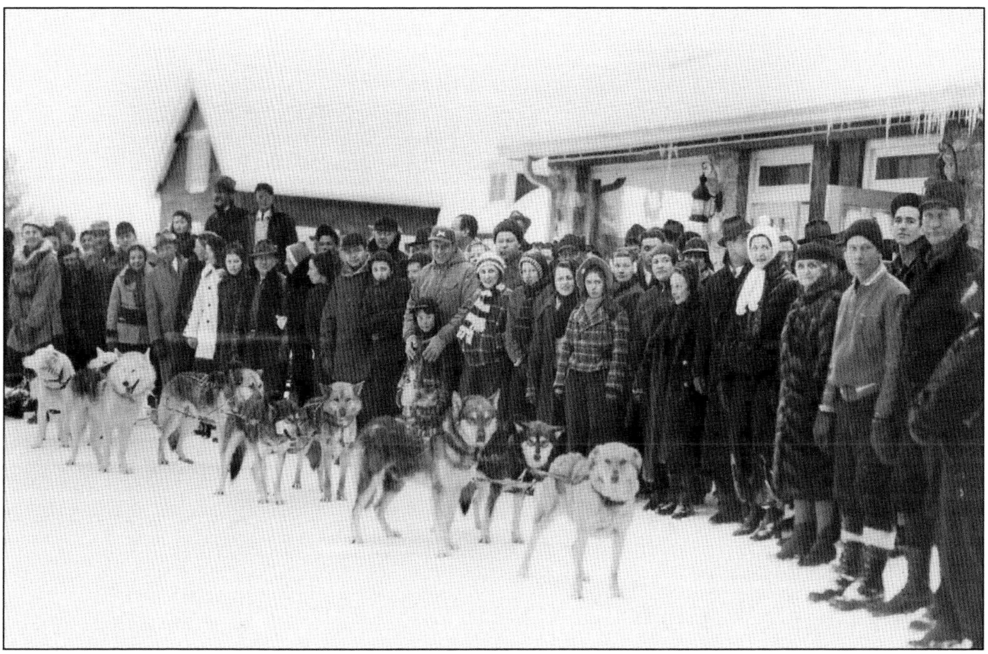

With many winter activities offered by the Gateway, tourism in Land O' Lakes remained strong through the winter. The popular dog sled team of Julius "Dude" Dodge, pictured here, introduced both residents and visitors to this unique method of winter transportation. (Courtesy of Gerd Klausmeyer.)

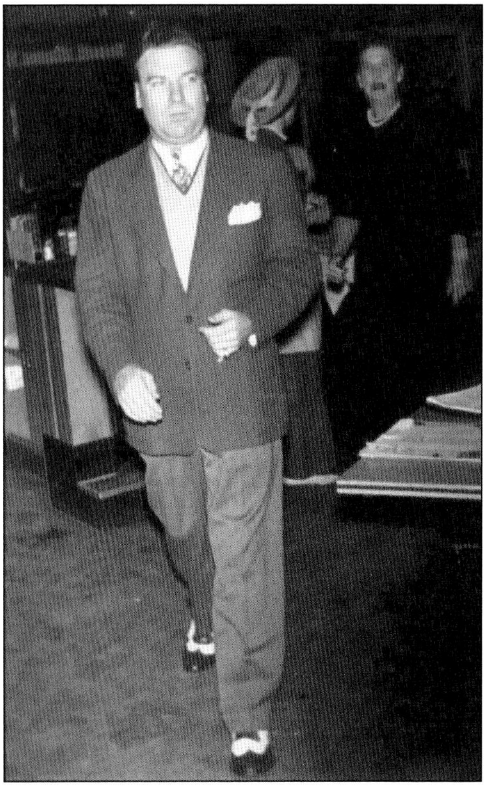

Former World War II Navy pilot and Gateway manager John Garber was one of the most renowned hosts in the area. Most evenings, dressed impeccably, he personally attended to the well-being of guests and visitors. He lived in the stone house just west of the Dari-Maid, and it was said he never forgot a name. After John King's widow sold the Gateway complex in 1961, Garber moved to Las Vegas and managed the Tropicana.

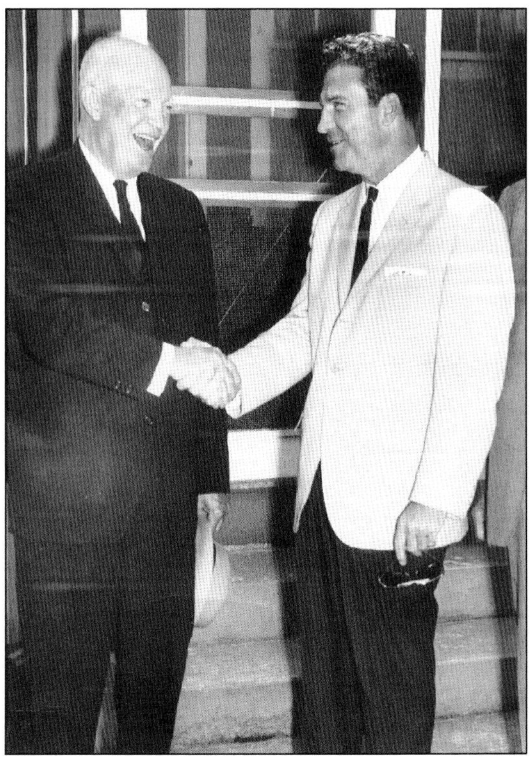

Gateway manager John Garber greets Dwight "Ike" Eisenhower at the Gateway Lodge. Ike was a frequent visitor to the Gateway but he rarely spent the night, preferring to stay with friends at private lake retreats. Ike's brother Milton, however, often vacationed at the cabin behind the Gateway Lodge on the west side of the road to the airport. Locals dubbed it the "Eisenhower Cottage."

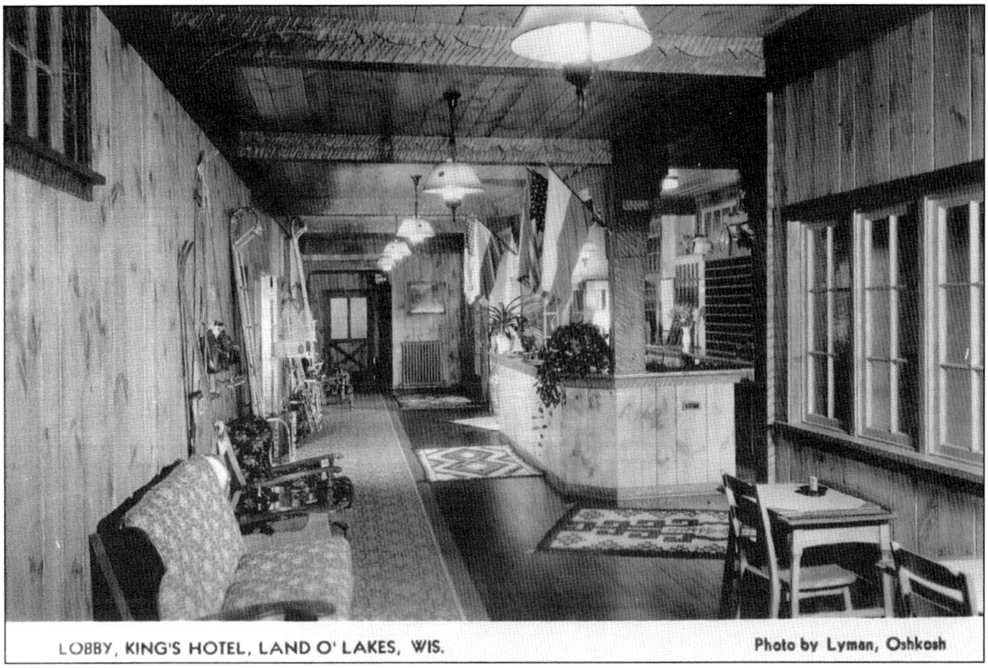

When the Gateway Lodge opened in 1939, the reception desk was located in the east portion of the hallway separating the dining room from the large fireplace/lounge hall at the main entrance. The wall at the left is now decorated with historic Gateway memorabilia and photographs. (Courtesy of Cindy Pekrul.)

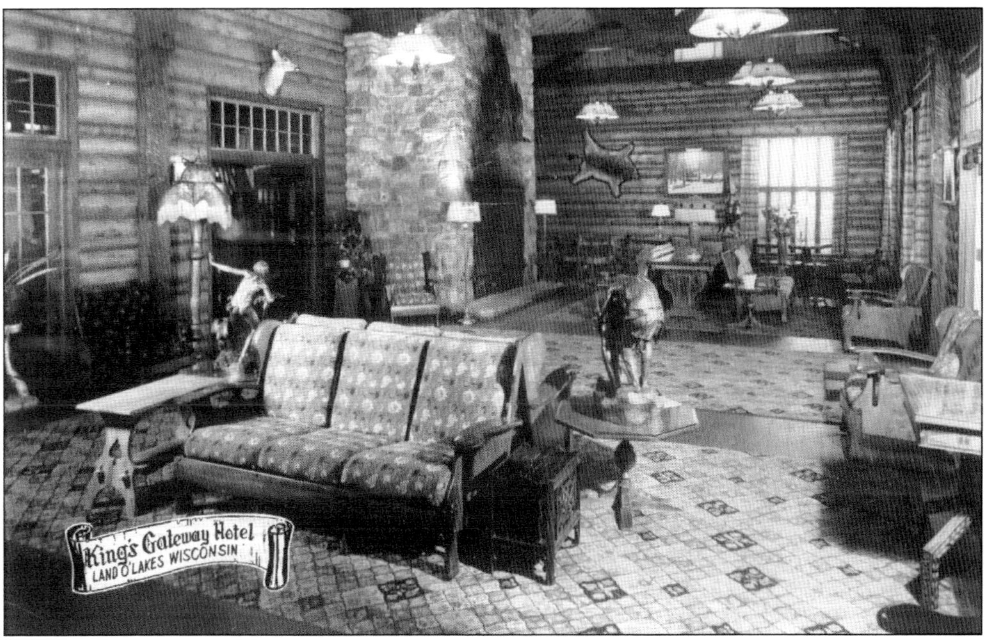

When the Gateway suffered financial difficulties in the 1970s, most of the furnishing of the grand entry hall (pictured) and other public rooms were sold at auction. Also sold were the many framed and personally signed photographs of celebrities who either visited or performed.

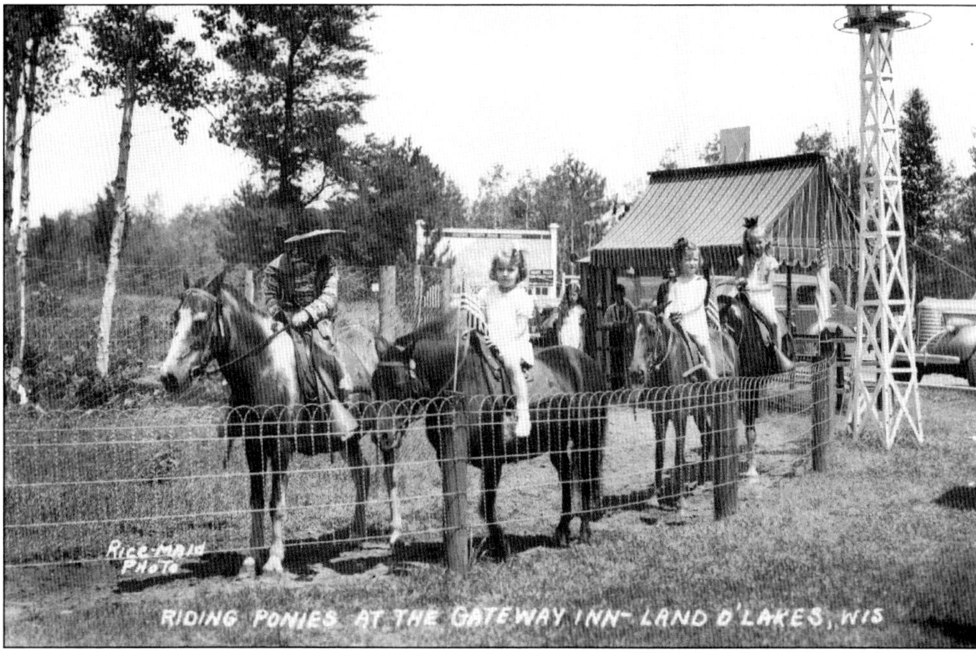

Both the Gateway riding stables and employee housing were northeast of the lodge on Crystal Lake Road, although this pony ride was located next to the inn along Highway 45. In the 1940s and 1950s, the Gateway Resort complex was the largest employer in the region.

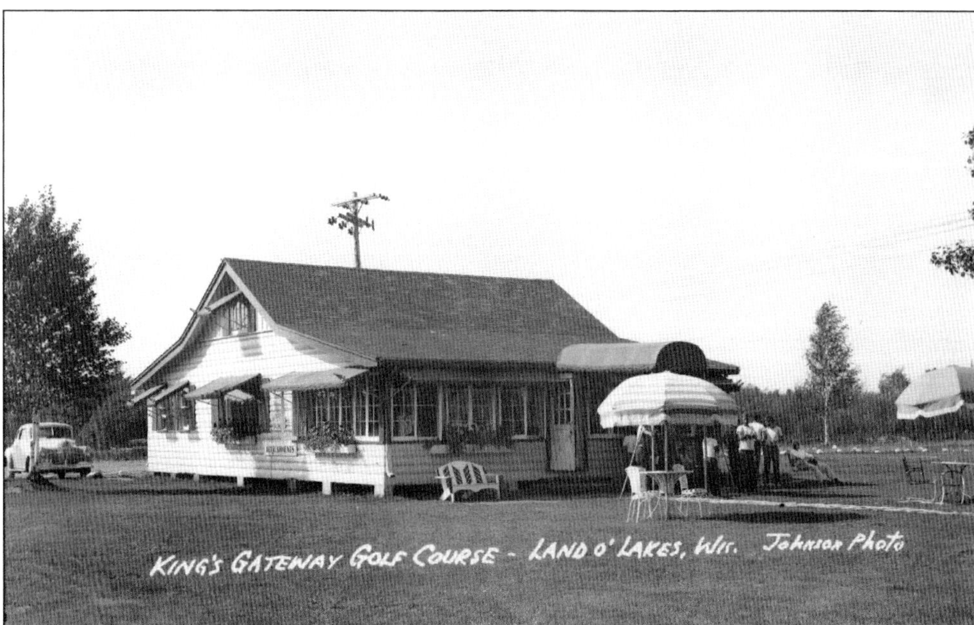

The Gateway golf course clubhouse originally served as the King's Gateway Airport terminal. It was moved to its present location in 1954 when King's widow, Sug, donated the airport to the town.

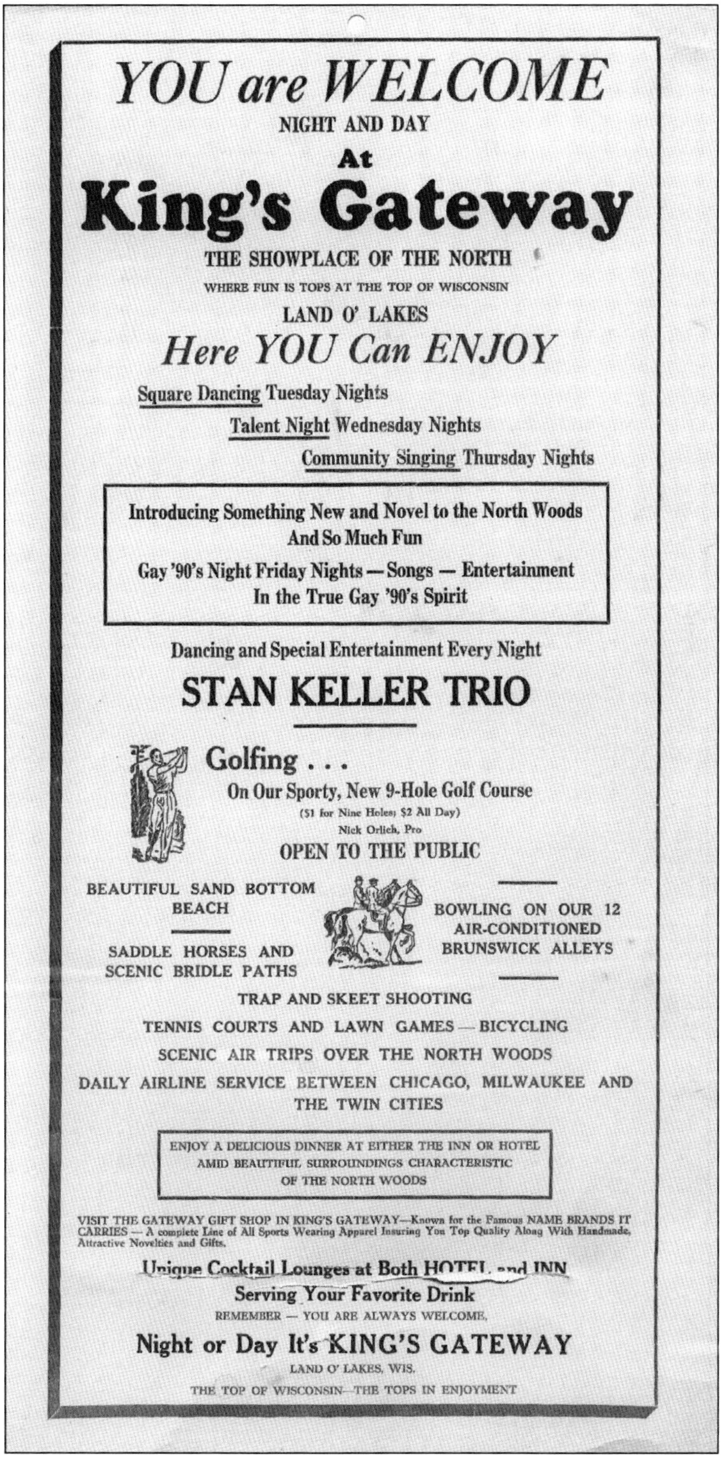

YOU are WELCOME
NIGHT AND DAY
At
King's Gateway
THE SHOWPLACE OF THE NORTH
WHERE FUN IS TOPS AT THE TOP OF WISCONSIN
LAND O' LAKES

Here YOU Can ENJOY

Square Dancing Tuesday Nights
Talent Night Wednesday Nights
Community Singing Thursday Nights

Introducing Something New and Novel to the North Woods
And So Much Fun
Gay '90's Night Friday Nights — Songs — Entertainment
In the True Gay '90's Spirit

Dancing and Special Entertainment Every Night
STAN KELLER TRIO

Golfing . . .
On Our Sporty, New 9-Hole Golf Course
($1 for Nine Holes; $2 All Day)
Nick Orlich, Pro
OPEN TO THE PUBLIC

BEAUTIFUL SAND BOTTOM BEACH

SADDLE HORSES AND SCENIC BRIDLE PATHS

BOWLING ON OUR 12 AIR-CONDITIONED BRUNSWICK ALLEYS

TRAP AND SKEET SHOOTING
TENNIS COURTS AND LAWN GAMES — BICYCLING
SCENIC AIR TRIPS OVER THE NORTH WOODS
DAILY AIRLINE SERVICE BETWEEN CHICAGO, MILWAUKEE AND THE TWIN CITIES

ENJOY A DELICIOUS DINNER AT EITHER THE INN OR HOTEL AMID BEAUTIFUL SURROUNDINGS CHARACTERISTIC OF THE NORTH WOODS

VISIT THE GATEWAY GIFT SHOP IN KING'S GATEWAY—Known for the Famous NAME BRANDS IT CARRIES — A complete Line of All Sports Wearing Apparel Insuring You Top Quality Along With Handmade, Attractive Novelties and Gifts.

Unique Cocktail Lounges at Both HOTEL and INN
Serving Your Favorite Drink
REMEMBER — YOU ARE ALWAYS WELCOME.

Night or Day It's KING'S GATEWAY
LAND O' LAKES, WIS.
THE TOP OF WISCONSIN—THE TOPS IN ENJOYMENT

The Gateway featured a different activity every day, and live music and dancing happened nightly. The nearby airport was also an event; when the afternoon North Central Airlines flight arrived, the parking area was crowded with onlookers waiting to see who disembarked.

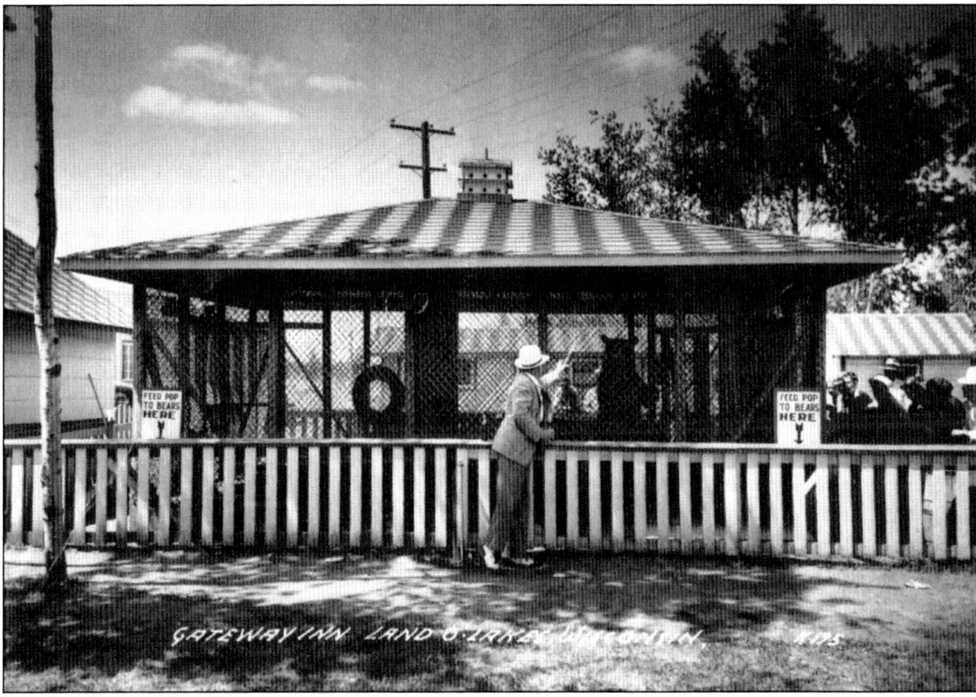

When John H. King bought the gas station property from Harrington in 1937, he expanded and improved the bear cage and built a protected area for the animals to hibernate during the winter. King loved the north woods animals, and early guests of the inn remember fawns mingling with diners at suppertime.

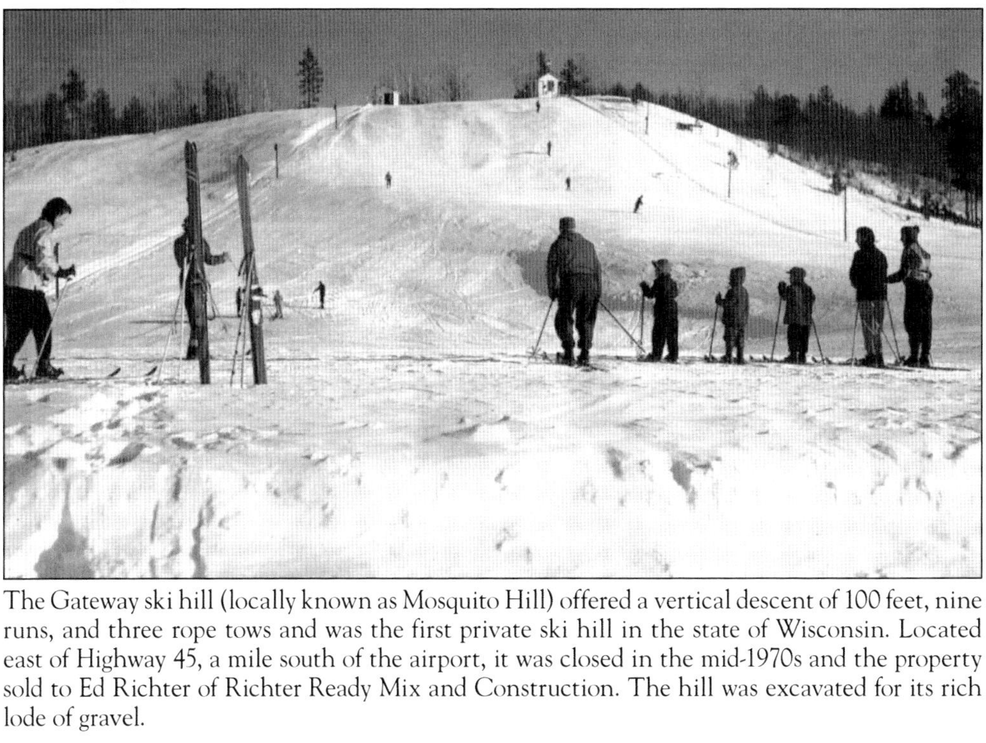

The Gateway ski hill (locally known as Mosquito Hill) offered a vertical descent of 100 feet, nine runs, and three rope tows and was the first private ski hill in the state of Wisconsin. Located east of Highway 45, a mile south of the airport, it was closed in the mid-1970s and the property sold to Ed Richter of Richter Ready Mix and Construction. The hill was excavated for its rich lode of gravel.

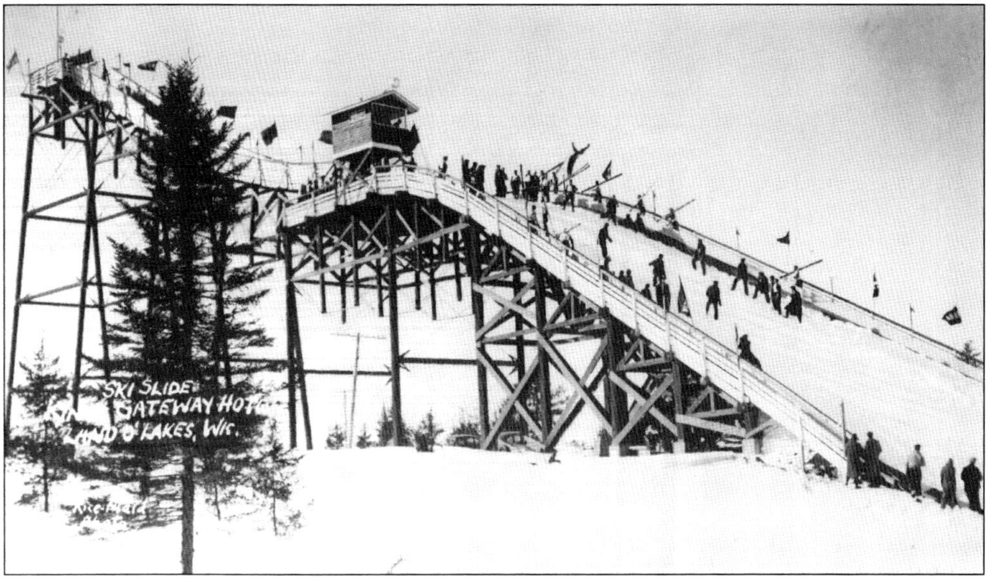

The King's Gateway ski jump was constructed in 1938, and during its time was the only ski jump in the state of Wisconsin. It was dismantled in 1957, and the timbers were reused to build private homes as well as the original teepee portion of Red Man Supper Club on Highway 45.

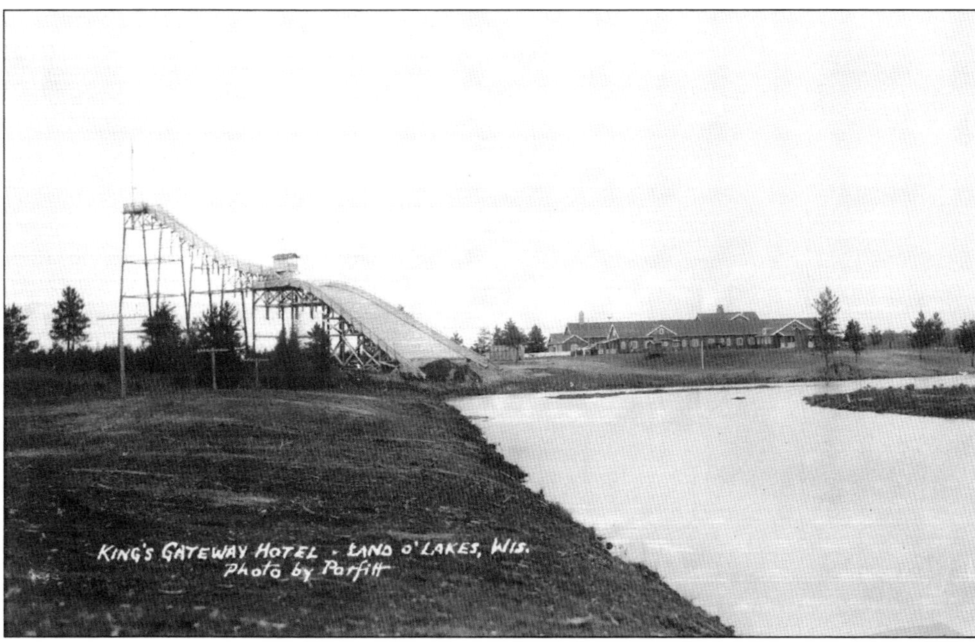

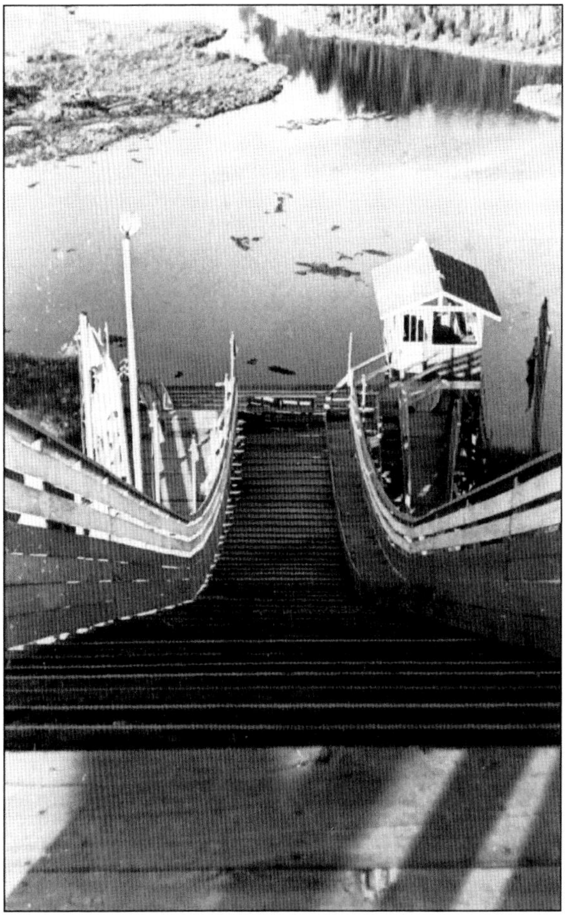

This rare photograph was taken from the top of the Gateway Lodge ski jump in the summer. In the winter, the frozen pond offered jumpers ample room to coast to a stop. The four concrete foundations of the jump's primary support pillars are still visible today, just to the east of the airport road.

Pomp and circumstance was often the preamble to ski-jumping competitions at the Gateway, seen in this c. 1944 image. Patriotism during World War II was especially vibrant, and flag ceremonies often included saying the Pledge of Allegiance.

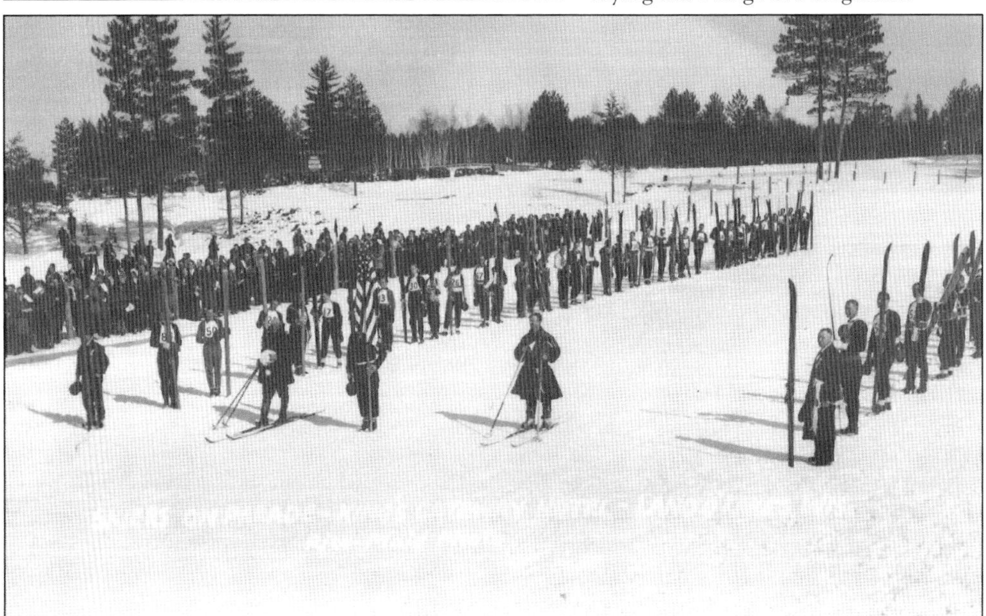

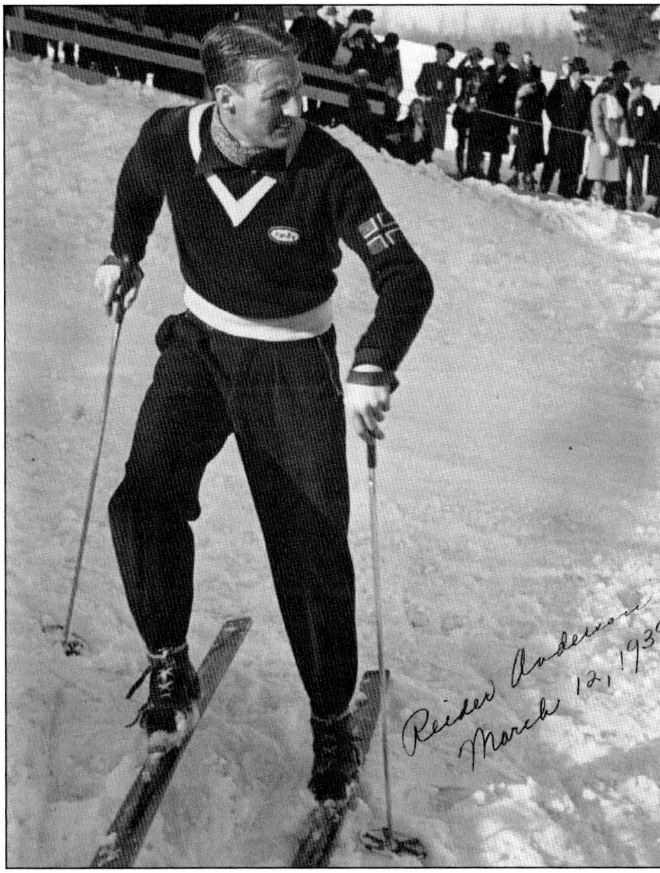

Norwegian world champion ski jumper Reider Anderson regularly competed at the Gateway ski jump. This photograph was taken on March 12, 1939, when Anderson set a record hill jump of 100 feet. The 93-foot-high structure brought many of the world's best skiing athletes to Land O' Lakes for competitions.

During World War II, the Gateway ski hill served as a training ground for the 10th Mountain Division of military ski operations. The pictured group of soldiers is being trained by Olaf Thornvald of Norway, the Gateway's renowned ski instructor, who was generally regarded as the finest in the Midwest. The division was rumored to be headed to the mountains of Italy for combat.

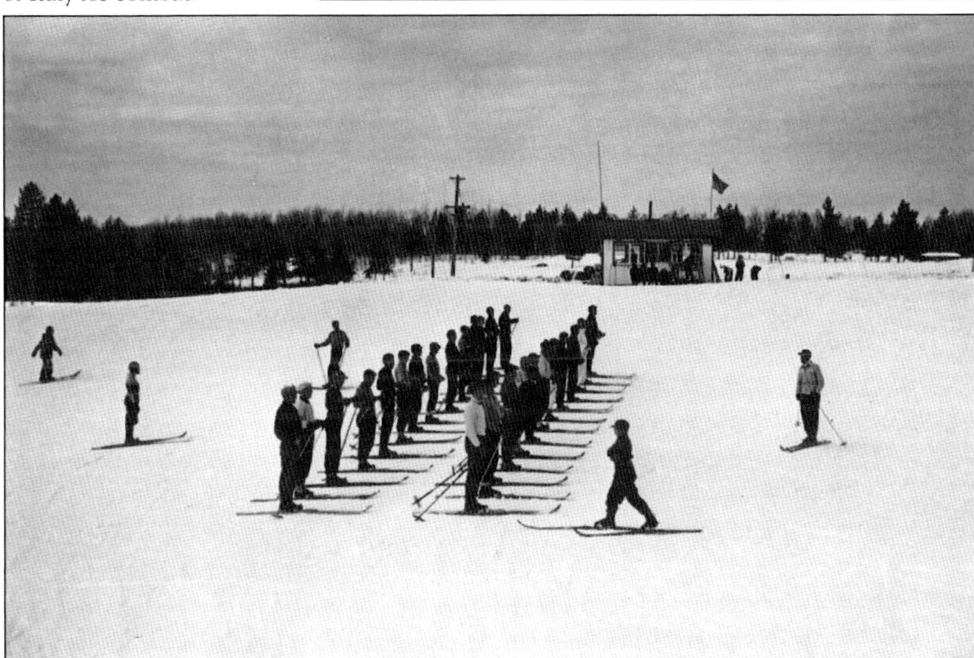

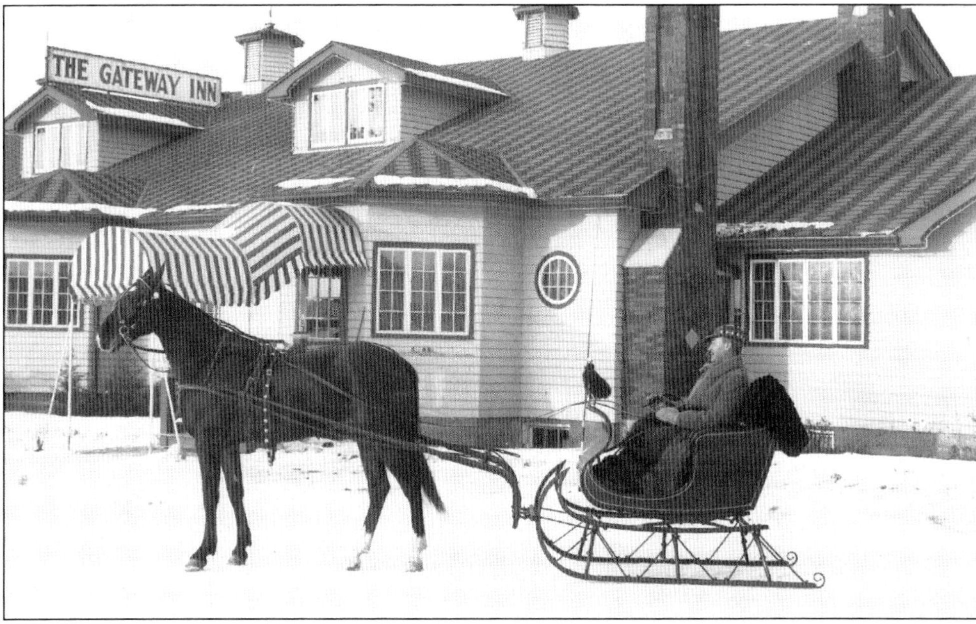

Horse-drawn sleighs were used by the Gateway to transport guests into town or on pleasure trips through the woods. John King (not pictured) took great delight in personally giving sleigh rides to children.

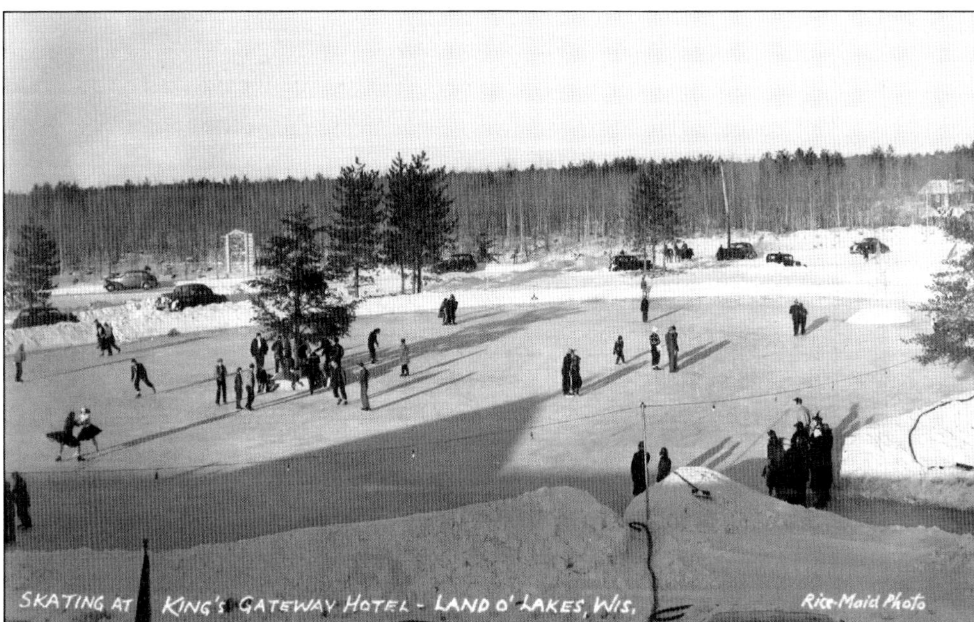

In the winter, the Gateway's ice-skating rink was enjoyed by guests and the public.

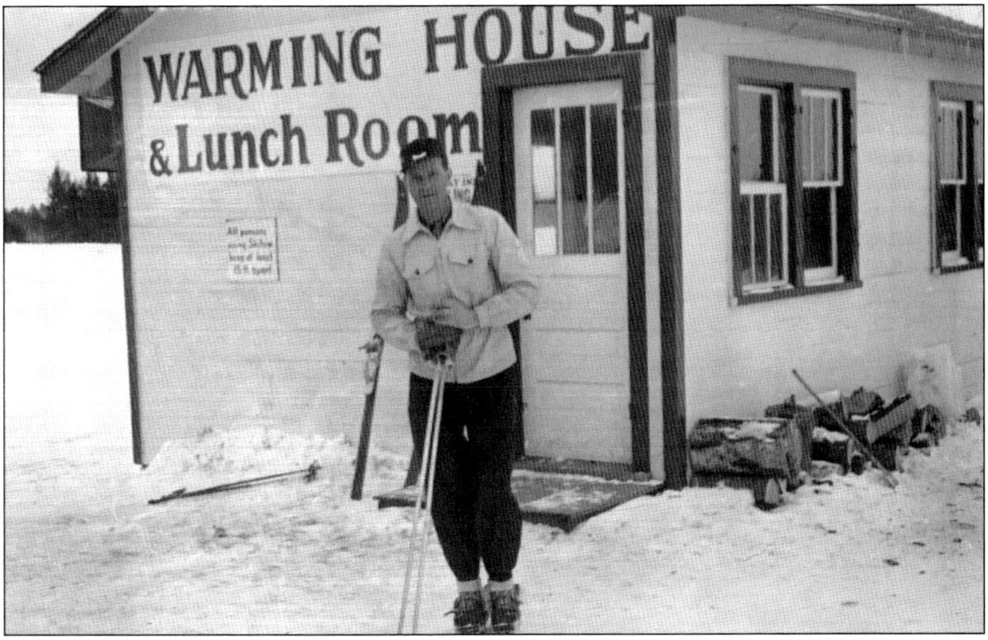

The Gateway ski hill opened before the large ski chalet was completed. During the first winter of operation, this warming house was the ski hill's only facility. When the chalet was finished, the building was moved to the top of the hill and became one of the rope tow stations.

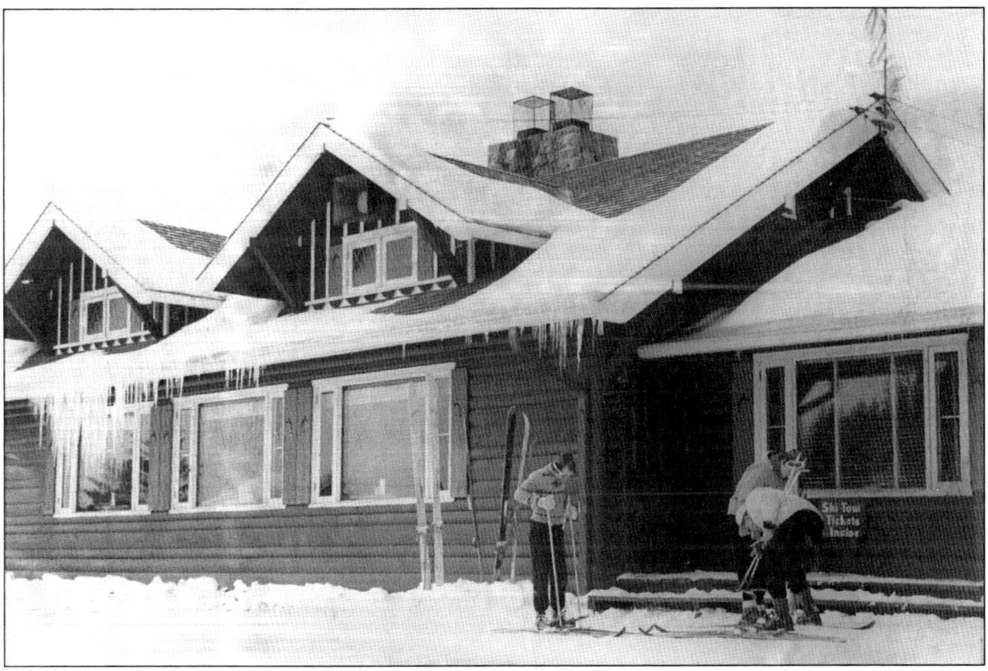

The Gateway buildings, including the ski chalet, pictured here, were designed by Milwaukee architects Henry Messmer & Son. After the hill closed in the mid-1970s, the chalet remained vacant until the winter of 1996–1997, when it was donated to the town by Donna and Ed Richter. It was moved to downtown Land O' Lakes with money donated by Frank Ferry Jr., and in 2001, it reopened as the Land O' Lakes Historical Society NorthernWaters Museum.

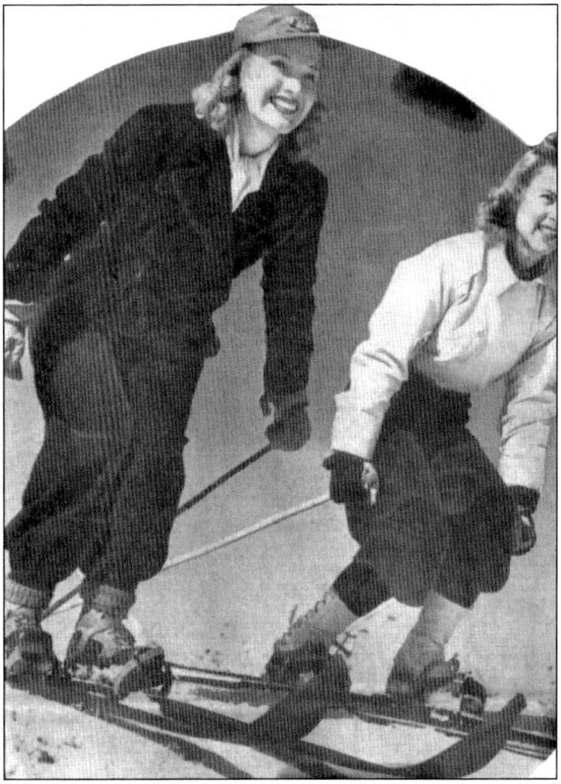

The significant media connections of John King resulted in articles and full-page photograph spreads about Land O' Lakes in the Milwaukee, Chicago, and Detroit newspapers. Both professional models and local residents were used in the photograph shoots.

Wisconsin senator Joe McCarthy and his wife were frequent guests of the Gateway. This publicity photograph shows him at the Gateway Lodge fireplace after successfully running for reelection in 1952. (Courtesy of Wisconsin Historical Society).

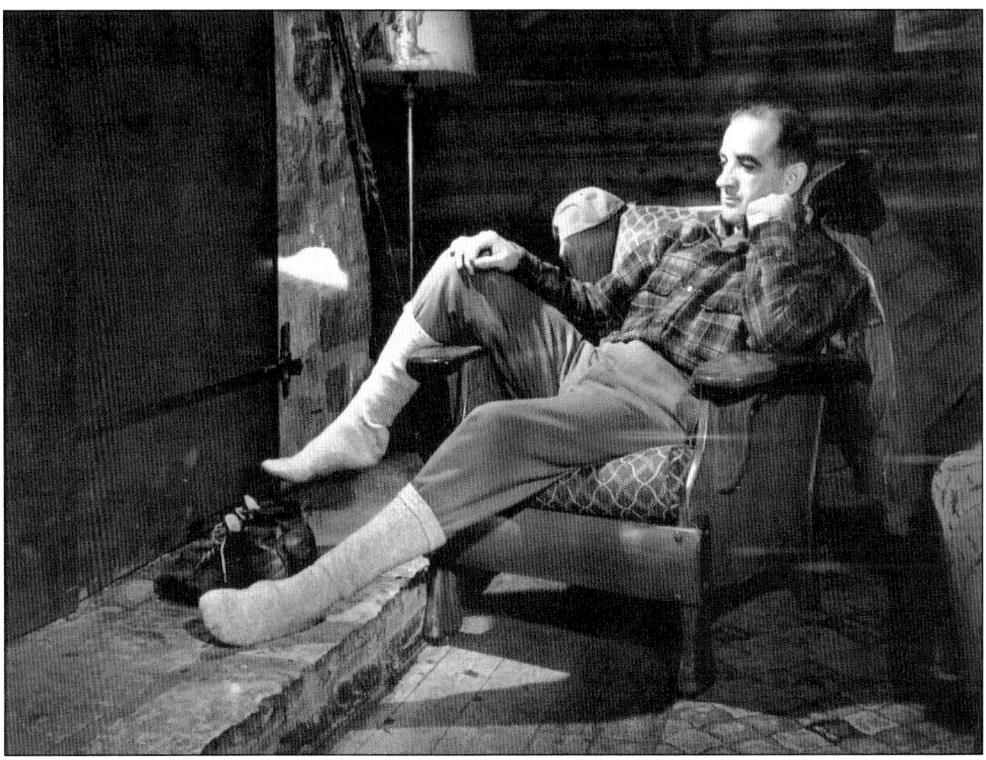

Five

The Historic Resorts

Fishing, Hunting, Swimming, and Boating at the "Top of Wisconsin"

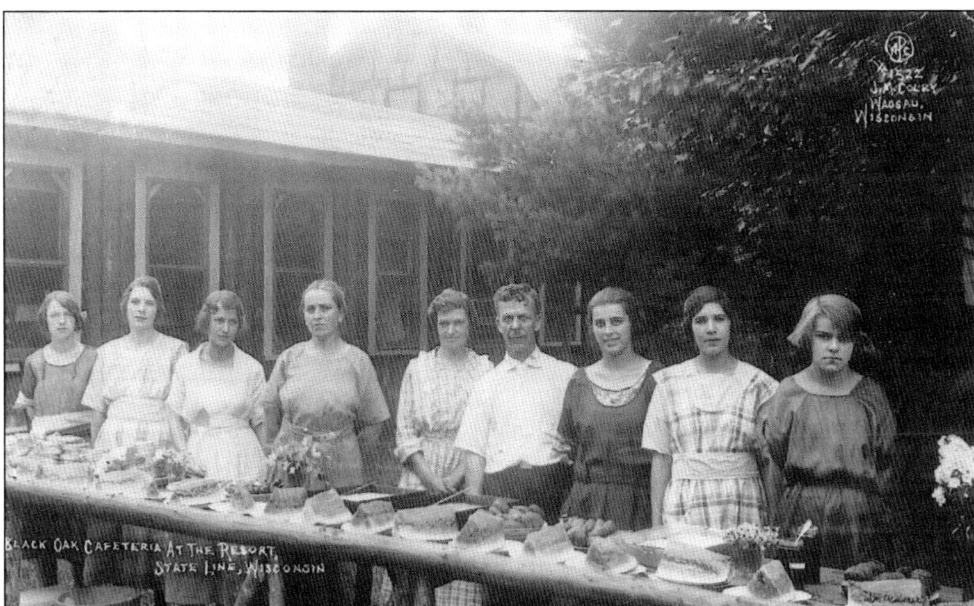

George St. Clair, founder of the Black Oak Lake Resort, stands behind a lunch buffet with resort employees. His wife, Nellie, stands to his right. In 1906, St. Clair bought 92 acres and 1,300 feet of frontage on Black Oak Lake and began a resort and commercial potato farm. St. Clair also served as the town clerk for Land O' Lakes for 14 years.

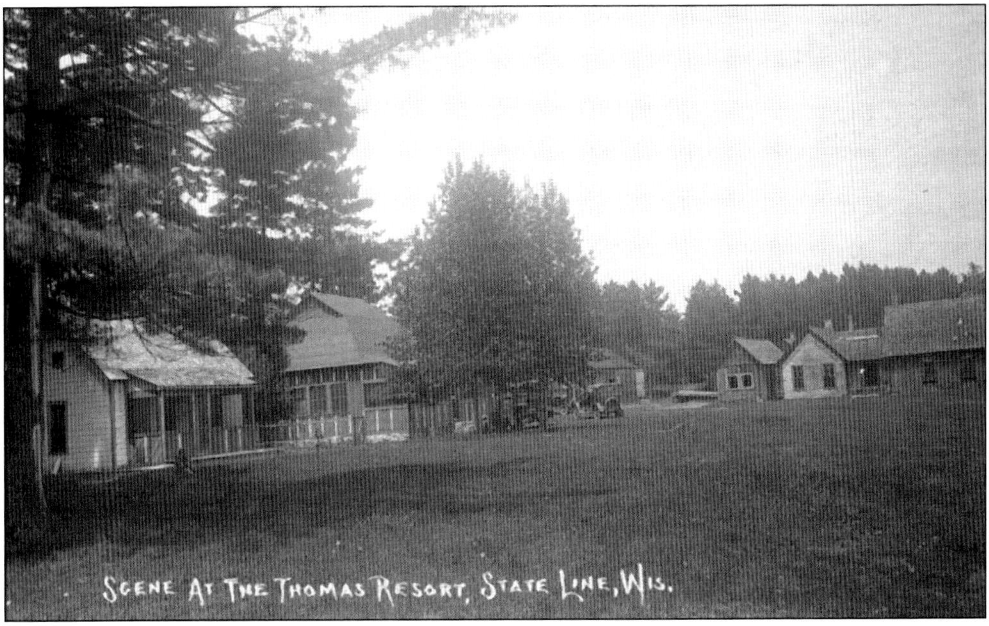

In 1884, Leonard Thomas opened the Thomas Resort, seen in this c. 1922 image, on the southwest shore of Lac Vieux Desert. The resort offered room and board to fishermen and was the first operating under the American plan in Wisconsin. Thomas was married to the daughter of G.L. Draper, the area's first white settler. The resort exists today as the Sunrise Lodge.

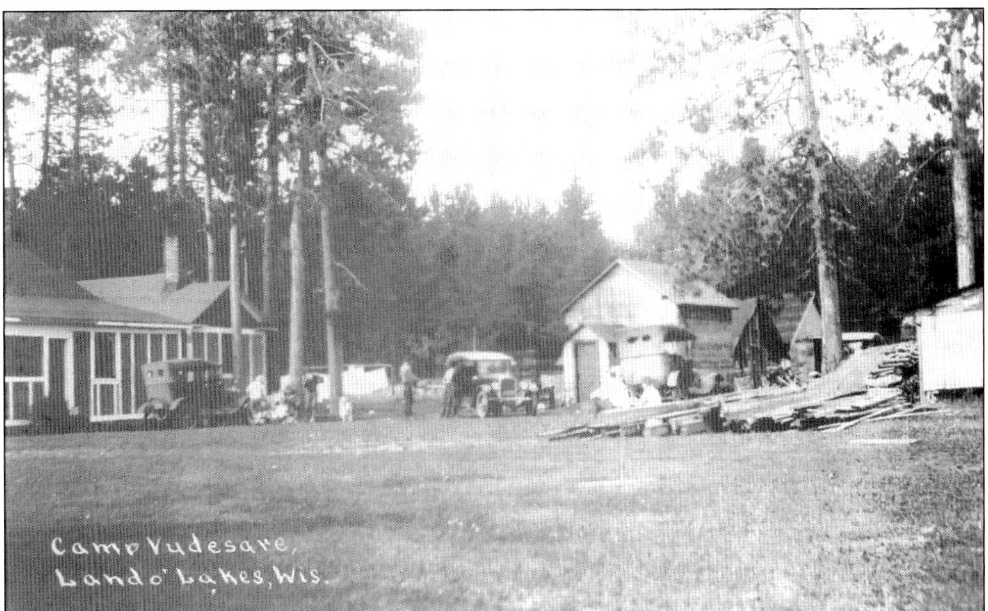

When Leonard Thomas passed away in 1898, his son Louis eventually assumed control of resort operations and renamed it Camp Vudesere. Louis was taught to read and write by his father, and as an adult Louis saved his money to further his schooling. He eventually earned a degree in commercial law from Norman University and returned to build the resort into one of the most successful in northern Wisconsin.

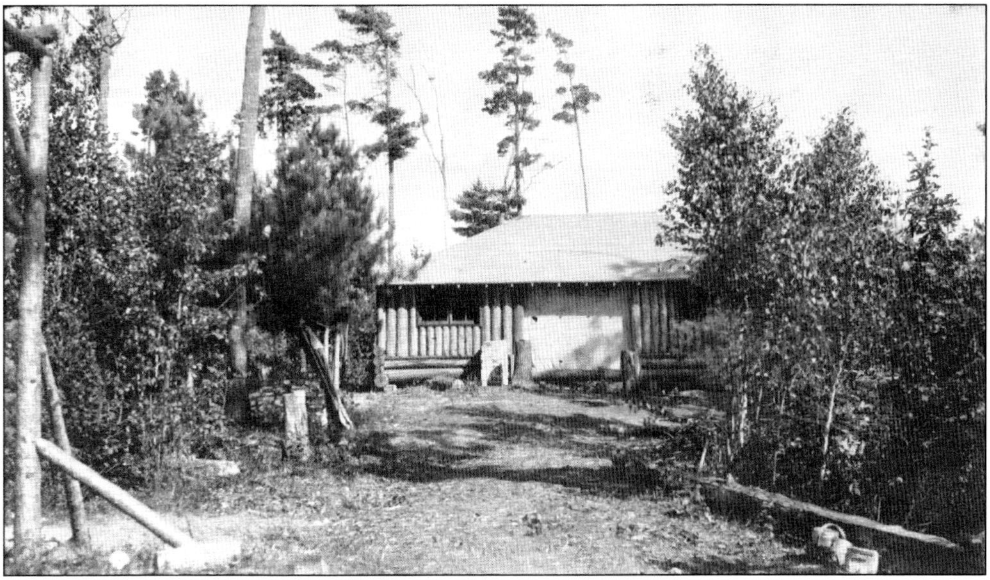

The Mockesair Lodge on Moccasin Lake was completed in 1919. For many years, it was owned and managed by Jerry Kessler, who also operated the Land O' Lakes bowling alleys (currently T&M Lanes) and a music store. Kessler sold the lodge to Alice and Don Ort in 1950. Today, the Jill and Steve Graf family operate it as the Enchanted Loon.

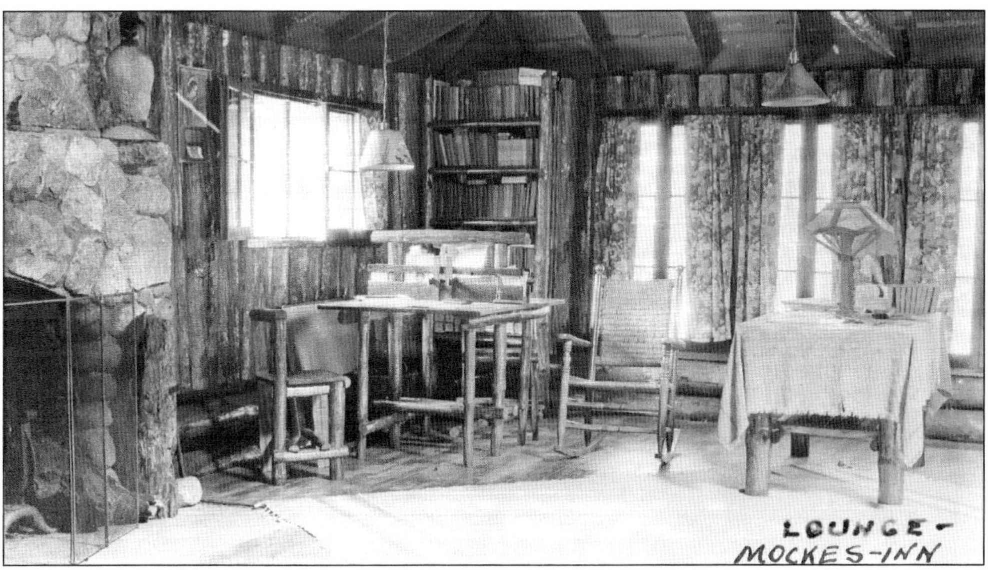

Much of the furniture in this c. 1930 image of the interior of the Mockasair Lodge survived ownership transitions and remains today in the same resort, now operating as the Enchanted Loon.

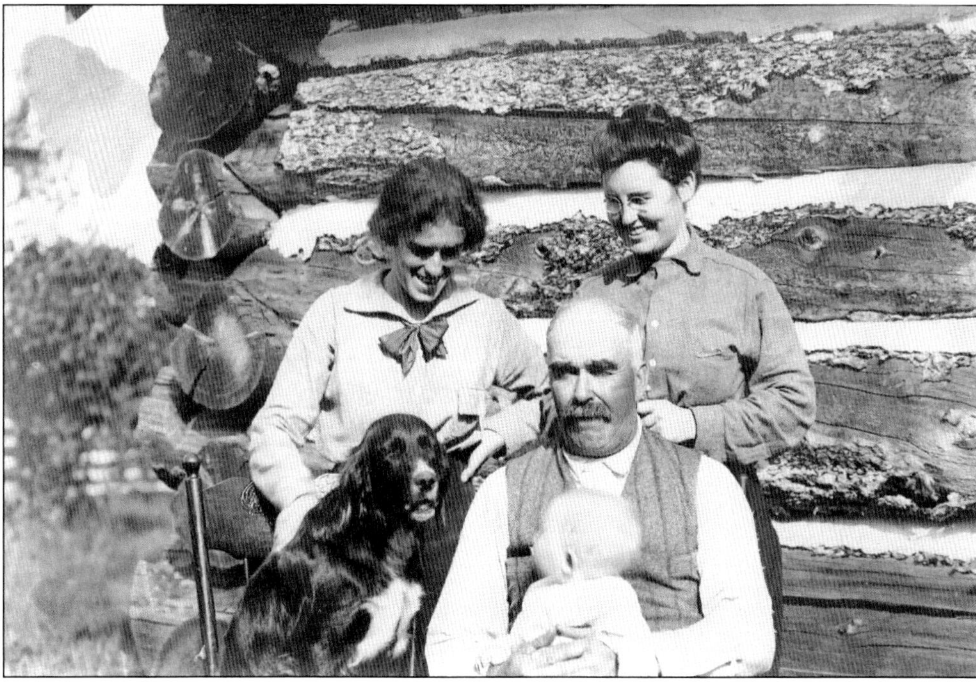

Charles Bent poses for a photograph with his daughters Elsie and Polly. Bent established his resort on Mamie Lake, where in 1896 he built guest cabins and a dining hall for summer visitors. In the winter, he was a game hunter for local lumber companies. Bent, a passionate conservationist, led efforts to manage the deer population and also helped improve the tote road, now Highway B. (Courtesy of Paul and Lisa Stemen.)

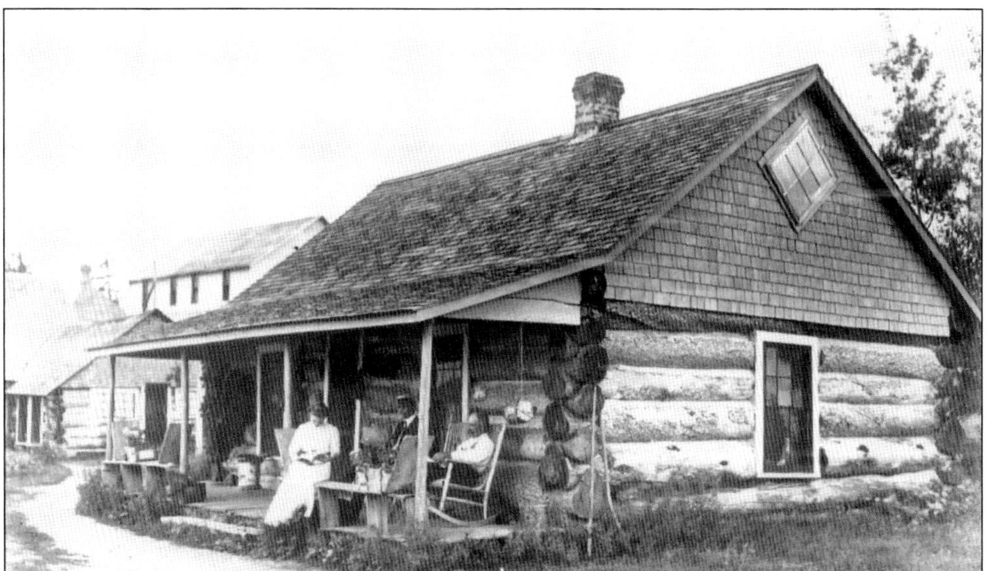

Named Lakeview, this cabin served as Charles Bent's residence, office, and eventually a guest cabin after Charlie built a bigger cabin for himself. Lakeview was one of the first camp buildings and still stands today. Over time, the lakeside porch was screened then moved to its present location on the cabin's right (west) side. (Courtesy of Paul and Lisa Stemen.)

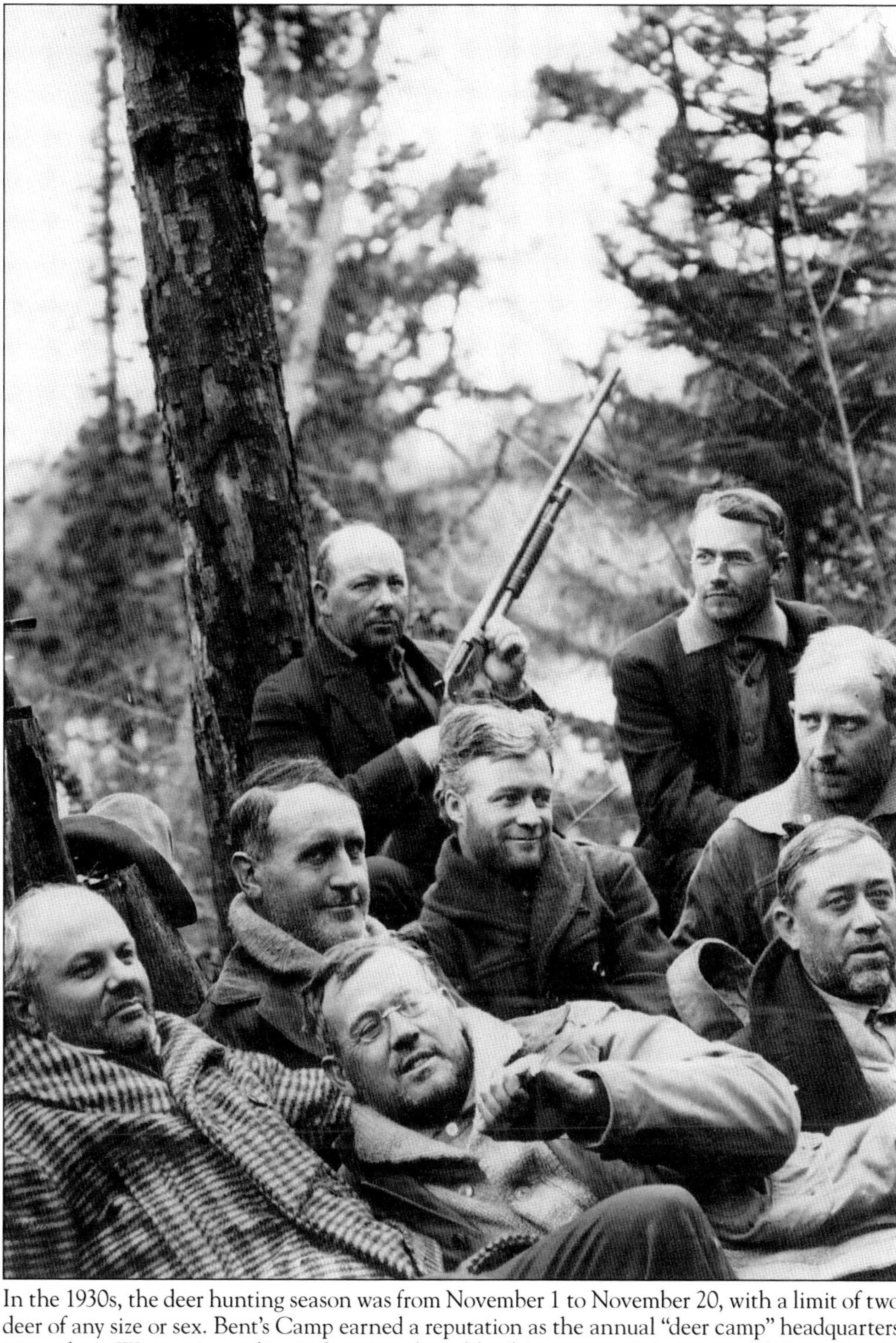

In the 1930s, the deer hunting season was from November 1 to November 20, with a limit of two deer of any size or sex. Bent's Camp earned a reputation as the annual "deer camp" headquarters in northern Wisconsin, and many hunting clans, like this one, spent their annual hunt at Bent's. (Courtesy of Paul and Lisa Stemen.)

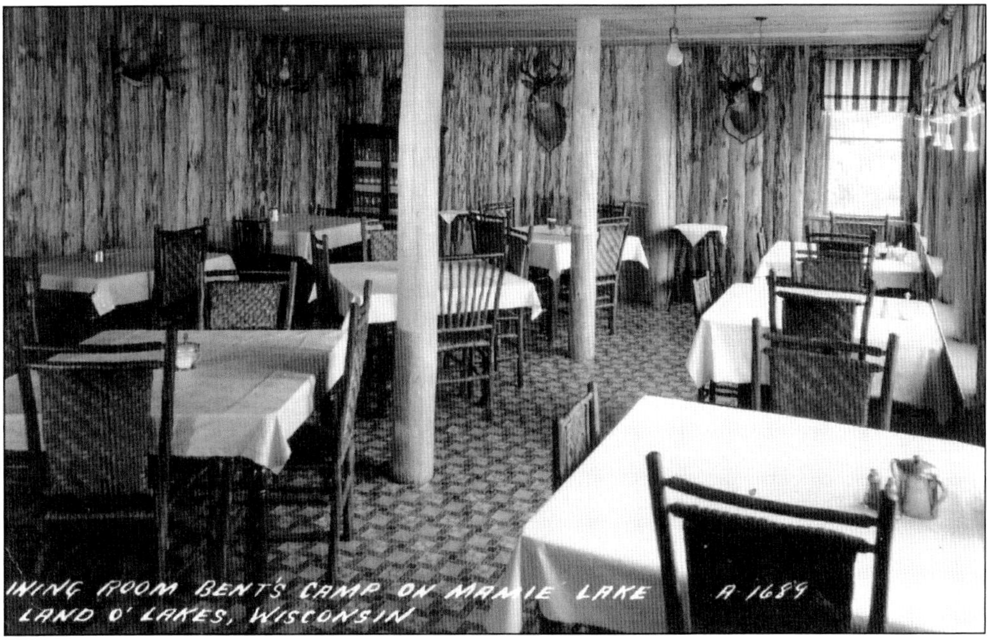

This postcard shows the dining hall of Bent's Camp in 1940. On Thanksgiving, Elizabeth "Lizzy" Bent, wife of Charles Bent, served extravagant Thanksgiving dinners in this room, with venison tenderloins, turkey, vegetables, and pies. Guests and locals would engage in "wild talk," singing, and dancing until the wee hours. The reverse side of this postcard (below) reads, "Hello: This sure does look inviting, doesn't it? I'm enjoying myself very much will be seeing you soon. Ray Seidlik."

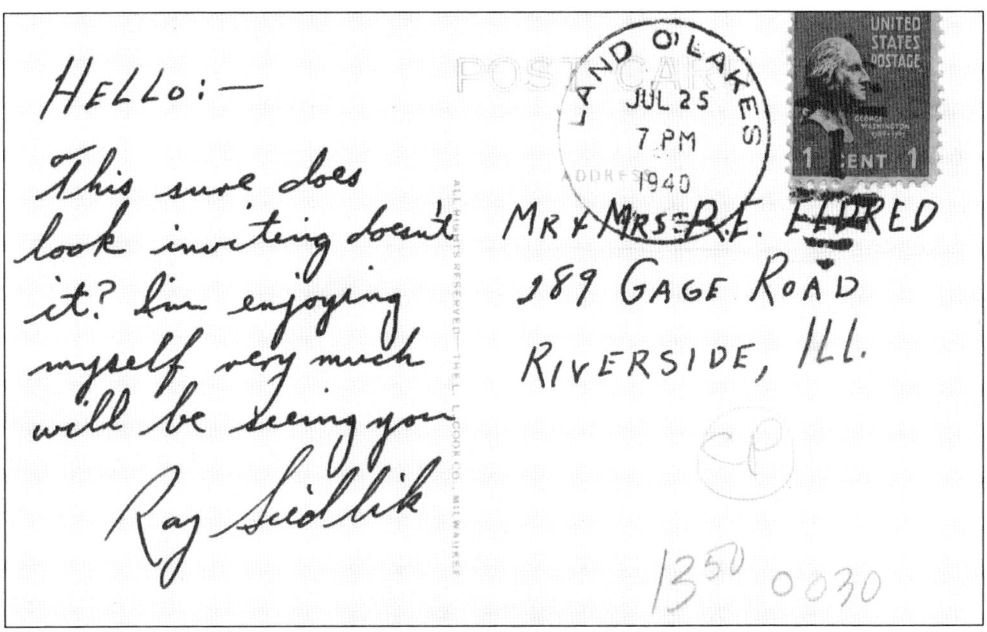

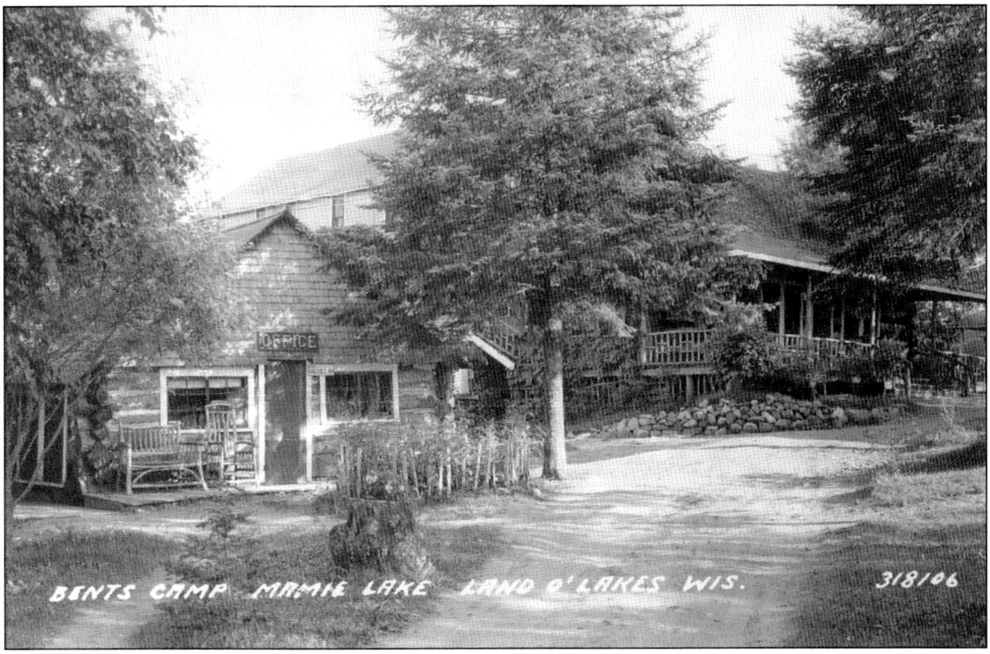

Pictured is the office of Charlie Bent, and behind it, the magnificent Bent's Camp dining hall, which no longer exists. In the distance is a portion of the building that houses the current restaurant, which formerly had three stories.

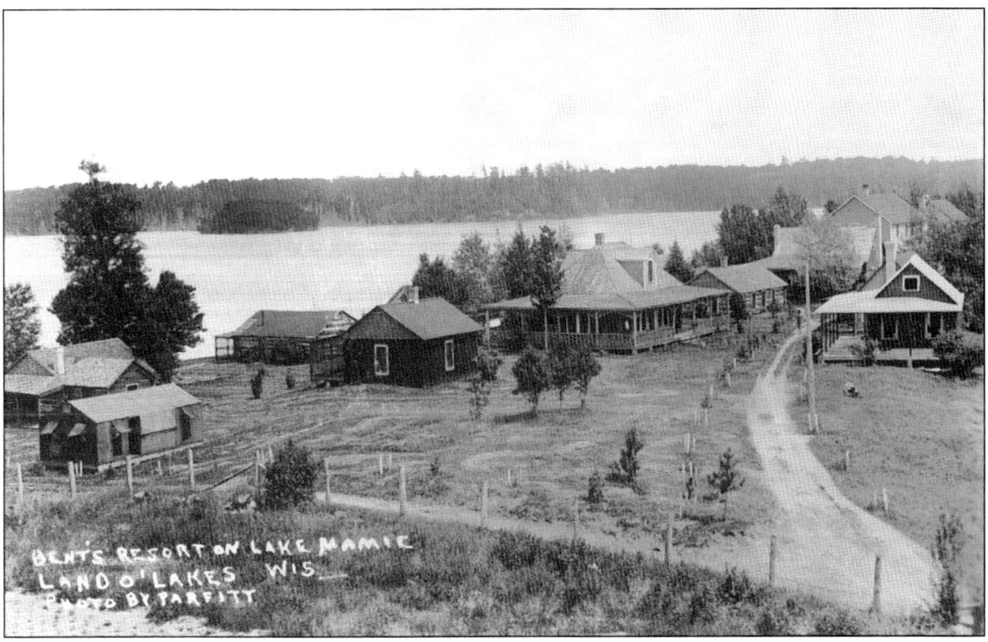

By 1924, Bent's Camp resort had been electrified and included a main lodge, 12 cottages, a family home, a guides' quarters, stables, an icehouse, a boathouse, and 30 rowboats and canoes. Few of these pictured buildings remain today. (Courtesy of Paul and Lisa Stemen.)

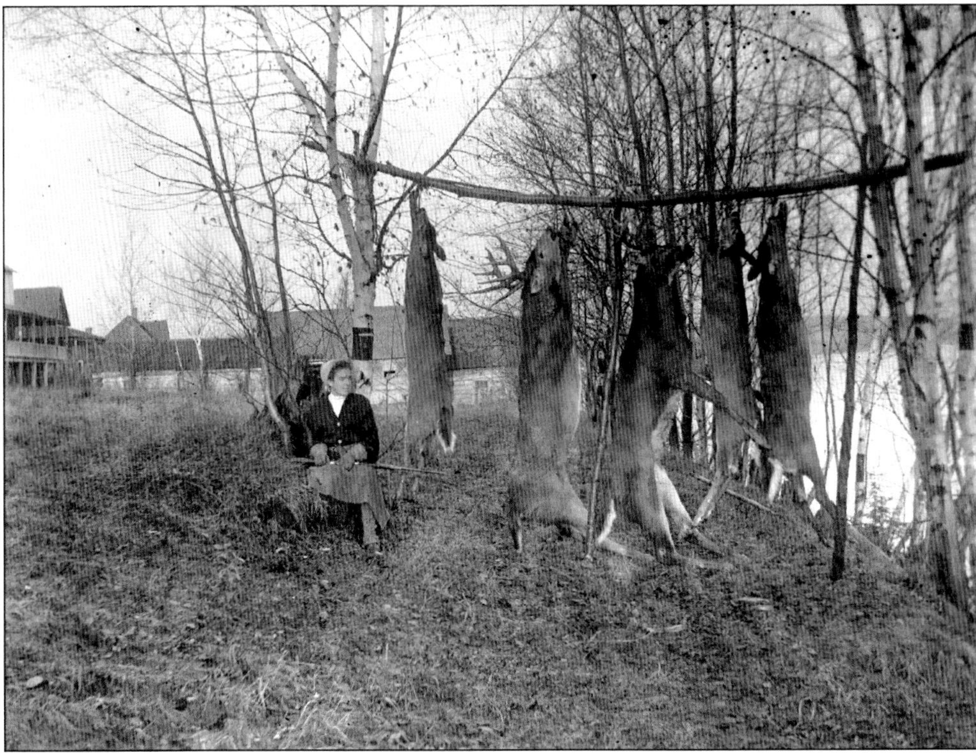

Charlie Bent's daughter Elsie was an avid hunter and often joined the hunting parties with great gusto. Cy Young, the famous pitcher for the Boston Red Sox, was a long-standing member of the "Clow Clan," a group of hunters from Illinois who annually hunted from Bent's Camp for over 40 years. (Courtesy of Paul and Lisa Stemen.)

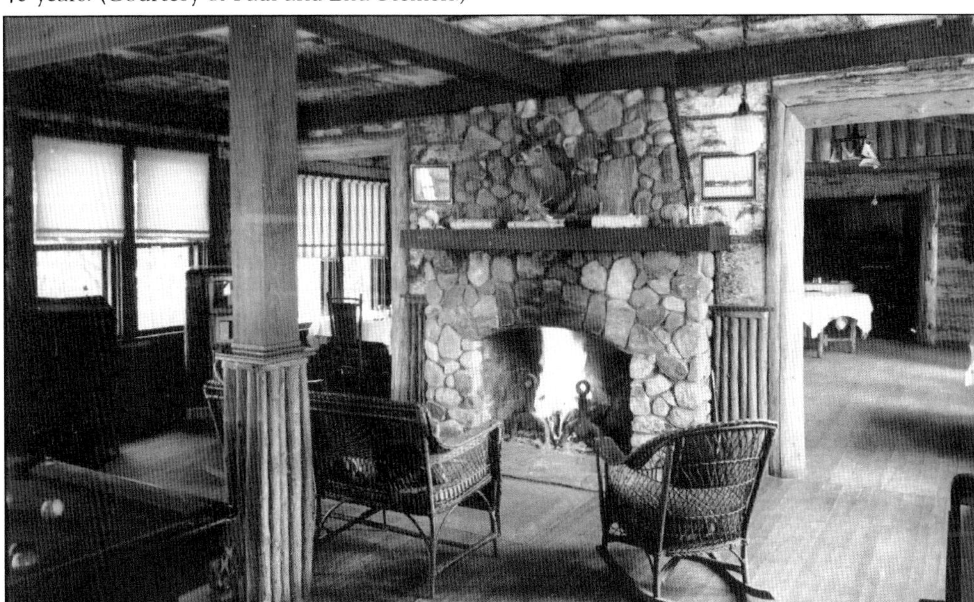

The original Bent's Camp pool hall and lounge is today's barroom. It still contains the same fireplace, wood pillars, floor, ceiling beams, and birch bark paneling. (Courtesy of Paul and Lisa Stemen.)

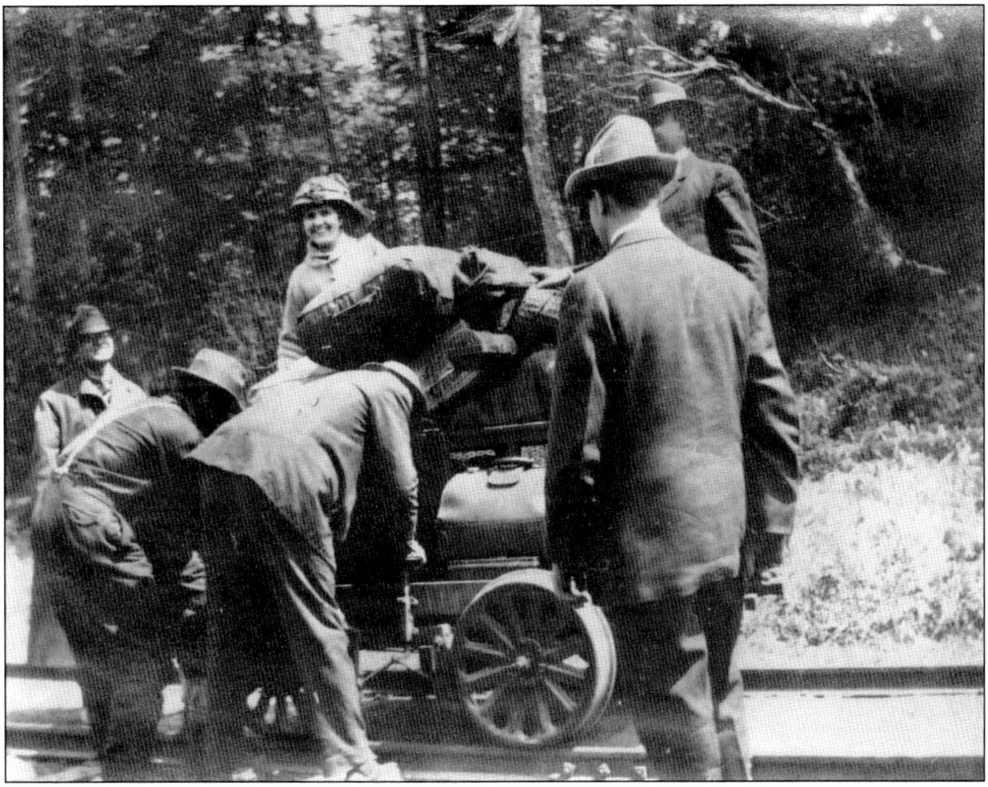

If the horses were lame, the wagons broken, or the roads washed out, handcars were employed to transport guests and their luggage to destinations via rails formerly used by the lumber companies. (Courtesy of Paul and Lisa Stemen.)

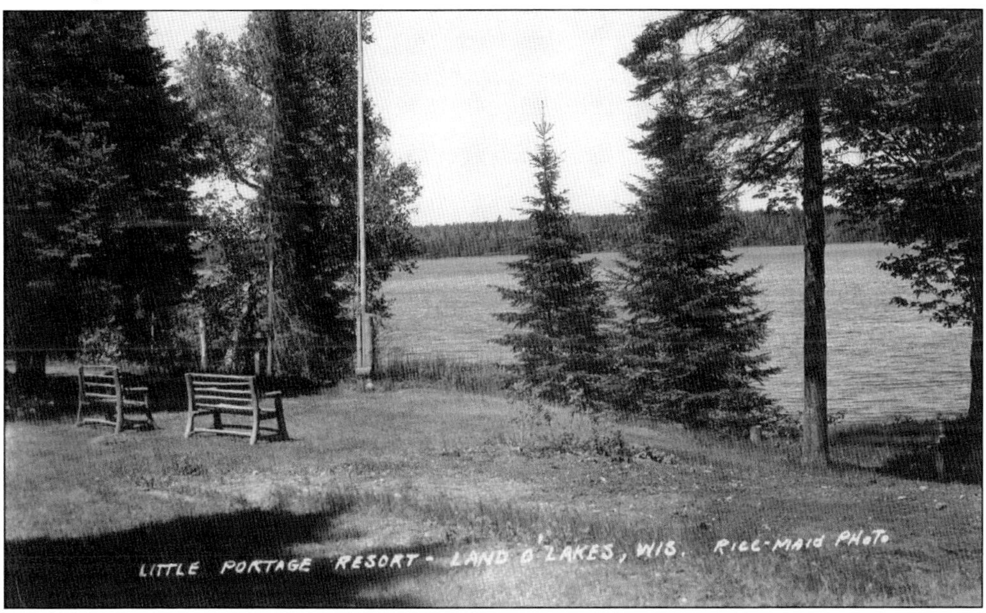

A small resort operated on Little Portage Lake between 1910 and 1950. It was owned by Marsh Johnson.

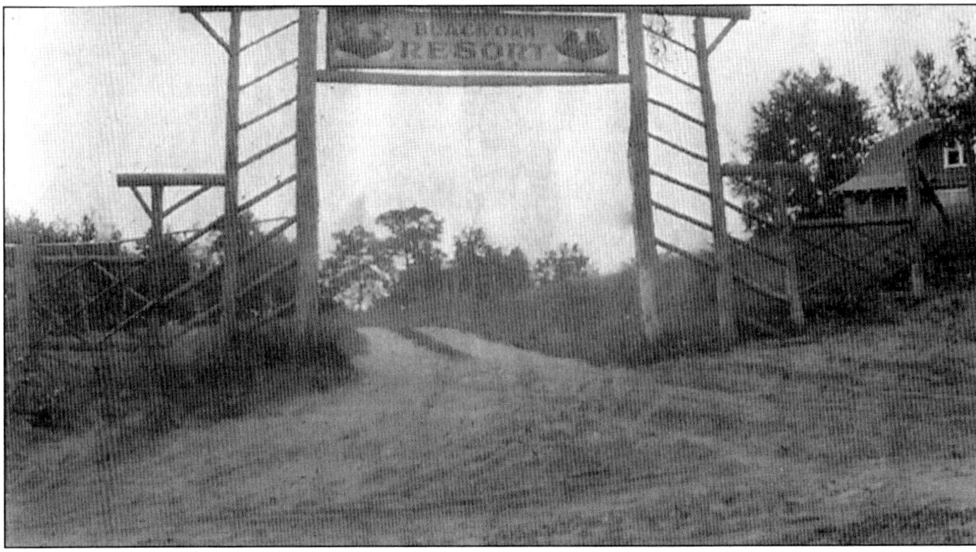

The entrance to the Black Oak Lake Resort on the southwest shore of Black Oak Lake was a welcome sight after hours of travel via train or automobile. In the 1930s, resort rates were $5 a day for a room and three meals, or $2 a day and $1 per meal. Many guests arrived at the resort via horse-drawn wagons dispatched from the State Line railroad depot.

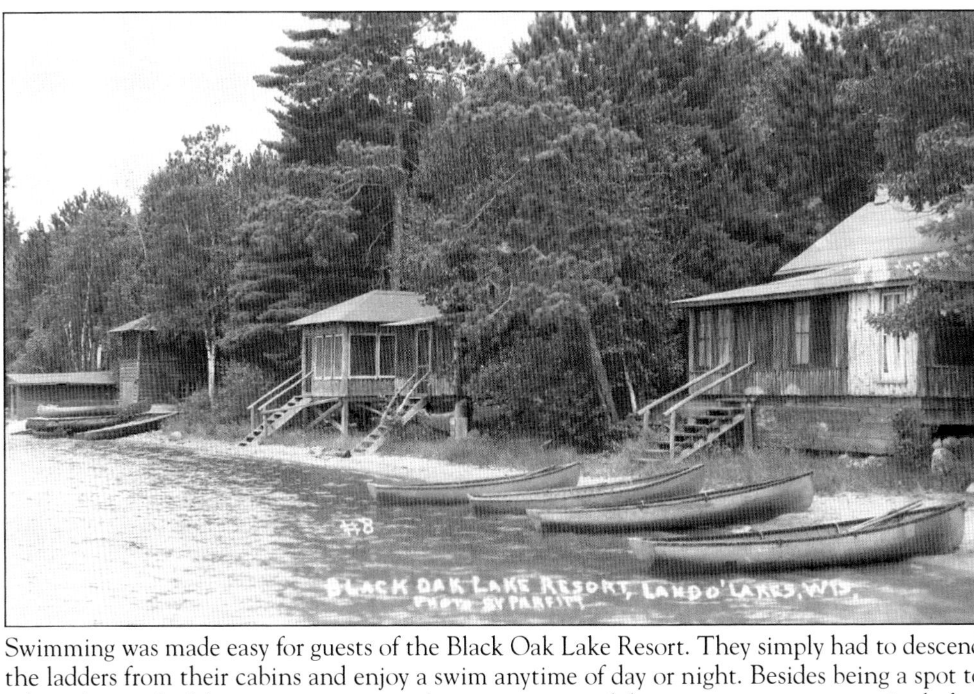

Swimming was made easy for guests of the Black Oak Lake Resort. They simply had to descend the ladders from their cabins and enjoy a swim anytime of day or night. Besides being a spot to take a plunge, the lake was a convenient place to soap up and shampoo, a common practice before indoor plumbing became mainstream.

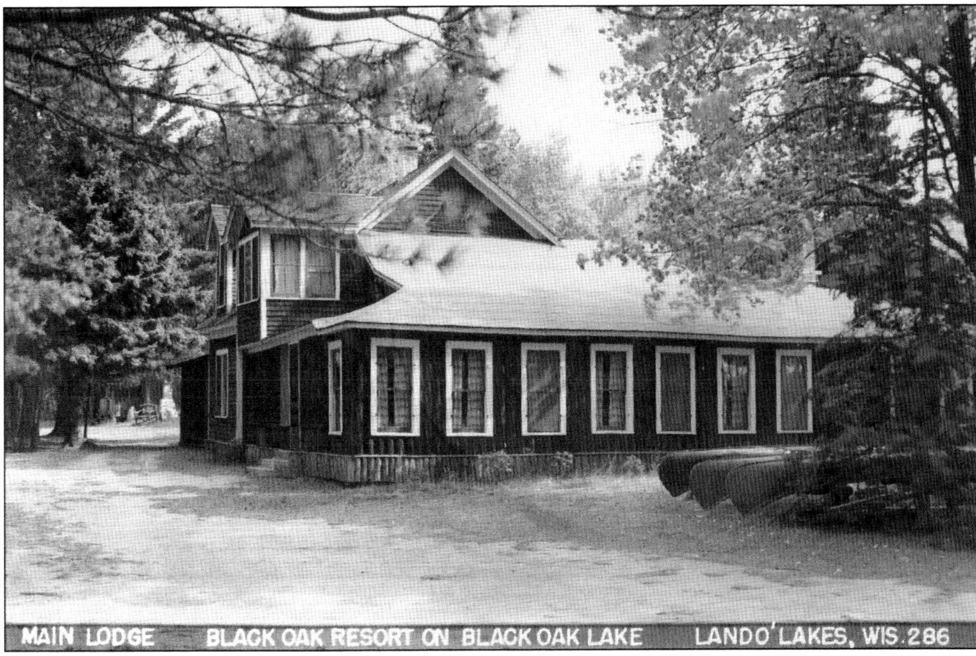

The main lodge of the Black Oak Lake Resort was the social center for guests. In 1974, George St. Clair's son Robert sold the property to the first owners outside of the St. Clair family. Facing immense costs to bring the old resort up to current safety codes, the new owners sold most of the buildings and furnishings, which were in great disrepair. Only the fireplace and chimney of the main lodge remain today.

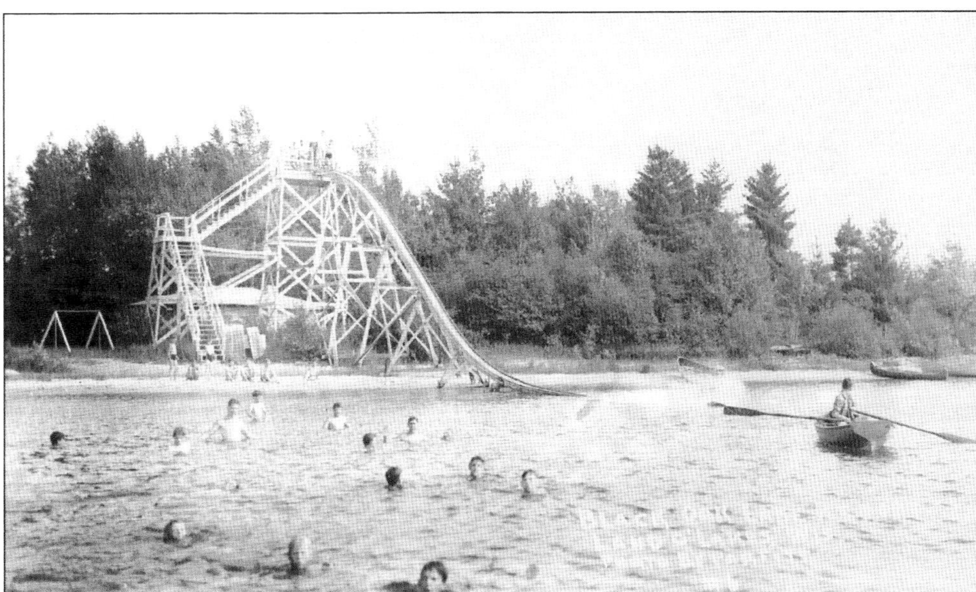

The thrilling water toboggan slide of the Black Oak Lake Resort plunged guests into the water via wheeled, wooden sleds on iron tracks. A sign at the top of the slide read, "Two to a Sled, No Standing." This photograph was taken in 1935. Nobody knows for certain when the slide was dismantled.

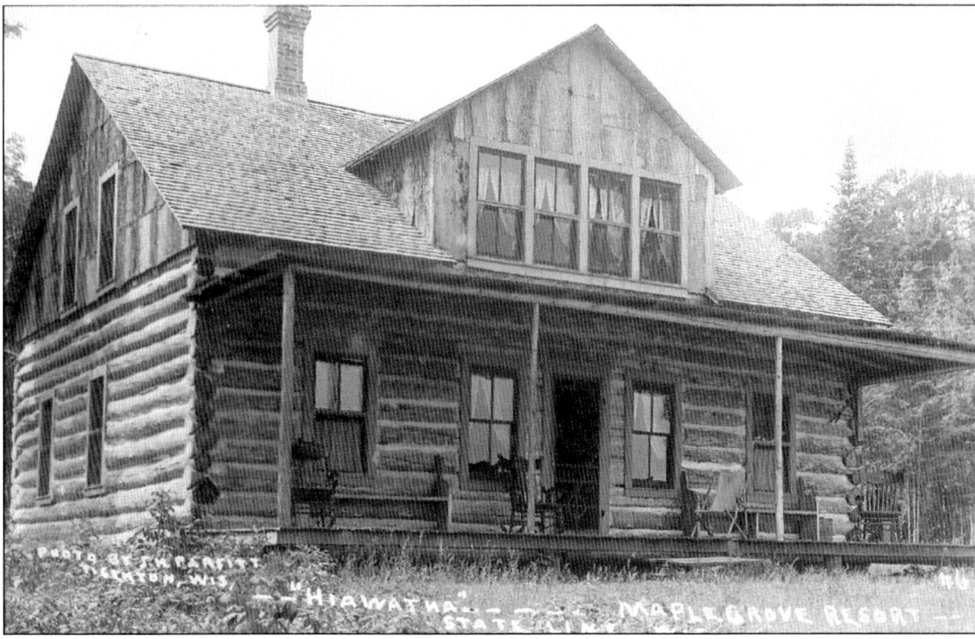

In 1898, Harry Frank began construction of the Maple Grove Resort on the southeast shore of Lac Vieux Desert. The resort operated under several owners until the 1970s, when most of the cabins and land were sold to private owners.

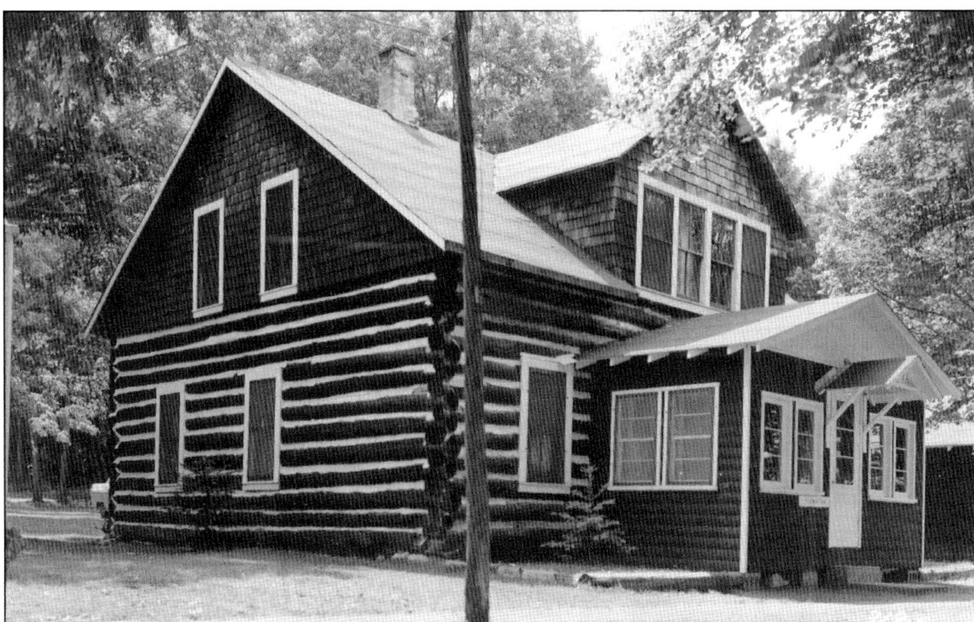

Over time, the main lodge of the Maple Grove Resort experienced several upgrades. This 1940s photograph shows the improvements made on the original building (pictured above).

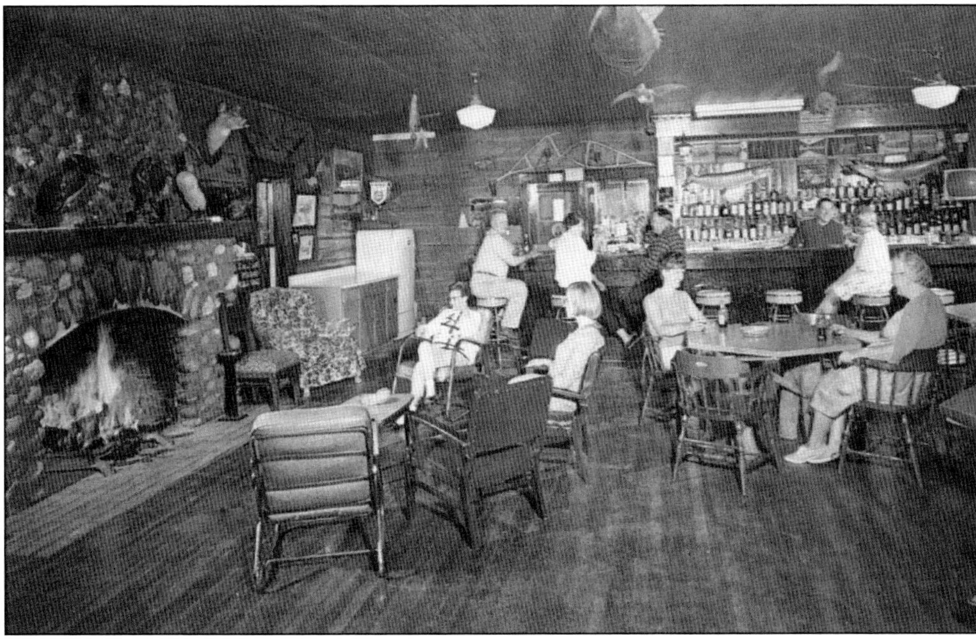

The main lodge of the Maple Grove Resort on Lac Vieux Desert offered a public dining room, cocktail lounge, and recreation room. This postcard is from the late 1960s, when the facility was operated by the Hartmans.

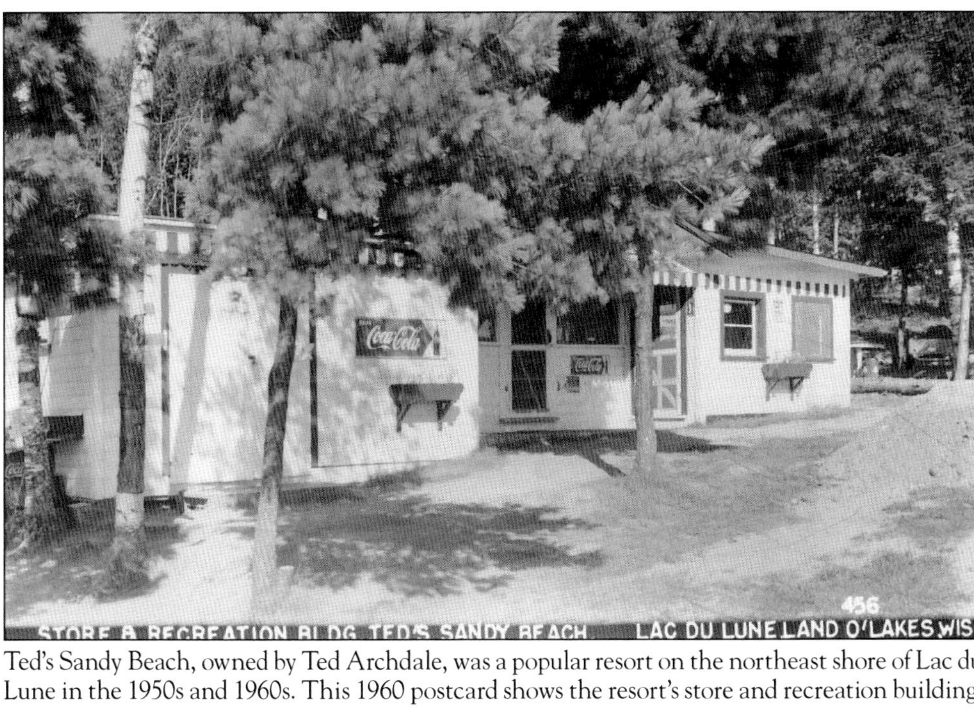

Ted's Sandy Beach, owned by Ted Archdale, was a popular resort on the northeast shore of Lac du Lune in the 1950s and 1960s. This 1960 postcard shows the resort's store and recreation building.

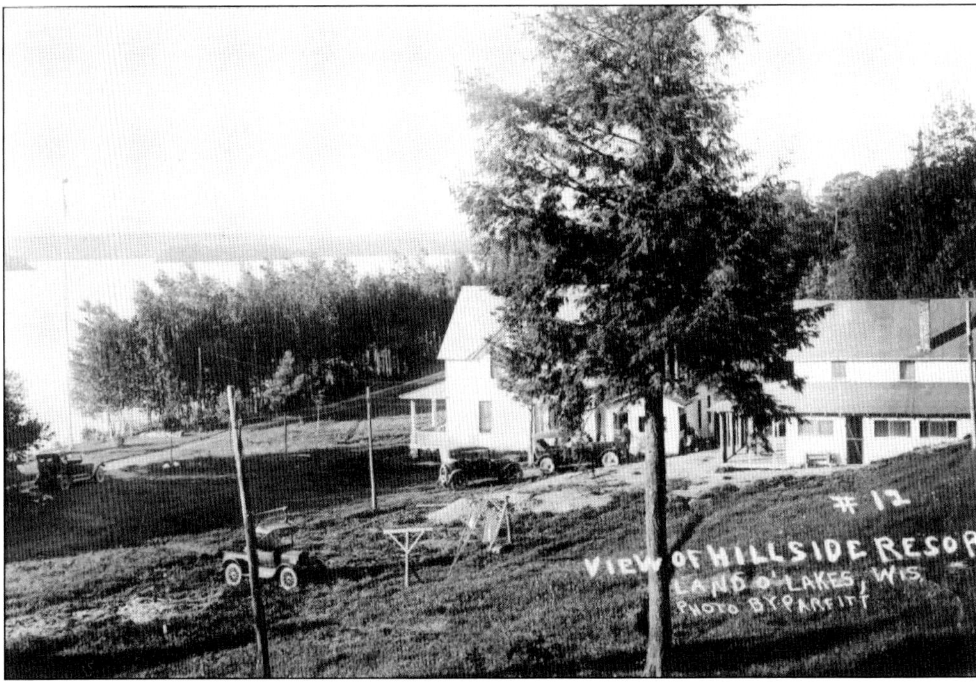

In 1912, John Jaud purchased 12 acres on the south shore of Lac Vieux Desert and established the Hillside Resort, hiring Finnish builders to construct the facility. In 1921, Jaud sold to William H. Love, who added cabins, a grass tennis court, saddle horses, and electricity. This photograph is from around 1926.

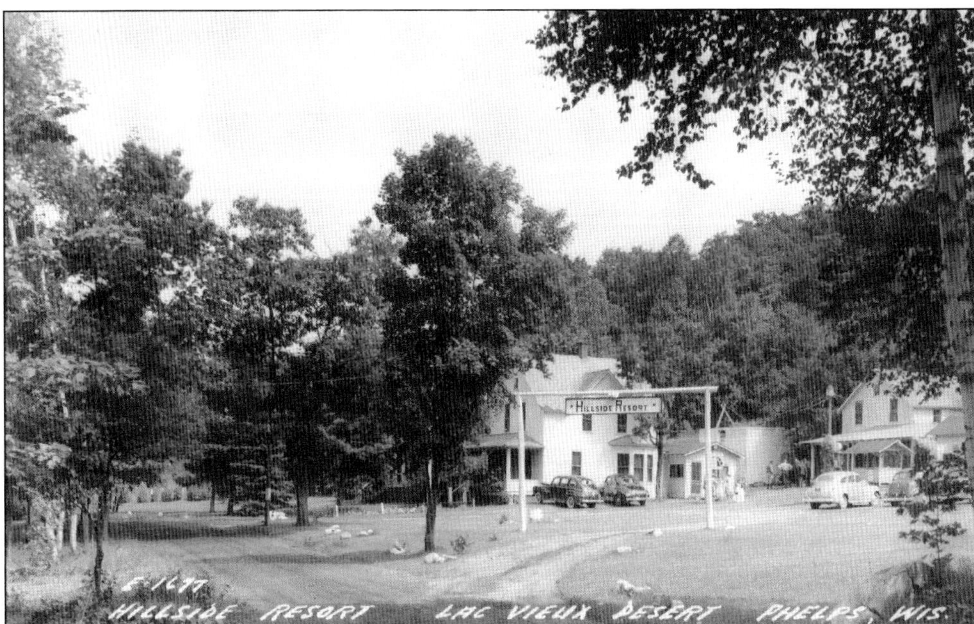

This photograph shows the entrance to the Hillside Resort in 1948. The main home (center) still exists.

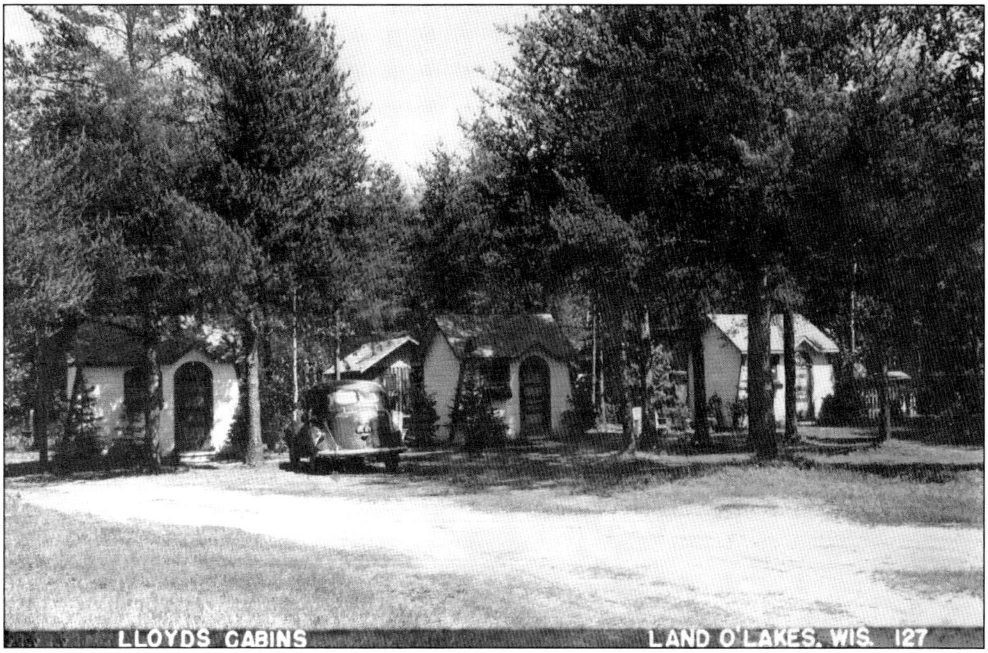

In the 1940s and 1950s, the Lloyd family rented cabins in what is now the Borderline RV Park just south of the Wisconsin River Bridge along Highway 45.

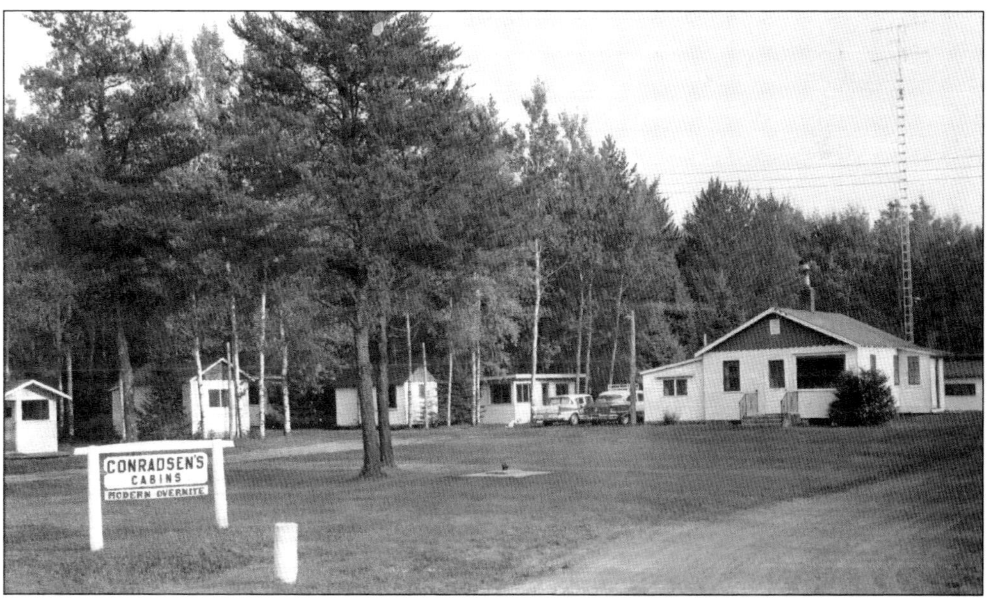

Gus Conradsen's cabins were popular place to stay in the 1950s. Located on the south side of Crystal Lake Road about a quarter-mile east of Highway B, only the large building on the right remains today.

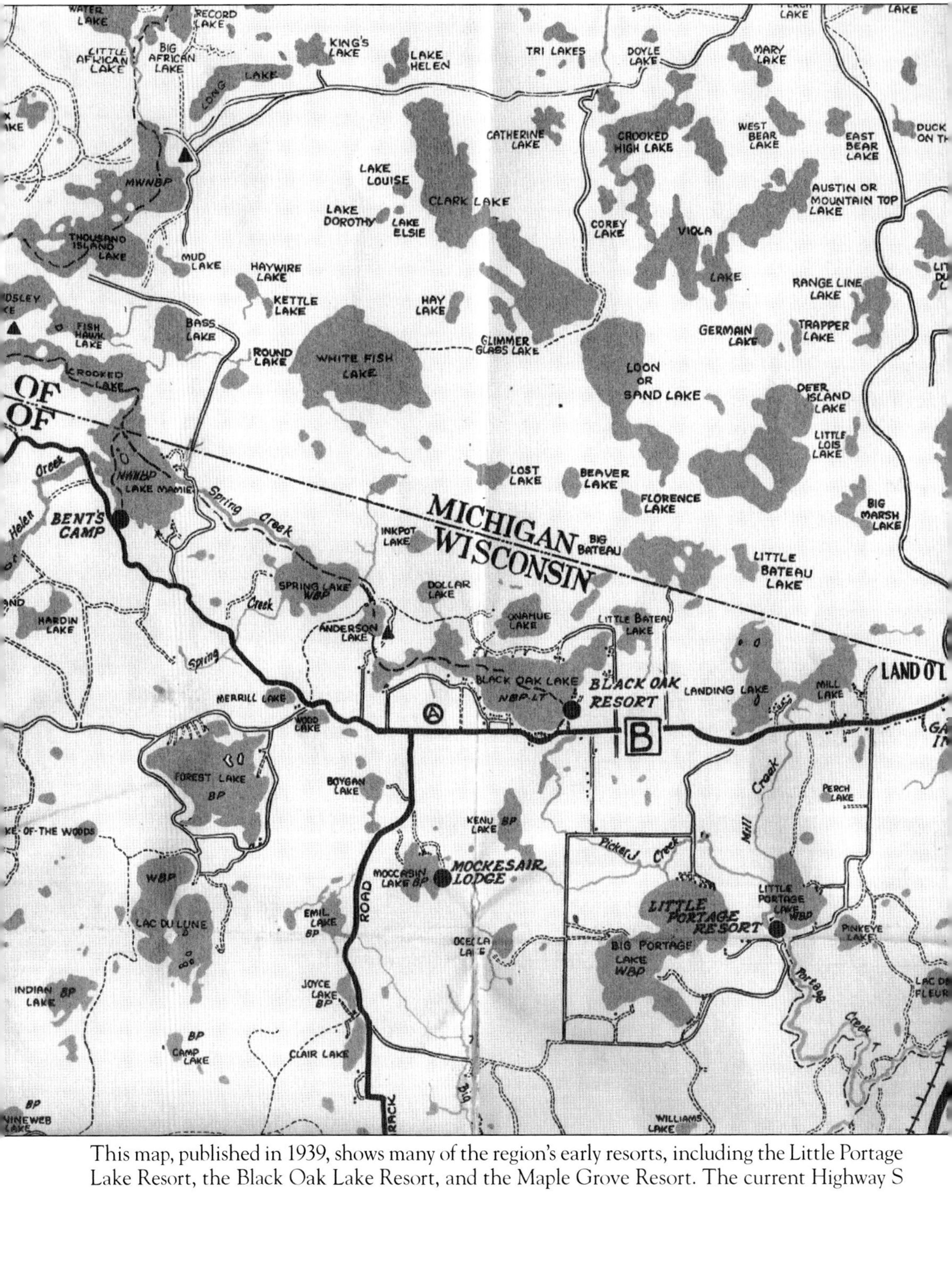

This map, published in 1939, shows many of the region's early resorts, including the Little Portage Lake Resort, the Black Oak Lake Resort, and the Maple Grove Resort. The current Highway S

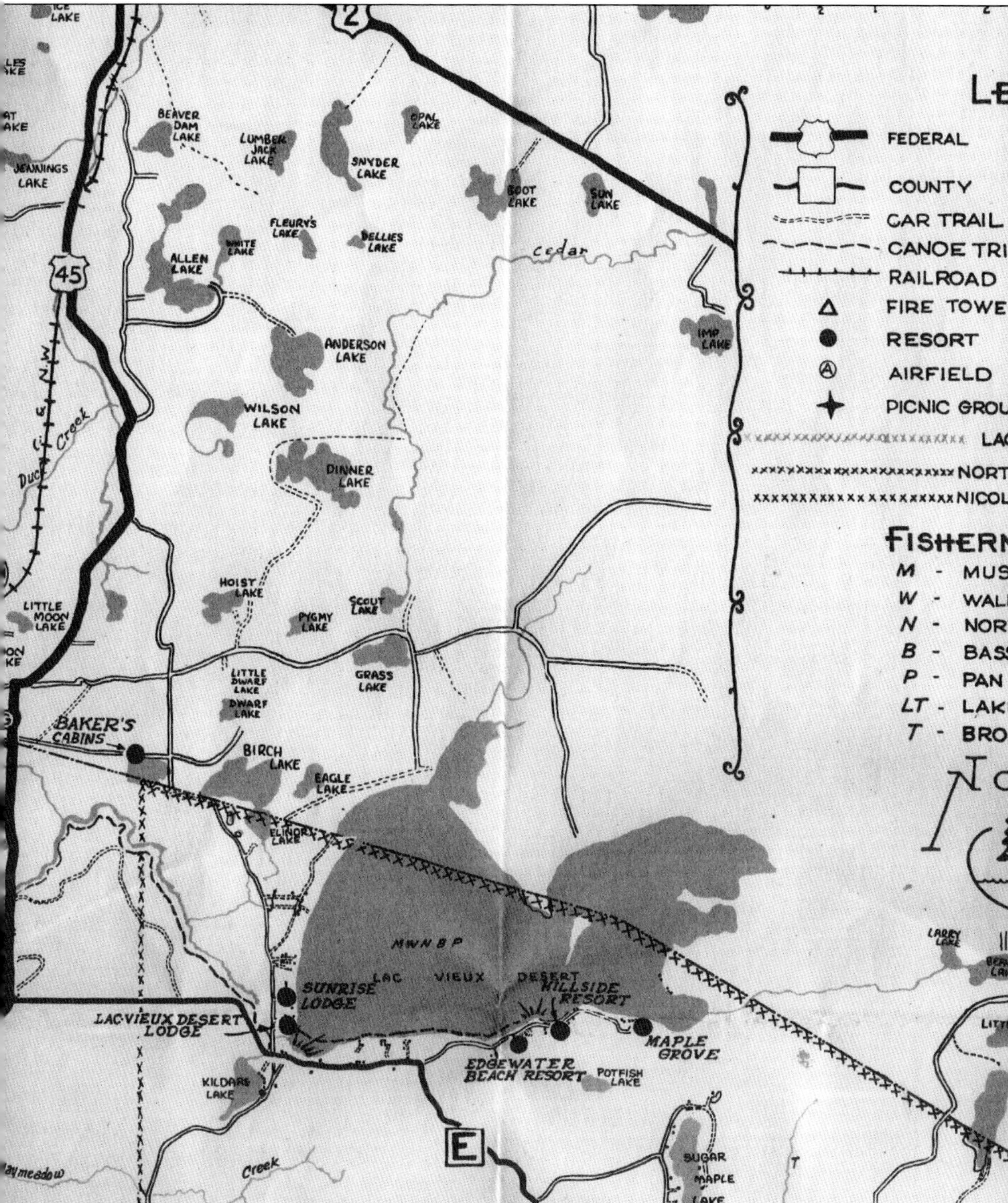

is named Tamarack Road, and the present Sylvania Wilderness was still privately owned. Note the airfield identified on the southwest shore of Black Oak Lake.

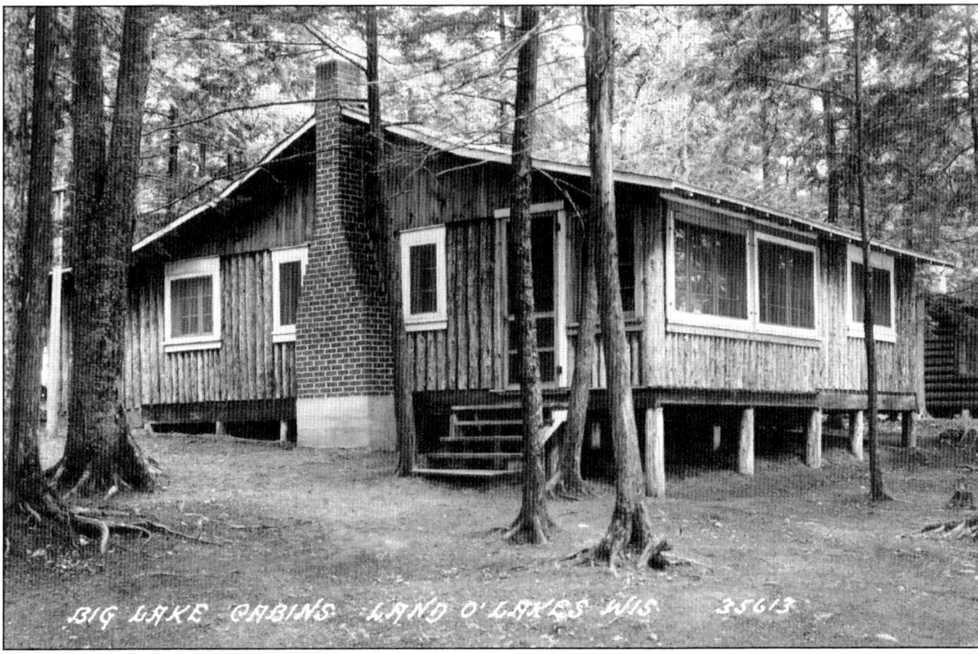

Throughout the 1940s, Lilian and Bert Carlson operated Carlson's Big Lake Cabins, with seven cabins, a main lodge, and a boathouse. This photograph shows "Thousand Island Cabin." Most of the facilities were built by Ray Hoock, camp boss of the Stange Lumber Company. Today, the pictured cabin, a second cabin, the main lodge, and the boathouse remain.

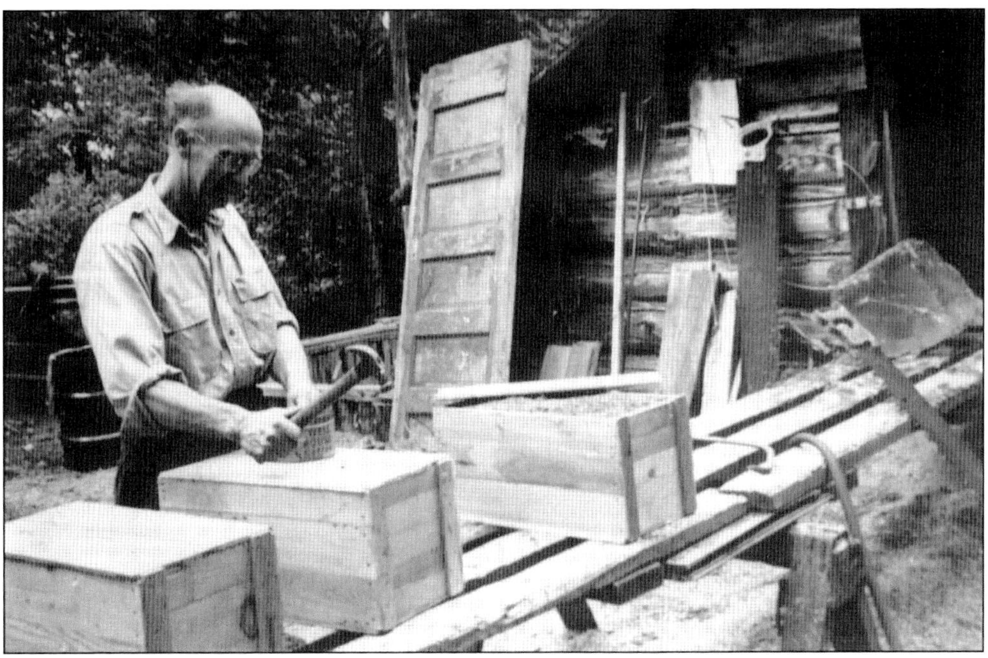

Fishing was so good that guests of Carlson's Big Lake Cabins often took their catches home. Bert Carlson (shown) packed the fish in ice and put them in moss-lined wooden boxes. The boxes were nailed shut, identified, and shipped home on the train with the guest's luggage.

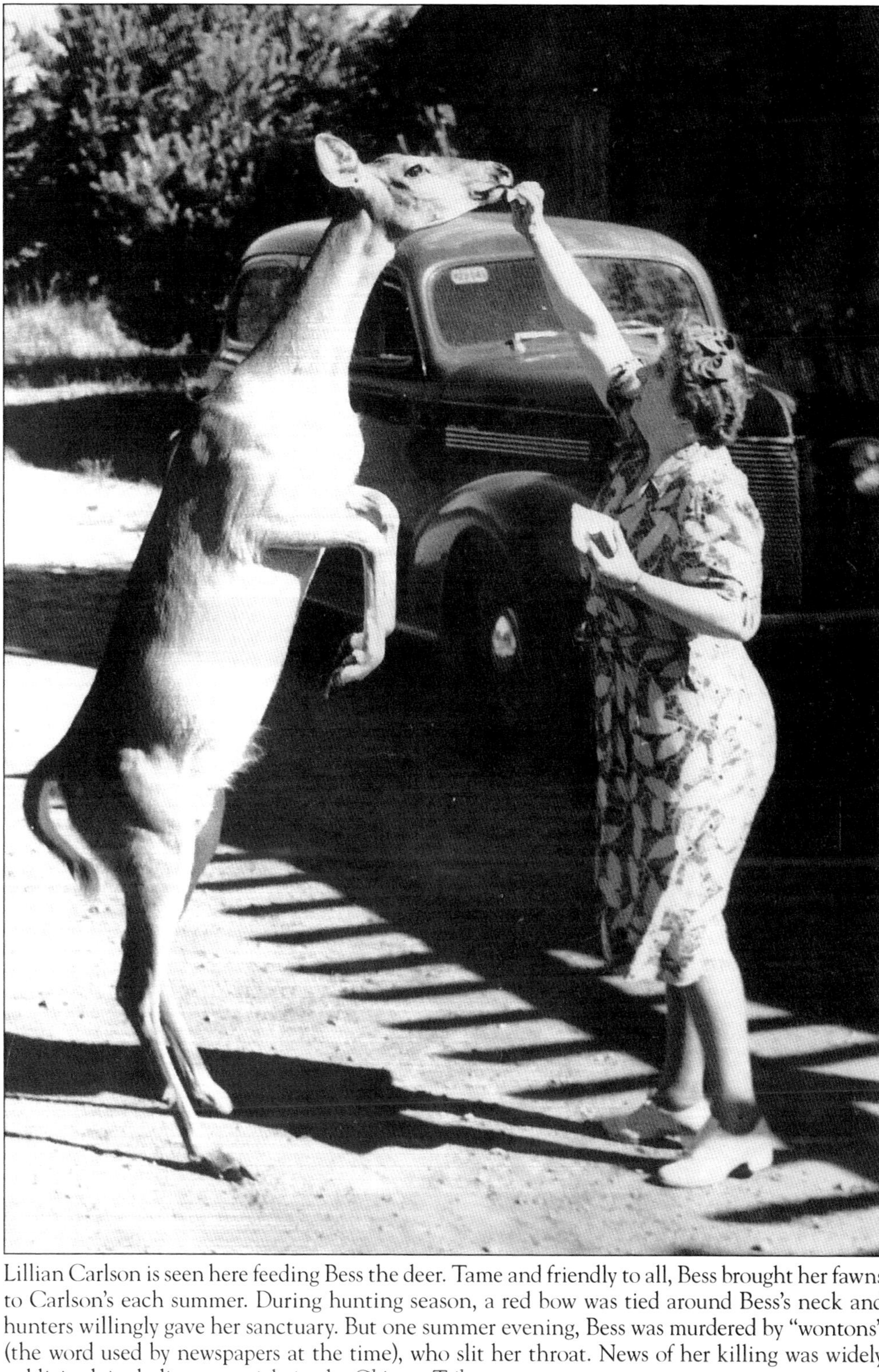

Lillian Carlson is seen here feeding Bess the deer. Tame and friendly to all, Bess brought her fawns to Carlson's each summer. During hunting season, a red bow was tied around Bess's neck and hunters willingly gave her sanctuary. But one summer evening, Bess was murdered by "wontons" (the word used by newspapers at the time), who slit her throat. News of her killing was widely publicized, including an article in the *Chicago Tribune*.

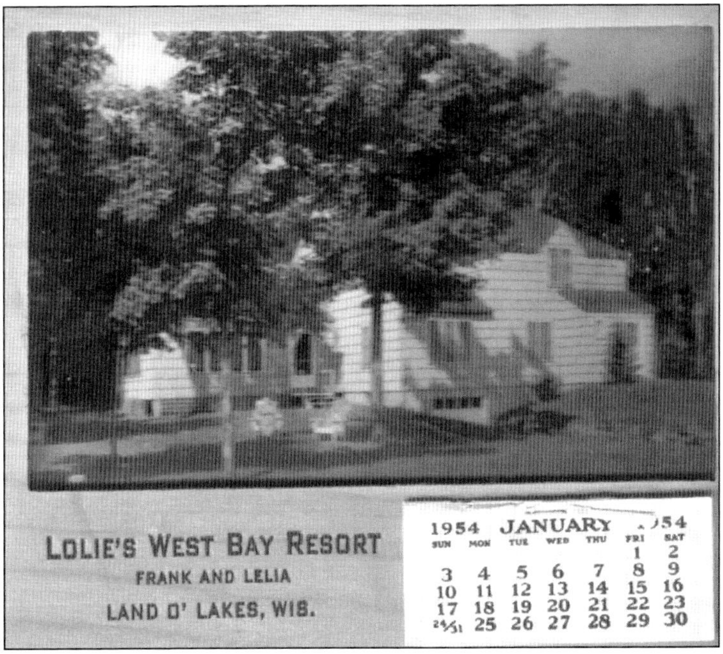

In the 1940s and 1950s, Frank and Lelia Lolie operated Lolie's West Bay Lake Resort on the Cisco Chain. In the 1920s, Frank Lolie worked as a yardman for Robert P. LaMont at the supposedly haunted "Summerwind" mansion, also located on West Bay Lake. The resort is now condominiums.

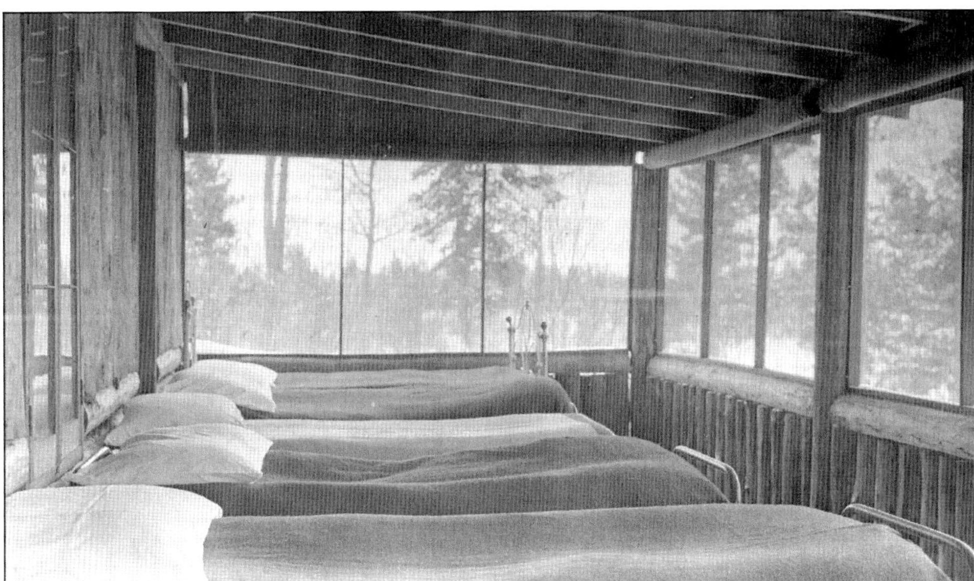

Before air-conditioning, a refreshing night's slumber was often enjoyed on screened porches. Here, resort guests could not only feel the cool evening breeze but hear the loons, the wind through the pines, and the howls of coyotes and wolves.

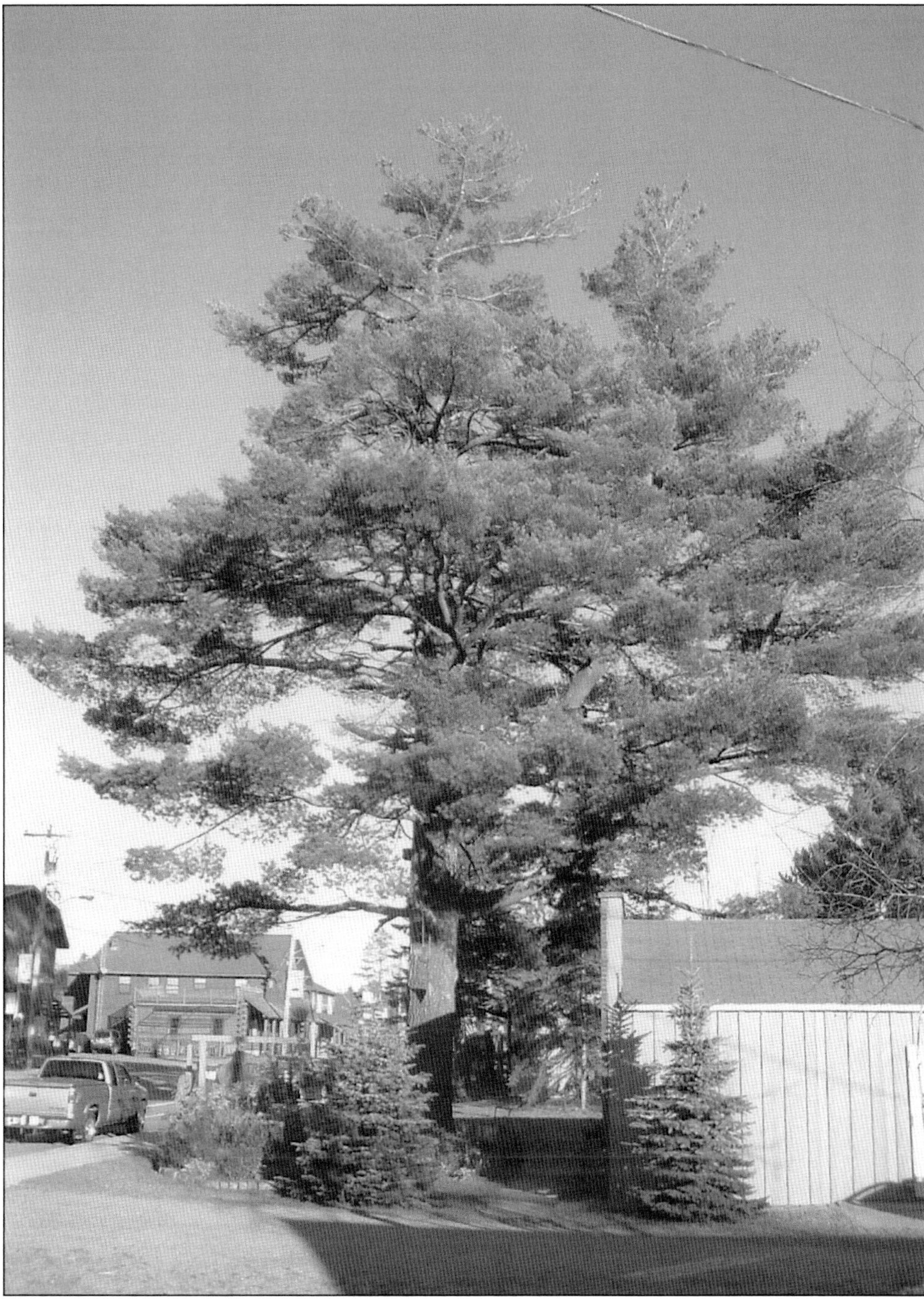

This great white pine, located in downtown Land O' Lakes, stood watch over Land O' Lakes for nearly 150 years. It saw every person, witnessed every development, and endured every storm. Perhaps the loggers spared it from the ax, knowing that State Line needed a guardian. It appears in many of the photographs in this book. (Photograph by author.)

The Land O' Lakes Historical Society and the NorthernWaters Museum

The Land O' Lakes Historical Society NorthernWaters Museum was dedicated in July 2001. Its mission is to present aesthetically appealing, interactive, and educational exhibits that honor, interpret, and preserve the unique stories of the Land O' Lakes area for visitors of all ages. It is located on Highway B, just west of downtown, in the former Gateway Lodge ski chalet.

The Land O' Lakes Historical Society was founded by Ann Bates, Barbara Nehring, and Cathy Nordine in 1995. The society's website is www.landolakeshistory.org.

About the Author

After independently exploring more than 60 nations, Jon Helminiak admits, "I've seen enough lakes, rivers, and oceans to know that the Land O' Lakes region is among the most beautiful and spiritual places in the world."

Jon has lived, worked, and canoed in Land O' Lakes and Vilas County for most of his life. He has authored six other published books.

Jon has pioneered several remote global destinations, including solo sea-kayaking expeditions among the island of the Raja Ampat Archipelago near Papua New Guinea and along the coast of Oman in Arabia. He is also a scuba diver, inspirational speaker, documentary video host, photographer, and instrument rated pilot with over 2,600 hours of pilot-in-command time.

His website is www.adventurequestproductions.com.

Consistent with our mission to preserve history on a local level, this book was printed in South Carolina on American-made paper and manufactured entirely in the United States. Products carrying the accredited Forest Stewardship Council (FSC) label are printed on 100 percent FSC-certified paper.

MADE IN THE USA